082892

LP   Cameron, Alexander
            Vet in the vestry.

Vet
in the
Vestry

Vet in the Vestry

ALEXANDER CAMERON

Thorndike Press • Thorndike, Maine

Library of Congress Cataloging in Publication Data:

Cameron, Alexander, 1926-
  Vet in the vestry / Alexander Cameron.
  p. cm. *90-B6248*
  ISBN 0-89621-993-3 (alk. paper : lg. print)
  1. Cameron, Alexander, 1926-   . 2. Church of Scotland--
Clergy--Biography. 3. Presbyterian Church--Scotland--
Clergy--Biography. 4. Veterinarians--Scotland--Biography.
I. Title.
[BX9225.C25A3   1990]   90-10793
285'.2'092--dc20   CIP
[B]

                17.⁹⁵

Thorndike Press Large Print edition published in 1990 by
arrangement with St. Martin's Press.

Cover design by James B. Murray.

**The trees indicium is a trade mark of Thorndike
Press.**

This book is printed on acid-free, high opacity paper.

To my parents, who sacrificed so much for their family, and to my wife, who has shared to the full in my "two lives"

Contents

In the Vestry

Preface

Away back in the late fifties, a Scots veterinary surgeon travelled from his practice in Devon to Glasgow for an interview, with the purpose of being accepted for training for the Church of Scotland ministry. It was a hard, indeed reluctant, decision to take, but I felt driven by a constant conviction inside me that this was the way I had to go.

I was interviewed by a bevy of professors and senior ministers with complete courtesy, but also with a sense of amazement, even amusement. Apparently there had never been a former vet in Scotland's Kirk before (though there are at least four now) and the mix seemed a strange one to the committee. I was to find over the years that the general public also thought it unusual, for on hundreds of occasions I have been asked to speak on my two lives, to every conceivable organization. Many kindly suggested that I should write a book about some of my experiences – the interest, the humour, the pathos. So this book was eventually born.

I am very conscious that many will think I am trying to copy James Herriot, whose books have put the work of a vet on the map — and on television — and have given pleasure to millions, including myself. But this is not an effort to 'do a Herriot', for two reasons. First, there is only one James Herriot, and I don't think his work can be equalled. Secondly, eighty per cent of this book was written during convalescence from a lengthy illness years ago, before any of the Herriot books had appeared. It was only recently that I hauled the manuscript out and felt I ought to finish it.

There are bound to be echoes of what another vet has written, for each vet in a general practice treats the same kind of cases, but part of this book is also about my many years as a minister.

I send it out with the hope that it will provide even a small proportion of the pleasure and interest that the books of my famous colleague in the Yorkshire Dales have given.

A.C.

1

The Devil They Know

Andrew warmly shook my hand, helped me off with my gowns, neatly folded them and put them back in their case.

'You'll be the seventh minister I've dressed every Sunday,' he announced. I was startled. I had already realized the general public's idea of a minister was a pretty wet, helpless creature, but I was unaware somebody had to dress him, and looked my surprise. He explained: 'Weel, ye ken, help him on and off with his robes.'

'Hold on,' I said, 'I'm not your minister yet; they've got to vote on it,' a procedure that was at that moment being conducted in the church.

'Ach!' said Andrew, investing the exclamation with such force and vigour that it would counter any argument, 'Ach! Efter that the day there's nae fear.' Then he added, 'You're jist like the gude ministers we've had before.'

I perked up, preened myself, and said that was a compliment indeed, recalling some of the fine men who had occupied that pulpit. I was ready for some more praise, so inquired in what way I resembled my predecessors. He told me . . .

'You're gey sweaty under the ocksters!'

So he had noticed. My shirt was in fact sticking to me, and might even have been steaming, a common experience of men who have undergone 'the weekly ordeal of public exposure' – even more of an ordeal when one is preaching for a charge and aware of the keenest scrutiny.

'Mind you,' Andrew went on, 'maist gude ministers sweat an awfu' lot. The yins that have the gift o' the gab an' just blether on when they've nothing to say don't sweat.'

Well, he should know, I thought, after a lifetime as a church officer, and in a way I was quite pleased that I had joined the elect band of the sweaty-shirt brigade.

'How long do you think they'll be?' I asked.

'No long,' he replied. 'Just you sit doon and rest yoursel' for a bit.'

I gladly obeyed. I had come to realize that preaching, contrary to public opinion, took it out of you, even if you didn't pound the bookboard and perform everything but handstands in the pulpit. Andrew peeped through the curtained window which gave a view of the church, a procedure he was to repeat every

Sunday thereafter, informing himself and anyone else in the vestry who, what and how many were in their pews. Everything Andrew the Beadle did was done with dignity, and somehow he managed to have his weekly peek and endue it with the solemnity of a sacrament.

'Aye,' he mused aloud, 'it's a while since I've seen the kirk sae fu'. Oh, that's them done noo; here comes the committee.'

The Committee squeezed into the small vestry, which also served as a choir-room and session-room, while Andrew discreetly withdrew. Rev. George, acting as Interim Moderator in place of Rev. Andrew, the appointed Interim Moderator who was on holiday, said, 'Well, Mr Cameron, after an open vote of the congregation, you'll be glad to know that the vote was unanimously in your favour. May I congratulate you, and wish you every blessing.' Then he gave a smile and added, 'I think this must be nearly unique – a vet in the vestry!'

I thanked him in stammering words; then the committee, led by Duncan the Treasurer, came forward to shake me by the hand or thump me on the back according to their inclination, and one and all to wish me well, in subdued or boisterous fashion.

'Of course,' said one of the committee, 'we never had any doot aboot it, but efter a gude sermon like that the voting was a formality.'

The congratulations over, some of the Elders turned to the important task of counting the offering. 'A gran' collection the day – notes in the plate,' said one.

I thought it time to depart before they passed the plate to me ... again ... so took my farewells and headed for my car, case in hand.

'Have you no' a hat?' asked one.

'Never wear one,' I replied. 'I did at one time, but you never saw anything like me in a hat.' Then, realizing I wasn't making much sense, added, 'I just don't seem to suit one, but you might see me in a cap sometimes.'

'Ah, times change,' sighed my questioner. 'I mind when Mr Macdonald came to preach for Moorton before the war, he arrived in a baby Austin wi' top hat an' tails on.' My mind grappled in vain with the picture of a car so attired, till he further enlightened me. 'Mr Macdonald managed to get oot o' the car withoot knocking his hat off, and he was as big a man as you.'

I just grunted 'Good for him,' realizing I would probably hear a good deal about Mr Macdonald in the years to come – a natural thing, for he and the speaker would have been young men together. I demonstrated that I too could negotiate a car with some elegance, albeit not wearing a hat, and was about to drive off when there was a hail as Duncan came up the church pathway in a 'pelting heat', as John Bunyan would have described it.

'I was busy with the collection,' he explained. 'There hasna' been one like that since Mr Cruickshank left. When you've no' a minister o' your ain, the folk don't come the same.'

'When the cat's away, the mice will play,' I suggested.

He agreed, reached in the car, warmly shook my hand and said, 'Man, you were jist gran' the day! Bring Mrs Cameron ower the morn an' we'll go through the Manse an' see what's to be done, an' you can pick some wallpaper. Though,' he added cautiously, 'we've no' got too much to spend. I'm the Treasurer an' it's me has to balance the books' . . . a phrase I was to hear often in the years ahead. But Duncan was a kindly soul, and with a final handshake from him, from yet another Andrew, the saintly old Session Clerk whose cherubic face just beamed, and from faithful Andrew the Beadle, I was off.

It felt good! I had just been voted their minister, in the democratic Presbyterian manner, by the congregation of Moorton, a humble country church but a church very much the centre of the scattered community it served, dwelling in the villages of Moorton and Waterfoot, and on the hundred farms in the sixty square miles of parish. It was also a historic church, founded in the 'killing times' and suffering greatly in those terrible yet valiant years when men fought and died for freedom of the faith. In a few weeks I would be ordained with due solemnity by the local Presbytery, but that was still ahead. I wondered, as I drove homeward, should I stop and phone Janet? However, I decided against it, and in fact pulled in to a lay-by for a few minutes to let it all sink in. I, Alexander Cameron, despite the odd letters MRCVS after my name, was now elected, and soon would be formally appointed minister of my first charge. Yes, truly it felt good! I was to come to love these kindly folks, and Moorton's storied past. But it was still unreal. What lay ahead, I knew not. Where, if anywhere else, we might be called in the future, I cared not. What was behind me I remembered well.

Three years ago I had been a country vet . . . now I was to be a country minister . . . as brother George had said, it would be a vet in the vestry. But was that any more odd than a doctor, teacher, joiner, farmer, company director, and a host of other occupations which had been represented at Divinity College? I remembered well the short interview I'd had with the selection board before they had decided that, subject to passing entrance exams in the Bible and in Greek, they would accept me.

'Were you really a vet, Mr Cameron? I mean,

did you practise?' asked the Chairman. 'Still do,' I replied, at which there had been smiles around the group and a murmur of 'Really!'.

For the life of me I couldn't see anything odd about it. After all, other vets had gone into other Churches. A fellow student had become a priest, and indeed the founder of my Devon practice was now a Canon in the Church of England. But everywhere there had been this same mixture of surprise and amusement, presumably because I was apparently the first of my kind, as far as people knew, in the Church of Scotland. I recalled being rudely interrupted during a Psychology of Religion lecture, in the midst of doodling, suddenly aware that I was being addressed.

'Perhaps, Mr Cameron, you could tell us of your experiences in this field with animals,' suggested the lecturer. Mr Cameron couldn't; I replied to the effect that I had never encountered a neurotic nanny goat or a schizophrenic sow, whereupon my pal Charlie passed along an instant portrait of a cow weeping copious tears, and saying: 'Cameron doesn't understand that what I need is a good psychiatrist!' But for the most part the banter was good-natured, and I usually pointed out that I would be doing the same job; only the species, *Homo sapiens*, was different. I was all in favour of men having had to work out in the big wide world, face difficulties, and understand the problems and trials of ordinary people before they tried to minister to them. It seemed to me that we had the best possible warrant for this, in that the founder of the Christian faith had worked as a carpenter to the age of thirty before becoming a wandering preacher. One thing I knew quite certainly, as I sat musing in that lay-by: I was still exactly the same person I had been as a vet, and if a halo was to be conferred to produce instant holiness on becoming a minister of the Gospel, then mine had somehow been lost in transit! I was the same fellow who had worn a calving-coat, even though now I would have a different uniform. I was no better a Christian for having become a minister – only a better informed and trained one.

Three months earlier my training had ended, and I had been cast adrift with my fellow students like so many ships seeking a harbour. I had been surprised to find that the way to reach a haven was to answer advertisements in the *Glasgow Herald* or the *Scotsman*, and these advertisements had really astonished and somewhat disappointed me. Churches vied with one another in offering the inducements of modern manses, up-to-date kitchens, central heating, beautiful outlooks, stipends so much above the minimum, and altogether proclaimed themselves as very desirable situations. I applied for a couple in the country, for with my background I would have been lost in a city, and meantime, to keep my family, I taught English in a comprehensive school. English included Geography, I discovered, and each night I swotted to keep one step ahead of the class. I thought I was doing rather well too, till one day, showing a film-strip and waxing eloquent about the Canadian prairies, I became aware of a disturbance behind me and discovered a good-going card school in the back seats. So much for my teaching know-how!

I hadn't long to wait, mercifully, for I had a wife and four children to maintain. In a month, the first charge for which I'd applied invited me to be their minister. After ten days' consideration, and feeling rotten about declining the honour these folk had paid me, I had to refuse, for the remoteness of the place was clearly going to present schooling and family problems. I'd applied for another charge in my native Ayrshire, and meantime, with the coming of the summer holidays, I was asked to take pulpit supply in various churches.

I first suspected that I had a visiting committee at an evening service in Kilmarnock. They were there again the next Sunday — and the next. On that third occasion, a glorious summer evening, few of the devout had come to church, no doubt preferring God's good sunshine to the Revised Church Hymnary, second edition, and my eloquence! But I had a congregation none the less; my visitation committee of four, and, almost at the front of the church, a group of about sixteen, all seated closely together. Obviously another committee – in force. But who were they? I don't know how I preached, nor indeed how I maintained any kind of concentration, for I was highly amused by the glances darting from one committee to the other and the intense scrutiny bestowed on me. I could almost read their thoughts: 'Does he read his prayers?' . . . 'Does his voice carry?' . . . 'Is he reasonably presentable in appearance?' (I'd heard of one student who was turned down because he had fiery red hair!) . . . 'I wonder if he believes in visiting?' . . . 'Has he a wife?' – the million-dollar question, this (one of my friends waited a year for a charge largely because he lacked this all-important attribute. Eventually he got a fiancée, and a church!). So the service proceeded, and at last, shaking hands at the door as was my custom, my regular four visitors whispered that they were holding a meeting a week on Tuesday, and that I was one of a short list of two. They were from the Ayrshire church to which I'd applied, it seemed. But who were the others?

I was not long left in doubt, for a deputation awaited me in the vestry. They explained they were from Moorton, and had only that morning appointed their committee . . . they had already fifty applicants . . . had I not seen their advertisement? If I was interested, would I apply, to keep the matter in order? I recognized one or two of them now, for Moorton was a neighbouring parish to Kilmarton, where I had acted as a student pastor during most of my three years at Trinity College (the minister there had died, and there were prolonged negotiations about union of the two churches). We had even lived in the enormous but very gracious manse, camping out in a few of its twenty rooms. This identification explained the far from charitable looks that had passed between the two committees, for clearly the farmers of Moorton recognized the farmers of the other parish, not twenty miles away. Here was a dilemma! I had applied for one charge, was one of a leet of two, it seemed, and was now being urged to apply for Moorton. What did one do? It all seemed so . . . what was the description . . . worldly? . . . materialistic? . . . all on the human level? I suppose I felt a dove should wing its way downwards with a message in its beak. And yet how could God work except through men and women, be they bishops or committees? As I thought about it all that summer evening, I recalled the words of Andrew Eastham, my parents' minister, who had

21

been, and was to continue to be, a friend, adviser, and father in God to me.

'Our system of electing ministers has its faults,' he said, 'but I honestly believe the Holy Spirit does guide in all this . . . and,' he added with a grin, 'that's a miracle.'

So I sent in the application for consideration, and left it there. I had no means of knowing whether I would be the selected one in the other short leet.

The following Sunday evening, preaching at Mochrum where I had begun as a young vet years ago, but a long way from Moorton, there was the Moorton committee again; seventeen of them this time, the whole lot. I've no idea how they knew where I was preaching, but the Scot is noted for his 'speirin' ', and someone had found out. The service over, I made a leisurely journey homewards, calling at my widowed mother's on the way to spend an hour or two with her. She greeted me with a message that I was to go straight home, since 'a minister and some men' (what ministers were in the human spectrum seemed doubtful!) were awaiting me and would like a word. The minister proved to be the Rev. George, the acting Interim Moderator, and every inch a man . . . the others were two of the Moorton Vacancy Committee. They explained they were from Moorton, had held a meeting that night, and invited me to be their 'sole nominee'. I listened carefully but with an assumed air of nonchalance, as if even St Giles wouldn't tempt me (I was learning fast), and subdued a smile when they, without giving a reason, asked, 'Could you let us have your decision before Tuesday?' Clearly farmers discussed other things at the market besides the price of beasts and the poor pig subsidies!

Janet had been valiantly supplying them with tea and making polite conversation till I arrived, and had withdrawn to let the men — and the minister — talk business. I asked that she should join us in the discussion, because from the beginning our Call had been a joint thing. I protested, I hope sincerely, that they had been less than fair to their other fifty applicants, some of whom were probably friends of mine from Trinity.

'Och, don't worry about that,' said one of the delegation. 'We decided we wanted somebody in his thirties, and we've been scattered like the Israelites across the face of Scotland this morning, hearing the ones we'd considered.'

'But you've heard me twice . . . and even more, for I preached at Moorton about a year ago when we were staying at Kilmarton. That's hardly fair to all the others,' I reiterated. 'Besides, I've applied for another church too, and it's possible they might be interested.'

They looked down, hesitated, then one said,

'Aye, we heard aboot the ither kirk, but we're unan . . . unani . . . a' agreed we'd like you.'

I assured them I'd think about it and let them have an answer within the deadline, and gravely showed them out. Then Janet and I hugged one another and did a few waltz steps round the room . . . most unseemly behaviour for a Sabbath evening! Somebody wanted us; maybe even two congregations. Still, we'd had no official approach from the other, and as we thought it over, prayed it through, and slept on it (a trinity of excellent actions) it seemed we should say yes.

That had been three weeks ago. Now, I thought in the lay-by, as I reached for the ignition key, it had come to pass. The congregation had endorsed their committee's recommendation. Maybe God did indeed work in mysterious ways . . . Anyway, it was time to pass on the good news to my waiting wife, and tell the boys something that was far more important to them. They could soon have the addition to the family for which they had been clamouring for three years, and to which I had always answered, 'You'll get it when Mummy and Daddy have a home of their own . . . you'll get your puppy then.'

There was jubilation on my return, my attempt to convey gloom and despondency signifying rejection being a flop. It felt grand to be wanted, to be settled, to be faced with a challenge, to be trusted by a congregation — even, my ego whispered, to be preferred to fifty others. The Rev. Andrew, when he returned from holiday and came to congratulate me, put the ego in its place when he remarked, 'I felt sure Moorton would go for you. You see, a congregation nearly always goes for the devil they know, rather than one they don't.'

That about summed it up!

PART ONE
Mainly the Vet

2

The Deep End

I was doing a surprising thing – in fact a daft-
like thing. I was sitting at a telephone and
longing for it to ring with news of trouble! Here
was I, Alexander Cameron, complete with the
letters MRCVS after my name, positively God's
gift to mankind – or at least to animal-kind, I
thought modestly – and the world out there
didn't seem to know what it was missing. Nobody needed me! True, in two weeks I would be
able to display my talents to the full, for I was
then to start work as assistant vet in the little
town of Mochrum, where I had completed my
schooling, and near where my parents still lived.
But that was two weeks away. Today, and for the
next fortnight, I was locum for Len Simpson at
Glenafton, where I'd been born and had lived
till I was fourteen, and where I'd seen most of
my practice as a student.

A student . . . my mind went back four days
to that scene at the old Vet College in Buc-

cleugh Street, and to the longest hour of my life. We had all just completed our oral finals, and had to wait for the results to be posted. With exaggerated nonchalance we wandered about to put in the time. We tried table tennis, but somehow that day the spins and smashes wouldn't work. Every few minutes we drifted back to the courtyard to glance at the notice-board or the clock. It must be bad, all this time they were taking! There were two theories about orals. One was that if you had not been asked many questions, you were clearly home and dry on the written and practical exams. The other theory was that few questions meant it wasn't worth the examiners' time quizzing you, for you were beyond hope and no amount of questions would alter the result; you were therefore doomed to re-sits, or maybe to repeat-ing the final year. We all tried to recall how many questions we'd been asked, and wondered what comprised a safe number. The air was thick with tobacco smoke, as men feverishly, with shaking hands, lit one cigarette from an-other. Nobody knew about the cigarette-lung cancer connection then, and it's questionable if it would have altered the position anyway in this frantic waiting period. At least the nicotine masked the odour of formaldehyde from the adjacent anatomy lab! We gravitated into small groups of the particular pals each had made over the years, and tried to console one another, but each of us, as time passed, was becoming convinced we'd failed the lot.

'They asked me how to treat conjunctivitis in an elephant,' said John. An elephant! We pondered that one deeply, and decided John was heading for Honours – or, wait a minute, maybe the wretched external examiners were taking the mickey out of such an appalling student . . .

'Twice when I answered, the Principal put his head down,' announced Joe. That sounded bad, but we tried to persuade Joe that the Principal was just tired after a long stint. As time dragged on, we became more cynical and 'Who cares anyway!'. The die was cast.

'There they go!' came a shout, and we looked up to see the two external examiners hurry away, to mingled cheers and whistles from about thirty suffering students. We knew now that we had about twenty minutes to wait, because it was decreed that no results be posted till the examiners were safely away – ever since an irate student who'd failed, and didn't think he should have, had assaulted and caused grievous bodily harm to one of the blighters in some past era. Never were more cigarettes consumed, nor such inane chatter uttered, in any twenty minutes since – well, since last year anyway! Some of the suffering throng had been there then, too. You could tell them by the extreme pallor of their cheeks, in thirty faces virtually devoid of colour – except for Bill, who'd had a few too many and was glowing pink. We all knew he'd passed because Bill was brilliant and had gained honours all along the way, and despite the fact that a friend had left him propped against his front door, out cold, the night before the written finals; he'd turned up seeing two exam papers, and had probably passed both with distinction.

But the longest day passes – as some of us had not – and eventually there was a sudden silence as the secretary emerged from the office, sheet of paper in hand, and headed, in a deathly hush, for the notice-board. Then there was an almighty rush, and a series of shouts of relief or groans of agony, as we studied that notice. No names appeared, for we all, like the prisoners we were, had numbers, and there, in an unrepeatable moment of ineffable joy, I had seen number 8 – me! If your number wasn't up – well, your number was up, if you follow me, and you were doomed to more months of suffering. I was quick, but I wasn't quick enough, for others had beaten me to the phones in college and in the surrounding streets. I hared across several Glasgow roads before finding an empty phone-box, and there, all pretence gone now, sent the glad tidings to my mother, forty-five miles away.

There was a hush at the other end while she swallowed a few lumps in her throat, and at last she managed to say, 'Well done, son! Your dad will be pleased!'

Then a mad rush back for the closing ceremony, a quick look at the notice — yes, number 8 was still there — and into the Board Room where I had missed all the speeches (no bad thing, maybe) and was just in time to get in the tail of the queue to pay the registration fee which made one a Member of the Royal College of Veterinary Surgeons. Since the college had not then been taken over by the university, which a few years later, for the same course in the same antiquated buildings, was issuing the degree of BVMS, with a full-scale graduation ceremony, we had to be content with a simple MRCVS, and pay for it. A bit thick, that, I thought!

Now I was itching to treat my first patient, but, as if fearful of what might befall their beasts, the farmers of Glenafton parish were lying low. I glared at the phone again, and a thought came to me; it could be the only explanation, so I picked up the instrument to find out.

'Number, please,' came a cheerful voice — too cheerful, I thought, in the circumstances.

'Er ... operator ... I think this phone must be out of order.'

'Why do you think that, sir?' she asked. That was better . . . 'sir'!

'Well, you see . . . eh . . . er . . . it hasn't rung for two hours now, and it's a busy number . . . rings a lot . . .' I ended lamely.

'What is your number?'

I told her.

'Oh, that's the vet's number, and I expect everyone knows Mr Simpson is away on holiday so they're not ringing,' she brightly answered.

'But *I'm* here!' It sounded a bit pathetic.

'Yes, but you are just a student or something, aren't you, so . . .' Was there anything these country operators didn't know, I wondered? A 'student' or a 'something' indeed.

'I'm not a student . . . I'm a qualified vet . . . I'm Mr Simpson's locum.' In my indignation I must have raised my voice, for back came the 'polite to the public' tone.

'I'm hearing you loud and clear . . . very clearly indeed.' I could picture her holding the earphones away from her head, and probably the whole exchange listening in. 'However, if you just replace your receiver, I'll ring you back.'

'Right-o,' I grunted, and put the thing down.

In a minute it rang. 'Aftonvale 153,' I said hopefully, though forlornly.

'Just testing,' came that wretched female

34

voice. 'The phone seems to be quite all right, Mr Cameron. I expect someone will ring you up eventually.'

She hung up, and I stood gaping. She even knew my name, and that 'eventually' seemed to imply that anybody would have to be pretty desperate to risk me. The wee besom, I thought, probably she had been to school with me – even worse, had been in a lower class. I gnashed my teeth at her condescension, took a few turns round the room, and flung myself down in a chair with the *Veterinary Record*. Flipping through the pages, I came to the 'Wanted' column and read: 'First-year student desires to see general practice, south Scotland preferred.'

That sent the wheels of memory whirling. A few years ago I had been a first-year student about to see my first cases. I recalled coming to this very house all eager anticipation, my shiny new wellington boots under one arm, lab coat under the other, and the only two instruments I possessed, a thermometer and a stethoscope, stuffed in a pocket. A long, lean, bronzed individual had answered the door, and hauled me into the room with the warmest of welcomes. I thought then that this figure, with his wiry frame, open-air face and aura of authority about him, exactly fitted my image of a country vet, the more so since he was dressed in riding-breeches and a tweed jacket. The impression I gained of Sandy Gray that morning was confirmed by the passing years – a first-class vet who had put up his plate and carved out a new practice by his skill, enthusiasm and warm personality. Farmers felt they could trust this man both on a professional and personal basis, and they were right. There had been two other students there that first time, a third-year student from Rhodesia, and Alec Milroy, a final-year student who, in contrast to most final-year men, treated first-year students like myself as fellow human beings with some common sense, and not as creatures from some lower order of the animal kingdom. Three students at one time was unusual, and I've no doubt I was simply a nuisance. I had as yet no theoretical knowledge, let alone practical experience, for the first-year vet course consisted of chemistry, physics, botany and zoology. I'd become an expert at cutting up worms and cockroaches, but since the number of these that a vet is called upon to treat is somewhat limited, I couldn't for the life of me see how they would help me calve a cow or treat a lame horse.

'You may not see much practice here, but you will see life,' said Sandy, an expression I was to hear him use with many students over the years. I did see life – but also a deal of practice too, and the list of case histories which had to be presented to the final-year examiners was wide and varied. At all hours of the day or night we would be on the job, and down in the book had gone cases ranging from every kind of presentation in calving – breech, head back, transverse, locked twins – to strange, bizarre events which baffled even Sandy. I remember the examiner picking on one of these, and asking in some surprise, 'What's this . . . plough handle in the stomach?'

It had been just that. A stirk maybe eight months old had been let out on grass for the first time after a long winter indoors. With its fellow Ayrshire stirks at Grassyards Farm, it had run pell-mell about the field, in sheer joy at this new world of freedom. The owner found it collapsed in the field, brought it in and phoned Sandy. From the beginning it was a puzzle, and also a very sick animal. Early on, Sandy had diagnosed a ruptured diaphragm (the sheet of muscle that separates abdomen from chest). It was weird to listen, with my brand-new stethoscope to the stomach, and hear respiratory sounds, and to the chest and hear gastric gurgles. Sandy had suggested he try surgery, but probably to his relief the farmer had declined, and decided 'jist tae leave her alane an' see hoo she'll dae'. We visited her every day for nine days, when – inevitably – she died. A post-mortem discovered a wooden plough handle in the abomasum or fourth stomach. The little stirk had, unknown to the farmer, run full pelt into a single-furrow horse plough sitting in the field, and the force of the impact had snapped off the handle, which had been forced between two ribs – we'd noticed this small wound in the chest but it had seemed of little consequence – and had then gone right through the diaphragm into the stomach. The farmer had missed his plough handle, but hardly expected to find it in a beast's stomach!

That case had been the first of many to illustrate the astonishing durability of bovines, as against almost any other animal. The stomach contents were actually sploshing about in the chest, one lung was completely useless, the other almost so, yet the stirk had lived for nine days! I could remember the quizzical look the examiner gave me when I explained the details. I couldn't blame him. For improbability, it beat any fishing story by a mile.

Two things I recalled about that first 'seeing practice'. One was doing my first pregnancy diagnosis – or rather, non-diagnosis. Sandy had, by rectal examination, felt the size of a cow's uterus through the rectal wall and pronounced her four months in calf. Alec Milroy had done plenty of PDs and didn't bother, but the third-year student and I were invited to have a go. 'Yes, about four months,' agreed the other, and I vaguely nodded when my turn came. I hadn't felt a thing except rectal wall, and cow dung going up my sleeve. I later asked the Rhodesian lad how he could tell it was four months in calf, and confessed that I hadn't felt anything I was supposed to. He grinned at me and said, 'That makes two of us.' I must say he was a superb actor, because he had emphatically concurred with Sandy's estimate.

The other big memory of that first time was Sandy's wedding. He had gone off on honeymoon to sunny Devon, leaving Alec Milroy in charge, it still being permissible for a student to act as locum. One night the phone rang, and on answering, I was asked by a distant voice if I would accept a long-distance call from Devon and pay for the call. I was still humming and hawing, not being familiar with the procedure of reversing the charges, when Sandy's voice came over the line. Clearly the operator in Devon had taken my grunts as signifying agreement – he probably thought I was speaking Gaelic! Sandy was brief and to the point.

'Alec,' he said, 'go into the top drawer of the dressing-table upstairs, get the three table-tennis balls there, and post them on. They've a table in the hotel here, but no balls.' In those closing years of the war, table-tennis balls were almost unobtainable.

'Oh . . . eh . . . right-o, Sandy. Everything's

OK here. We had a couple of calvings yesterday, a horse with colic and . . .'

'Cheerio, Alec, try and get those balls off
tonight.'

I looked at the phone in astonishment. What
a queer vet: he didn't want to know about the
work we'd done! Eighteen years old and still
starry-eyed with the novelty and excitement of
treating animals, I found it inconceivable that
he didn't want to know. Sure, it was his honeymoon, but I mean to say, we might be ruining
his practice, or stuck and needing his advice! I
had yet to learn how completely demanding
single-man practice was, and didn't appreciate
that this was the first holiday Sandy had enjoyed for years, since the day he'd put up his
plate. Yes, a queer phone call that!

Brm, brm . . . brm, brm . . . brm, brm. I sat
up with a jerk. The phone was ringing.

'Aftonvale 153,' I almost shouted, in eagerness.

'This is Polquhirter Mains. We've a cow to
clean tomorrow.'

'Tomorrow? Oh, I can come out today and
clean it.'

'No, tomorrow is the third day. We always
leave it till the third day.'

'Sure you're wise?' I queried. 'She's not off
her food or anything?'

'Not her! See you tomorrow.'

My hopes were dashed – tomorrow! Polquhirter Mains (pronounced, as any sensible person knows, 'Pa-whirter'): that was Mr Aird. I knew the farm, just half a mile from where we'd lived in Glenafton; in fact we'd bought our eggs there. A cow to clean – that was a nice easy case. I stretched out my arm and rehearsed the job, meticulously removing the afterbirth from the rows of cotyledons, known as 'berries', which stuck out from the wall of the womb in a cow. To remove the placenta was a bit like peeling about fifty little oranges blindfold, the cotyledons varying in size from a hazelnut to a smallish tomato. I shuddered when I recalled the student who'd just pulled the 'berries' off, and the cow had almost bled to death. Oh well, I couldn't get a much easier case for a first, I thought, but decided to check the car to make sure I'd put pessaries in. I'd already checked the contents three times. Why couldn't the case have been today?

I went back to my easy chair and looked round the familiar room, remembering. I recalled one incident which, even after three years, made me fidget uncomfortably. Like table-tennis balls, cars were also at a premium at that time, the waiting period for new ones being about five years. But Sandy had discovered that a particular make of sports car could be obtained with just a few months' wait. The time had passed, and daily he expected news of the car. Being a good vet and willing teacher (except for uninterested students, like the boy Sandy called for at his digs one evening to see a calving case, who had thanked Sandy with a smile and said, 'I'll not come, for I've seen one of those'), Sandy had a student almost every holiday period. That Easter there were three of us again, and on our way to the house on the morning of 1 April we thought it would be a fine idea to phone Sandy, say this was so-and-so's garage, that his new car had come, and would he collect it that afternoon? Being the only Scot of the three, I was appointed to disguise my voice and be the salesman. All went well; the fish took the bait, and when we arrived at his home Sandy was one big smile.

'Great news, lads! The car's arrived, and I'm going for it this afternoon.' We shared in his joy, and kept our faces with just the right amount of smile on them. All morning Sandy was in a ferment of excitement, wondering about the car's colour, what her top speed would be, how much she'd do to the gallon, and so on.

'It's just as well your holidays are nearly over,' he said thoughtfully, 'for being a sports job, there's only two seats. I'll need to take just one student after this.'

He was like a kid with a new toy, and we let him ramble on while we laughed behind our hands. What an April fool! He rushed through his cases to be free for the great expedition of the afternoon, when suddenly, in the car mirror, he spotted the two in the back seat sniggering surreptitiously. He liked a joke, and he asked us to tell him this one. We did, thinking ourselves pretty smart that we'd been able to keep it going so long. The car stopped with a screech of brakes and Sandy went crimson, then a deathly white. He was furious and really tore into us, which we deserved. He demanded to know who had made the call, and his wrath fell on me as I tried to curl up and look insignificant. Suddenly, we saw the thing for what it was: a rotten trick which had gone sour, and caused this man, whom we all respected and who had gone out of his way to help us, a lot of embarrassment. He had apparently rung his bank immediately after the 'garage' had called, and had arranged an overdraft. Students can be exceedingly thoughtless and cruel, and even with the passing of the years, I felt – as I deserved to – very bad indeed about it all. His anger soon passed, but clearly he had been deeply hurt.

So I still felt uneasy, sitting in that room where he had so often sat, and remembering all I owed him. He had even taught me to drive! Sandy was now a vet with the Ministry of Agriculture – a reluctant Ministry man, for he loved general practice. But it had almost cost him his life. Giving a horse a pill, or bolus as it was called — 'balling a horse', to the farmers — his hand had been badly gashed as the horse clamped down on him with its back teeth. He'd given the wound a dab of iodine, and then had gone on for a few days, calving and cleaning cows, lancing abscesses, paring horses' feet — all the day-to-day tasks of the profession. His wound became infected, a raging septicaemia developed, and in hospital, even with the new wonder antibiotics, his life hung by a thread for days, and his convalescence was slow and frustrating for him. His illness had illustrated the vulnerability of a vet in a single-man practice. All was well when you were fit, but there was just no time for illness or even regular holidays. So he'd advertised the practice and sold it to Len Simpson, and had taken a five-day-week job. I'd seen practice with Len once or twice, and while his style was quite different from Sandy's, he too had taught me much. As my course at college drew near its end, he increasingly gave me my head in cases. Now he was entrusting his practice to me for a fortnight, and I appreciated that, especially as there would be a wage at the end — my first pay!

The day slowly dragged on, with lunch providing a break from the monotony of the *Record*. I yawned my head off, and reconciled myself to the fact that in my first day on the job I'd done nothing. I wondered if this was some kind of record, when I was roused from my reverie by the phone. I couldn't believe it was a case, but it was — a cow with a torn teat at Mid Brockloch. I glanced at my watch: five o'clock. Oh well, better late than never.

It might have been a torn teat; I couldn't say, for we never found the teat. Where it had been was a great gaping hole in the udder, big enough to put your fist in, and pouring out a mixture of milk and blood. In fact, the dung channel ran red with the flow from that huge wound, for not only had the teat gone, but a great strip of udder skin was flapping about as the cow moved its legs. I kept my head down and looked at that wound for a long time, to allow me to get over the shock and think. Never before, or indeed since, did I have to cope with such an udder wound — and to think that all day I had been longing for trouble of some kind! Well, I'd got it now, big trouble. This was being thrown in at the deep end with a vengeance, and I was trying madly to think how to swim!

'How did this happen?' I asked, trying to gain a few more moments to think.

'She tried to jump a barbed-wire fence,' said Mr Barclay.

He was a quiet man and an excellent farmer,

one of the most respected men in the district, a church Elder, and would seldom criticize anybody. He had known of me since I was a wee laddie and must have realized that I was just very recently qualified, but he'd received me with his customary quiet courtesy as if I was some famous consultant who had come to treat his cow, and indeed had apologized for troubling me. Peter the dairyman had joined his boss and me at the cow, and had heard the explanation of the accident. He gave me the whole story.

'It was a young collie I'm training that chased her, the stippit dug. The beast's only a week calved, and just about our best milker. I hope you can dae something, veet.'

I hoped so too, and looked at Mr Barclay with added respect. Most men would have been cursing their dairyman and his dog, but no word of reproach had he uttered. He looked at me now, and said, 'I know it's a bad wound. I can only ask you to do what you can. What will you need?'

I shook myself from the mental paralysis which had seized me, and realized that this man of vast experience was awaiting the orders of a mere novice. At another time I'd have enjoyed this new position of power, but, truth to tell, that ghastly wound had so shaken me that I just wanted to crawl away.

'I'll need lots of hot water, soap and towel, a rope and two strong men.'

'Right,' said Mr Barclay, 'I'll get Bill the ploughman to give us a hand. Peter, leave the milking for now. The cows can wait.'

The dairyman nodded and departed to get the necessities I had listed.

'Bring a halter, too!' I called after him. 'Now, Mr Barclay, let's see where we can cast her — somewhere reasonably clean.'

He led me to the hayshed. 'Will this do?'

'First-class,' I nodded. 'Let's just make a good soft bed of straw for her.'

We did, and in rapid succession the dairyman's wife arrived with water, soap and a snowy white towel, Bill the ploughman came with a long rope, then he and Peter brought the patient, leading her with a struggle on the halter, to our improvised operating theatre. Meantime I'd laid out suture materials, needles, disinfectant and a great roll of cotton wool in gleaming white trays on top of some bales of straw. The trays wouldn't be white for long, I thought.

I'd never actually cast a cow myself before, but I had assisted often; fixing the ropes in Reuff's method around the cow, I told the men to pull. She went down exactly as the book said she should. That was encouraging. Soon we had her hind legs pulled forward, and she was trussed up like a parcel. I splashed disinfectant liberally into the bucket and started to clean the wound. I had only just cleaned away the outer crust of dirt and semi-congealed blood, when a great spurt hit me in the eye. Two large vessels were sticking out of that hole and were pouring blood. You could easily grip them with your fingers and temporarily stop the flow. I did not know what damage I might be doing to the udder's blood supply, but these big vessels simply had to be tied off.

'I don't remember seeing such a bad tear before,' said Mr Barclay.

'And I hope you won't again,' I replied.

'I admire you men, the way you can stand up to this kind of thing,' he said. He evidently couldn't hear the thunder of butterflies' wings in my stomach, and the cow's blood must have given me a nice ruddy complexion I didn't possess. I was slow, painfully slow, but then it was my first suturing. It had all been done on dead greyhounds at college, and they don't bleed! The flapping skin was first stitched back where it belonged. The hole was a different problem.

'I'm afraid I can't do much about where the teat was, Mr Barclay. I can only try to make the hole smaller, but the pressure of milk will be bound to keep it open.'

I put twenty-two stitches in her, puffed some

antiseptic powder over a now dry and reasonably neat wound, gave her a shot of penicillin, and said cheerfully, 'Right, you can take the rope off and let her up now.'

Sixty seconds later my cheerfulness had disappeared, for as the cow lurched to her feet, Peter's dog galloped out from some corner where he'd been lurking. The cow kicked up her heels, broke into a trot, and bang went half my sutures. There was an almighty hullabaloo, shouts from Mr Barclay and his men, and a weary moan from me. It didn't help now that the byreman had caught his dog and was kicking it round the yard. We'd to catch the cow, cast her again, and re-clean and re-stitch the wound. At last it was done – I'd been one and a half hours on my first case.

'Keep her in the byre for a few days, and I'll see her tomorrow . . . and keep that dog out of the way.'

So it was done. The first case was over. As I drove home I reflected that one thing about going in at the deep end was that you had to learn to swim mighty quickly, and were unlikely to be so shocked again.

The next day I cleaned the Polquhirter cow, and as he held the cow's tail the byreman remarked, 'I heard about that job you did at Brockloch yesterday. Sixty stitches, I was tellt!'

I modestly protested that that was a bit of an

exaggeration, and marvelled at the speed of the bush telegraph in the country. It appeared that others had heard too, for I was kept quite respectably busy for the next fortnight and the Brockloch cow was a frequent opener of farmers' conversation. It seemed that 'the student or something' had been accepted. The cow did fine and the wound healed without infection. On my last visit, Peter the dairyman grinned and said, 'She's the quickest cow to milk in the place. As soon as I put the teat cups on her, the milk just pours out that quarter in two minutes. You've got to be gey smart wi' a bucket to catch it. We use that milk for feedin' calves.'

One thing the case did teach me, a lesson I've never forgotten: never look at a phone or it might ring and do a Brockloch on you!

3

Growing Pains

'You'll have to stich it,' said the boss, holding out a hand encased in a dish-towel which was getting bloodier by the minute. 'We've phoned every blessed doctor in the place and they're all either on holiday or out and can't be reached.' He took the towel off his hand to reveal a badly gashed thumb, blood welling up in it and dripping to the floor, at which sight his wife fled, saying, 'I can't bear to look!' I felt like fleeing after her!

'I couldn't do that.' I quailed at the thought. 'I could drive you to the hospital. It's only ten miles.'

'And sit in Casualty bleeding like a stuck pig for two hours? No fear!'

'But I've done hardly any suturing,' I wailed. 'Besides, eh, er . . .' I paused helplessly, and he grinned and said, 'And I'm your boss so you feel on a hiding to nothing. Come on, Alec, I'm asking a lot, but you can do it.' He plonked himself down in a chair and said, 'Get busy!'

Then followed one of the most harrowing half-hours of my life, yet one of the most momentous of my vet career. I cleaned the wound, soaked it with ethyl chloride local anaesthetic, and, forceps in one hand, needle in the other, began. He jumped as the needle went in, so I said, 'Sorry,' and applied more ethyl chloride. Painfully slowly, I sutured his thumb, which was cut along almost its entire length. He must have felt it plenty, but said not a word except at the end, 'Well done,' as I finished tying on a bandage. I noticed there were beads of perspiration on his forehead, but they were nothing to the rivers of sweat running down my back. Never, I'm sure, did two men welcome more heartily the cup of tea that arrived at that moment.

The next morning he greeted me with the news that he'd been to his doctor the previous evening, and the Doc had said, 'A first-class job,' and had given him an anti-tetanus shot. I don't know whether the doctor said any such thing, and daily I waited for the boss to appear with his arm in a sling and say he had the beginnings of gangrene, or for his wife to inform me one morning that he'd been carted off in the night with blood poisoning. But no, it healed perfectly . . . and from that moment I was trusted with almost any kind of case. It was a sticky start and not one I'd recommend to any budding vet, but there's no doubt it was a turning-point in my career.

I'd been Mr Buchan's assistant for some weeks before 'the case of the boss's thumb', but all I'd had to do were very routine jobs – S19 injections in calves, cleaning cows, and all the cat work. He reckoned I couldn't do much damage with the first two, and the cats didn't matter! Mind you, I could understand his attitude. He had come into an almost dead practice some years before, and by his hard work, youthful vigour and modern methods had built it up to the point where it was too much for one man and barely enough for two. But it was still growing, and he reckoned that shortly it would keep two men fully occupied. Ian Buchan's clients had come to him because he was a good vet, and strong personality that he was, it was not going to be easy for him to trust another with his clients, or for the clients to accept anyone but himself. The position had been made worse by the one assistant he'd had for a few months – my immediate predecessor – who, by all accounts, had been a disaster. 'Pansy', 'cissy', 'dreep', were some of the words I'd heard used to describe him. I'd only met him once and could understand the epithets applied to him. A city-bred lad (which could have been forgiven), with long hair, foppish ways and superior manner, he had, to put it mildly, failed to impress the hard-headed farmers of Ayrshire.

Typical of the stories told me, no doubt by way of warning, concerned Mrs McQueen and her pigs. That worthy woman conducted the young vet round to her piggery, where he gazed vaguely and dreamily into the pen in question, and then took out his comb to sleek back his long hair. Mrs McQueen suggested he might like a mirror, to which he replied, 'Thank you all the same, but I'll manage.' The pigs' owner had then asked him if he knew anything about pigs, and he replied, 'Not much,' whereupon, being a woman of bold speech, sterling character and bulging muscles, she ran him off the farm.

So it appeared I'd succeeded a very bad vet and had come as an assistant to a very good one, certainly where farm animals were concerned. The two facts combined to explain why I had my cases hand-picked for me – that while the boss did eight cases, I was given two, and consequently spent much of my time making up stomach mixtures, scour powders, bloat drenches and the like. When the shelves were groaning with about a year's supply of the various remedies, I was given a supply of Westerns and a comfortable armchair to while away the weary hours. Many boring days I'd put in just sitting in the surgery (which was in fact an annexe of their bungalow home), the hours brightened somewhat by the appearance at regular intervals of Mrs Buchan with tea or coffee.

I told myself this was only to be expected, that these were merely the growing-pains of becoming a vet, and that eventually things would change, but they were not changing quickly enough ... till the thumb! During some of my colleagues' initiation into practice they had been rushed off their feet, while my gripe was that I was getting next to nothing to do. However, for a week the boss was limited in what he could tackle, and I had to fill in for him. It seemed as if that agonizing half-hour we'd shared had altered my position completely, and gained me his confidence. In that week, amongst other things I treated two milk fevers, calved three cows, including an embryotomy (where a bloated dead calf has to be dismembered inside the cow by means of a fine wire like a cheese wire) – an operation I had been dreading. Also in that week, I cleaned my first mare, at Mr Anderson's farm at Garpin. He patiently held the mare, and though he said nothing, I suspect he knew this was my first. It was with considerable satisfaction that I ran my fingers between the placenta and the wall of the uterus, and peeled off the placenta in one piece. I laid it out on the ground afterwards and saw with relief the 'pair of breeches' shape that had been described at college, with the warning that if we didn't have that, we'd left a bit behind, which in a mare (in complete contrast to a cow) could produce metritis and death in a short time.

But if I'd come good, at least to some extent, with my boss − though I still regarded him with an awe akin to fear − it was a different story with the farmers. I found there weren't many Mr Andersons about, either in courtesy or confidence. There was nobody like Mr Buchan to the farmers, and when I appeared on their farm their faces perceptibly fell. They would inquire if Mr Buchan was ill or away, and had I seen anything like this case before? It wasn't calculated to boost one's confidence, and the position was made more difficult by the fact that I'd gone to the local Academy with the sons and daughters of some of them. My parents still lived in the area, and in a little town like Mochrum ... well, 'a prophet hath no honour in his own country', so what hope was there for a vet?

But bit by bit, with a few cases under the belt on each farm, one came, at least, to be accepted. Mind you, there were many growing-pains to be endured, difficulties to be over-come. Attending a cow at Merkland one day, I diagnosed an impacted rumen (the first of a cow's four stomachs). I knew various stomach drenches would do the job of starting it churning over again, but that Carbachol would be quicker. So I got out my syringe and injected a few cc's into the cow's neck, and closed my case. The farmer continued to glance at me expectantly. Finally he asked, 'Are you no' goin' tae drench her?'

'No need now. That injection will do instead.'

He treated me to a look of withering scorn, and demanded, 'Hoo can a jag in the neck get tae a coo's stomach?'

'Give it twenty-four hours and you'll see,' I said, fingers crossed.

I looked in next day and he greeted me with a huge smile, and took my arm to conduct me up the byre. 'Man,' he said, 'that jag fair did the trick. There's a barrow-load o'dung ahin' 'er. See!' He pointed, and we both stood admiring as if it were gold!

One or two farmers were openly hostile. Many had pedigree herds of Ayrshires or Aberdeen Angus, most were first-class farmers, and the majority had some knowledge of the various diseases and their treatments; they tended to phone up and ask the vet to come and inject some particular drug, and you had to be mighty sure of yourself if you deviated from their stated orders.

Old man McNulty was like that. He was an obnoxious man, with a vile tongue, a cynical outlook on life and a superior air towards his fellow men. He seemed to think that he was doing the vet a considerable favour by calling him, and he should note that fact! My first brush with him was sticky. It happened to be afternoon milking-time when I walked up the byre, and I was looking round about me for signs of human life when a loud, gruff voice demanded to know, 'Who the hell are you, and where do you think you might be going?'

I told him I was Mr Buchan's assistant, and I'd been sent to see a sick cow. He didn't look at me – he looked through me, and, jabbing a finger in the air, announced, 'When I send for the veet, I expect the veet, an' no' a boy' (I was twenty-four!) 'just learnin' the trade at my expense!'

I explained that Mr Buchan was away at a calving case, and he couldn't cover all the work himself.

'Well, he kens damn fine to come himsel' to me' – which seemed either to imply that he was some close buddy of the boss or had very precious beasts indeed. I'd been sent to do a job, and I was going to try to do it, so I asked, 'Could I see the sick beast now I'm here anyway, Mr McNulty?'

'Och, it's no seeck, it's stawed – it just wants

a bottle o' your glucose. That's her, second frae the end.'

A 'stawed' cow in Ayrshire was a case of acetonaemia, very prevalent towards the end of winter, when beasts had been housed for six months and stall-fed on concentrates. I took her temperature. The old man spat derisively (it was soon apparent he was a spitting addict) and asked what I was playing at. I ignored him and took her pulse. Both were slightly above normal. I caught her by the horns and smelled her breath; there was acetone there all right, but I had a vague uneasiness about her, and wasn't satisfied that the acetonaemia was the prime cause of her going off her food. She had a pained look about her, back slightly arched, elbows pointing outwards. I gave her a poke just behind the diaphragm and got a decided grunt. The old man, meantime, was alternating between cynical laughter and derisive spitting at my antics. He really was a shocker!

'I'm not sure but there's something more than acetonaemia,' I said.

'And I'm telling you she's stawed! Get the glucose into her!'

'Oh, I'll do that all right, but I'd like to put the cintel on her.' (The cintel was our metal-detector: earphones and a sensitive diaphragm that picked up the presence of any ferrous metal — foreign bodies, as they were termed —

which might be lodged in a cow's stomach. At Glenafton we had, in fact, made do with an old wartime mine-detector.) 'I think she's got a wire or nail in her.'

'Damn the fear o' it!' he answered.

'I may be wrong, but I'd like to see what Mr Buchan thinks.'

'Well, see he comes himsel', an' disnae charge me for twae visits.'

The boss was just back from his calving when I walked into the surgery. I told him of old man McNulty and his cow.

'I'll nip up with the cintel after tea,' he said. 'Away you home and get yours and don't worry about either McNulty, father or son.'

So I departed for home, three miles out in the country where my father was stationmaster of two small railway stations. My times off-duty were strictly limited to Friday evenings, and one weekend a month. Otherwise I was on duty at the surgery, or on call, which meant I had to be by a phone. The summons came about eight. 'Rumenotomy at McNulty's; come and give me a hand,' said the boss.

In those days, when straw and hay was held in bales by wire instead of string, and in an area where there were principally wire fences instead of hedges or dykes, a foreign body was quite common. Indeed a rumenotomy was the 'in' operation of the time. What happened was that the cow, a non-selective feeder, would scoop up a piece of wire or a nail in hay or grass, and this would make its way to the reticulum or second of the four stomachs and there would sometimes – but by no means always – cause trouble. A long list of unusual objects, including an umbrella frame, had been found in cows' stomachs, many of these foreign bodies only being discovered at slaughter, apparently having caused no discomfort to the beast. The only unusual object, apart from nails and wires, that we'd so far found was a sixpence, which was causing no trouble, but which had some bits of wire for company, which were. Anyway, the sixpence was better in the vet's pocket than the cow's stomach! Symptoms of the presence of a foreign body only occurred when it was actually lodged in the wall of the reticulum, and causing pain and sepsis. But the real danger was that a fall, or some violent muscular effort like calving, would force the metal right through the reticulum and diaphragm, and into the pericardeum (the sheath surrounding the heart). Many a sudden death in an apparently healthy cow was due to the object reaching the heart itself, the distance between reticulum and heart being a matter of a few inches. A rumenotomy was only successful when the foreign body was still in the stomach and could be removed. If it had passed into the chest cavity or pericardeum, it could not be reached and the cow was doomed.

I drove with the boss up to the farm where the whole squad was mustered – the old man, who neither looked at me nor spoke to me the whole night, the son, who briefly nodded, plus two farm labourers, who were still human enough in that sour farm to raise a smile of welcome. The rumenotomy proceeded normally; an opening was cut in the cow's left side (under local anaesthetic), the contents of the massive rumen were removed and carted away in a barrow, and then, reaching through the incision in the rumen wall, the vet searched about in the reticulum for whatever he could find. The boss nearly always did this part of the proceedings himself, and in this case, after a few moments, he gave a grunt of satisfaction and brought forth a three-inch nail.

'It was through almost right to the head. A few more days and we'd have been too late, Mr McNulty,' he announced, and went on: 'In fact we might still be too late, for that nail may already have set up a pericarditis – that's an inflammation round the heart. But with a bit of luck she'll be all right.'

Old man McNulty was examining the nail feverishly, running it round in his hands, holding it up to the light. In fact he did everything but test it with his teeth. I think he'd have liked to have accused me of planting it, but that being impossible, he rounded on his two workers.

'Damned carelessness, you lazy devils! One of you must have left that lying when you were fencing. If that happens again, I'll have your hides and then it will be doon the road for the pair o' you.' He meant he would sack them, but with his choice of words I had a picture of two skinless men walking down the road, like something horrific from the realms of science fiction. In fact old McNulty was horrific enough, with a face as black as thunder, and the oaths spilling out of him like an overflowing sewer. He was the kind of man who must always have someone to blame.

'Well done, Alec,' said the boss as we headed away. 'I'll charge the old rascal double for doing the operation after hours. He insisted it be done tonight. You should have seen him when the old cintel started buzzing. He nearly had a fit, swore for five minutes, and then demanded that I do something right away. You made a good job of the suturing, by the way.'

I appreciated that. Having got the nail out, he had very pointedly told me to stitch her up to show that he at least had confidence in me, even if McNulty hadn't.

'Och well, I did my practice sutures in a nice tender skin!' He grinned.

A few days later we had another rumeno-

63

tomy, but the atmosphere and circumstances were totally different. For a start, it was at Willie McCulloch's farm, and that meant we were welcomed warmly, for Mr and Mrs Buchan and the McCullochs were very friendly and socialized together. Willie was a gentle, canny soul who would seldom speak ill of anybody. He had a droll manner, and having been endowed with a rather long face by nature, when he had the cares of the world on his shoulders his expression was positively lugubrious, not unlike a friendly bloodhound. Mr Buchan had told me that when the McCullochs' child, now a growing boy, had arrived, the baby had cried more or less solidly every night for two years! Father and mother took night about walking the floor with him, and on one occasion Mrs McCulloch, at her wits' end, appealed to her somnolent spouse, 'What will I do with him?', to which she got the weary reply, 'Throw him out the window!' However, Willie had survived the rigours of parenthood, though it was maybe significant that they had but the one child.

It appeared that often a deal of leg-pulling went on between Willie and Mr Buchan, and on the occasion of the operation the boss decided to play a trick on Willie. At the appropriate moment when he withdrew his arm to clean and re-soap it before the search in the reticulum, I was to slip him a great long, thick spike, something like a tent-peg in appearance, which I duly managed to do without Willie spotting me. The boss played up well, muttering to himself as if perplexed, and finally shouting explosively, 'Good life! What have we here?'

'What is it, Ian?' demanded Willie excitedly. 'Have you found something?'

The spike was slowly and solemnly brought forth and handed to Willie, whose large eyes opened another couple of inches while his face fell another foot, making him look more than ever like a sorrowing bloodhound who has just seen his quarry escape up a tree. It was some time before Willie found speech.

'Would you credit that! Nae wonder the beast was no' weel,' he pronounced at last. The boss had meantime turned his face cow-wards and was guddling about in the reticulum, while I discovered I had to bend over the bucket for some time and slowly wash my arms, each thus successfully managing to hide our humour, for Willie's expression would have made the dourest mortal laugh. A piece of wire was found – genuinely – and removed, and the boss could hide his joke no longer, for in truth the situation had become solemn.

'I'm sorry, Willie, we had you on. There was just the wire,' he said.

It was some time before this dawned on

Willie, who was still gazing awestruck at the spike. 'So it wisna' this at a'?' he finally managed.

'No, Willie, it was the wire,' said the boss, 'and though I'm not certain, I think, Willie, that's just a bit of it, and there's another bit already broken off in her chest. Keep your fingers crossed.'

Stories should have happy endings, as most authors would agree, but in real life it is not always so. In this instance old McNulty's cow survived, while likeable, friendly Willie's beast died a few days later; which maybe supports the old Scots maxim that 'the de'il's kind to his ain'!

4

'Go and learn to be vets'

'Go out now from this college and learn to be vets,' our Principal had said to us as we left with the letters MRCVS after our names. We had smiled at his paternalism: 'Dear old boy . . . learn to be vets, indeed . . . what does he think we've been doing for five years? . . . we *are* vets . . . we know it all now.'

So youth, in its innocence or arrogance, has always answered. But after some months as an assistant vet in a general, mainly farm practice, the words had come back to me and hit me smack between the eyes. Every week I was realizing there was a very great deal still to be learnt. Much I was learning from watching my boss at work. Some of it I was finding out by trial and error, and getting away with it. A great deal I was learning the hard way. The growing-pains were still mighty sore at times.

The boss came in chuckling one morning. 'You know wee MacFarlane down the road at

Blackbyre?' he asked. I nodded. 'I was out there at a milk fever this morning and as we were coming out the door he stopped and pointed up at a beam in the roof. "Do you see that?" says he. "Do you think I could reach it?" "Never," says I. "Oh well, I reached it last nicht," he told me.

'Seemingly he and his dairyman had just come out to start the evening milking, when the bull came at them. He'd broken his chain, and you know he's a treacherous brute. Well, they both turned and ran for the door; the dairyman got there first and slammed it behind him. So, with the bull breathing down his neck, MacFarlane jumped, caught the beam, and sat there looking down at his bull glaring up at him and pawing the floor. Eventually MacFarlane walked along the rest of the beams which go on into the next byre and got out the door there. It was some jump, Alec. It's amazing what you can do with a bull at your back.'

He paused, lit his pipe, then went on. 'I mind when I was blood-testing the herd at Dalwhinnie − I don't think you've been there yet − but the couple there have a wee boy who's a mongol child. They've also got a notorious bull. The wee fellow didn't like me "jaggin' his coos," so he walked away saying, "I'll get somebody that'll sort you." He did too, for he came back leading this big brute with a piece of binder cord through its ring. He led him right up the byre to me and said, "There he's, Jock – get him." I looked round for the farmer, and he was already up on the milk pipe out the road.'

'What did you do?' I asked.

'Stayed put where I was, between two cows where the bull couldn't get at me. The farmer spoke quietly to his boy – but still hanging on to the milk pipe, mind you – and at last the boy went away, and that bull followed him like a pup on a lead.'

'How do you account for something like that?'

'I don't know, Alec, but I think it's just that these kids don't know any fear, and the animal senses it. Take Spike' (his springer spaniel). 'You know how he'll let nobody get in the car unless I'm there?'

'I know fine; he nearly took the hand off me the other day when I opened the door.'

'The only person who ever got in there without me was wee James McKendrick.'

'And he's a mongol, too.'

'He is, and the first time I was on the farm, I said to his father he'd better keep James away from the car or Spike would go for him, but the old man shook his head and said, "I don't think the dog would touch him." "Well, you don't know Spike," says I, and off we went to the byre. When we came back, James was sitting in the car and Spike was licking his hand. I was flabbergasted, and asked his father how he had known the dog wouldn't harm him. He told me that one day when he came into the farm close, he couldn't find James. He looked about and saw the stable door open, so in he went, and there was James actually standing between a horse's front and back legs – and that horse would let nobody but a certain ploughman near him, not even McKendrick himself. "Animals don't hurt James," was all he said.' He paused, puffed at his pipe and reflected, then said, 'Maybe there's something in the saying that there's a special Providence that looks after drunk men and helpless bairns!'

I thought about those stories as I set off on my morning round. I knew plenty about Ayrshire bulls. As a boy I'd spent a lot of time going about farms and I knew of several instances where bulls had attacked their owners, in two cases actually killing the farmers. I made a mental note again to tread warily when around bulls. But pigs now, they were safe. Or so I thought as I drove into Applegrove, a bonny wee farm run by two sisters. I had been told that the patient was a pig about six weeks old, one of a litter of eight.

I rang the farmhouse bell, got no reply, so

walked round the buildings shouting: 'Hello! Anybody about?' I couldn't find a soul, so went looking for the patient and came to a pen with a sow and seven piglets. 'Aha,' I reasoned, having 'O'-level maths, 'I bet the patient's the one that makes eight. It will be lying in the house.' It was a typical pig-pen with a concrete exercising yard and feeding trough, and the pig-house built on to it with a low door for the pigs to get out and in. There was another door round the back, but it seemed to be all blocked up; so I jumped into the pen and crawled through the wee low door, my black case in my hand. Sure enough, there lying on the straw was a piglet. He wasn't all that sick, for as soon as I'd inserted the thermometer into his rectum he hollered loudly, there was a great snort from outside, and in came mother at the trot, mouth open, heading straight for me. She had a fine set of teeth, and she evidently meant to use them. I leapt to my feet as she took a snap at my leg. She missed, but only just, and got a mouthful of corduroy trousers. She stood looking at me, as much as to say: 'The corduroy is just for starters, now the main course,' while I eyed her, fending her off with my case.

I licked my lips and glanced around nervously. The proper door was blocked up with bales of straw, and I wasn't going to turn my back on that wild beast to remove them. I sort of sidled along the wall towards the low door

I'd come in. The sow sidled along too. It was stalemate, and for some time we just stood and watched each other, neither of us liking what we saw. When I thought her eyes wavered just a fraction from me towards her offspring, I made a sudden dive for that door and crawled through it. No rabbit ever disappeared down its burrow quicker than I exited from that pighouse. I didn't stop to look behind me, but with coattails flapping and black case bursting open, I leapt the wall. I just made it too, as she came after me for another tasty bite. Evidently the first taste of my trouser leg had whetted her appetite. I was vaguely aware of a figure standing before me as I jumped. It turned out to be female, and it was bent double with laughter. I assumed — rightly — that this was one of the Miss Wilsons, and she was having the best laugh she'd had for a long time, it seemed.

'Miss Wilson?' I inquired, with a sort of 'we are not amused' note in my voice. She nodded, and then laughed some more, her large, well-padded frame quivering like a jelly. 'If you'd seen yourself . . . ha, ha, ha! A vet six feet tall jumping a wall, chased by a wee pig; oh . . . ho, ho, ho!'

'She nearly had me, too,' I said in an aggrieved tone. 'Look at my trousers!'

She did, sobered up, and then said, 'That will teach you, young man, never to molest a piglet when its mother is about.'

It did; ever afterwards when handling babies that were likely to squeal, I made sure there was a good stout door between the sow and myself.

Yes, some things were learnt the hard way, like being too casual, even with seemingly quiet animals. Just finishing a herd tuberculin test, at the end of a hard day, I came to an obviously ancient beast, with great spreading horns. Thinking her quiet, I got a bit too near her head and she came round in a flash and caught me on the jaw with the base of one horn, sending me staggering into the middle of the byre. Cassius Clay would have been proud of that left hook. I honestly thought my jaw was broken, but though it felt like it for days, apparently it was only bruised.

Being too confident was just as risky as being too casual, I discovered. I'd gone to McNulty's to inject a cow for foul in the foot, known in Ayrshire as clit-ill. For some reason, McNulty seemed to get a lot of it. It was summer, there wasn't a man about the place, but Mrs McNulty told me I'd find the cow in the byre, the only beast there. I'd injected many beasts before in the mammary vein, but if the animal was hale and hearty, in full possession of its faculties, as this one was, I usually got some-body to push the beast's tail straight up or have its nose held, both traditional means of restraint. Today I just boldly went forward, flutter-valve on the sulphamezathine bottle at the ready, and stuck the needle into the vein. The next moment I was flat on my back in the middle of the byre. I'd never even seen the foot come up, but I sure felt it. Getting kicked by cows, or having one's toes trodden on, was an almost daily occurrence, but that was the father and mother of all kicks. She looked round to see the effect of her nifty back-heeler, then went on chewing the cud, satisfied she'd done a good job and had given, in the old man's absence, a typical McNulty welcome. I searched round the byre for some time before I found the needle, shuddering to think what the old boy would say if a further rumenotomy disclosed a hypodermic needle. Taking a clean one from the box, I injected the drug subcutaneously behind her shoulder, a safe position half-way between horns and hind legs. I didn't know whether the drug was effective this way, since it had always been given straight into the bloodstream before, to hit the bug hard and produce a knock-out blow, emulating the cow's style! Apparently it did work, so that was one fact I'd learnt, and — more important — never again to attack the mammary vein of a fit, unrestrained cow.

What with the risk of contracting brucellosis, anthrax, rabies, psittacosis, mange, tapeworms and a host of other cheerful things, I was finding that my profession was somewhat hazardous. But it was fascinating too, and as I bumped along the side-roads of my native county I was learning all the time and was content with my lot. I was even learning how to handle the car I'd been given. It was an ancient Standard whose back springs were gone, so that cornering produced a decided tilt, a horrible rubbing sound and the smell of tortured rubber. In fact, it was not unlike the motion of a ship, and to add to the nautical illusion there was a regular splash of water. Just above my head was a hole in the roof. I kept it stuffed with a rag, and when it rained, which it does quite a lot in Ayrshire, I'd become expert at rolling down the window, pulling out the dripping rag, squeezing its excess moisture out of the window and stuffing it back in the roof, all with one hand, meantime keeling my torso sufficiently far over to prevent the rain pouring straight down my neck through the unguarded hole. It gave one a new slant on the passing scene, and made driving interesting! The boss was impatiently waiting the delivery of a Land-Rover, when I would fall heir to his Ford Prefect. Meantime the Standard staggered on.

Compared with the old Austin at Glenafton, however, my car was positively hale and hearty. We had a visit from my friend Mike, who had gone as Mr Simpson's assistant at Glenafton, and he arrived with a roar one evening to see us, driving the same old car in which I'd learnt to drive and which I'd used when acting as locum. It was now in such a state that it was in line for being declared a disaster area. I wondered why Mike came out the passenger door, until I saw the intricate arrangement of string and wire keeping the driver's door still attached to the body. There was a hole in the floor which no doubt helped ventilation but provided a water hazard from beneath. To start the car, Mike laid a brick on the accelerator pedal, cranked the starting handle like mad, then leapt into the driver's seat, removed the brick and replaced it with his foot. If he didn't manage this without the engine stalling, he had to begin the brick work all over again. Apparently the brakes, long suspect, had now all but given up the ghost.

Mike enlivened the evening by telling us some of his experiences in his brakeless car, chief of which was an occasion when a bus drew into a stopping place to pick up the waiting passengers. Coming in the opposite direction was a car, and just behind the bus came Mike, hauling like mad on the Austin's handbrake, which slowed him sufficiently to allow him to swerve on to the footpath and nip out in front of the bus, to the astonishment of passengers and driver. Yes, in those days before MOT tests for a car's roadworthiness, there were as many dangers to the budding vet just driving to the farm as awaited him when he arrived. I suppose it all came into the category of learning to be vets.

The days were full of interest and incident, with new cases and the occasional new client. Came the day when I gained one. Mrs Buchan came through from the telephone looking extremely worried, and not for the first time I realized what a strain was imposed on the wife in a practice which could not afford a receptionist/secretary. It seemed that Mr Wallace had a cow which had choked on a potato and was badly swollen with the build-up of gas. He had phoned for his own vet who was miles away and unable to be contacted, as was Mr Buchan. Now, Mr Wallace was an important man in the area, being an employer of many men, but he also farmed. So I could understand Mrs Buchan's anxiety when she asked me if I could come out, and if I knew what to do. I knew all right, but didn't tell her I'd never seen, far less treated, a choke before. However, after throwing a probang, trocar and cannula into the car, I hurried at the Standard's full rate of knots to the farm. I was received somewhat suspiciously by Mr Wallace himself. He was used to experienced vets, and I could read the doubt in his glance as to whether this young fellow knew what he was about. The case was fairly desperate; the cow was badly bloated and on the point of collapse. I got the long probang over the beast's throat and gave the potato a few taps, but it was stuck fast, and the animal was ballooning by the minute to bursting-point.

'I'll have to stick her,' I said.

'I think you will,' he agreed.

So, recalling from our college lectures how to work out the spot for stabbing the rumen, I tried, and only then realized how tough a cow's hide could be. I couldn't get the trocar through the skin, so had to use a scalpel. The cow never felt it; she was in too much agony in other ways, liable either to float up into the air or explode in our faces, it seemed to me. The skin cut, I plunged the instrument in, withdrew the trocar, and, like a dam bursting, the gas came hissing out of the cannula. When she had reached reasonable proportions again I had another go at shifting the potato, and with the inside pressure now considerably reduced, it went first shot into the stomach. Mr Wallace looked at me and said, 'I bet you were sweating the first time you had to do that.' I smiled and agreed that I had been, omitting to tell him this was it.

When I got back, the boss cross-examined me on the case. Clearly he had been hoping to get a foothold in the Wallace establishment for some time; he was obviously pleased, and said so. This helped to increase his confidence in me, it seemed, for soon after that he began asking me which cases I'd like to do. He phoned one evening shortly afterwards, and cheerfully announced I could take my pick between lambing a ewe in a blizzard of snow up the hills at Greenwell, or driving twelve miles to treat a mare with colic. I knew which one I preferred, but thought it prudent to say, 'Whatever you like.'

'I'll do the lambing, then,' he decided – which I had hoped he would, for it really was a perishing night. The colic proved to be quite a violent one, with the mare sweating, and kicking every few minutes at her abdomen. I listened, and could hear plenty of gurgles and squeaks; in fact I reckoned there was about as much wind inside her as even now would be blowing round the boss up at Greenwell. However, to be certain there was no twist, I did a rectal. All seemed straightforward – an ordinary flatulent, spasmodic colic, treated with a jab of pethidine, followed by some Carbachol. Fairly quickly the pethidine brought relief; I felt that she could safely be left, and that during the night there would be sundry explosions coming from her rear, and by morning, a good load of dung.

The weeks and months sped past, full of interest now. Except on that precious Friday evening off, it was strictly duty. However, if there was nothing pressing I could stay at home in the evening and have any calls relayed. But one day the boss decided it would be a considerable asset to have a few kennels in a small brick building at the top of his garden, so for some time there were few evenings off. I'd never been a bricklayer or plasterer before, but the kennels shot up in no time — it's amazing how quickly you can work just in order to keep warm! With two of us working, and with only a small number of kennels, the boss was able to encourage the small-animal side of practice, something he'd wanted to do for a few years. An evening consulting hour was started, the first boarders arrived, and dogs could be kept for a couple of days after whatever surgery they had undergone. Small-animal operations were always done in the evenings; sometimes it being ten o'clock before we were able to start. The boss initially did all the surgery; I was anaesthetist and general factotum. I thought him a good surgeon, and certainly he was with farm animals. Comparing him with Kenneth later, Ian was not in the same class in the field of small animals — but in relation to both of them, I was a complete dud. My fingers were all thumbs, and my general surgical technique left a lot to be desired.

I recall the evening when the boss told me to spay a cat, and he would assist. A simpler operation can hardly be imagined, and I'd seen him do a fair number. With my patient safely anaesthetized, I made my incision, and poked about looking for ovaries and uterus. I kept finding loops of small intestine, but no uterus. I looked at the cat again to make sure it was a female, then enlarged my incision and groped and guddled some more. Finally, with sweat blinding me, I said to the boss with what dignity I could muster, 'I think there must be something abnormal about this cat. Maybe you'd better do it.' He took over and found ovaries and uterus immediately. So much for my abnormal cat!

This business of learning to be a vet could be humiliating, as well as dangerous. I had my failures, too, on the farms. Twice I'd had to admit defeat at calvings, which went against the grain, but those were both great big, ugly bulldog calves, an abnormality certain strains of Ayrshire threw up occasionally. In each case, I'd had to ask the farmer to phone the boss, and felt very small indeed when he managed to complete an embryotomy where I'd failed. In both cases, he'd tried to console me by saying, 'It was a right stinker!', but needless to say, this didn't help my reputation with these particular farmers. Having learned that danger was part of my profession, seeing this man at work made me realize that dedication and sheer determination were also necessary. I pledged myself after that second defeat that henceforward determination would be part of my make-up – and so it became. Many, many times there at Mochrum, and in the years to follow in Devon, I was on the point of giving up at a calving, having lain on my side and had each hand and arm in turn numbed by the pressure of the calf on them, pinning them to the pelvic bones. More than once I felt like saying, 'Phone for Mr Buchan,' if only to get relief after maybe two or three hours' hard labour – but sheer cussedness kept me going. I'd learnt to grit my teeth and fight on, and gradually, over the two years there, I came to be accepted by all but a few farmers and there would be a welcome 'Hello, Alec!' or 'Good morning, Mr Cameron!' It felt good. The apprentice was gradually becoming a tradesman – but now and again something would turn up, knock the pins from under you, and cut you right down to size. There was one particular instance, and it was horrific.

Now that we had the kennels, if a client turned up with a dog through the day Mrs Buchan would sometimes put it in a kennel till one of us came in. This particular morning I arrived, and was told there was a labrador in kennels, to be destroyed. For some reason, the boss liked to use a humane killer for large dogs. The gun was one of the captive bolt type and I hated it, but an assistant has to do as he's told, so I went into the kennels with the humane killer, brought out a handsome-looking labra-dor, held him firmly by the collar, put the weapon to his head, and pulled the trigger. At the very last moment he jerked his head, let out a howl as the gun went off – then he was off, and I was left with his collar in one hand and a smoking gun in the other. I'd forgotten to make sure the outer door was properly closed, and he was out, down the drive and away. It was horrific, for I knew the bolt had broken the skin and drawn blood. As white as a ghost, I'm certain, I ran after him, weapon still in one hand, collar in the other. He was headed for the town, and had anyone been about, very likely they would at once have phoned the police or the nearest lunatic asylum, with a wild-looking man charging about the place with a gun. Fortunately there was not a soul on the street; equally fortunately, I had been told the dog's name was Rex, so hollering 'Rex . . . Rex . . . Here, boy' I kept going and, miracle of miracles, he eventually stopped at the sound of his name. I slipped the collar back on him, tried not to look at this poor beast with a small hole in his skull spurting blood, then took him back to kennels, shut the door and finished the job. I had to grit my teeth to do it, and felt the biggest rotter in creation. That trusting dog had stopped at the sound of his name, let me lead him back to a place of terror – and there I'd betrayed his trust. Ugh! I must have looked pretty ghastly when I went in the surgery door, for Mrs Buchan asked me what was wrong, and I told her the tale. She also said 'Ugh!', then poured a strong cup of tea. Later in the day, the boss cornered me.

'I've been hearing about your experience this morning, Alec,' he said.

'I made a right mess of it . . .' I began, but he interrupted.

'Now, I've been meaning to talk to you about this. You're far too careless in these kennels. You must always shut the outer door, as I do.'

I nodded dumbly.

'We can't have escaped dogs running all over the town. It will give the kennels a bad name . .' Especially when they have a hole in their head, I thought. 'Don't you agree, Alec?'

'Yes . . . oh yes, I'm sorry. It was sheer carelessness.'

'Well then, we'll say no more about it.'

A few mornings later, as I was heading towards the surgery to begin another day's work, I met the boss driving furiously down the hill that led to Mochrum's shopping centre. A pretty urgent case, I thought. I got into the surgery, hung about for a time, and finally Mrs Buchan came through and said that I should just make a note of where I was going, and carry on.

'Ian isn't here,' she said. 'He was taking the dogs out of the kennels this morning to exercise them, when three got away from him. He might be some time.'

He might indeed, I thought, searching the town for three runaways.

'How did it happen?' I asked ingenuously.

'He didn't stop to tell me,' she answered, truly innocently.

No word was spoken about the runaways, but I knew, and the boss knew I knew — he'd forgotten to close the outer door!

Yes, this learning to be a vet could be a long process, I thought.

5

New Beginnings

'Mr Cameron,' a lass said to me the other day, 'Brian and I are getting engaged a year come the first of June, on my birthday.'

I had a quiet smile to myself at her earnestness, but when she had gone, I sat at my desk and thought back over the years. That girl seemed part of the modern way: you fix your engagement in advance. It seems so matter-of-fact, so staid, so planned, so apparently lacking in romance.

My mind went back over the years to a bright summer day in June. Janet and I had gone to the Heads of Ayr for a swim, a picnic, an afternoon away from the grind of veterinary practice and teaching maths. On the way back up over the hill to the car, as I watched her swinging on ahead of me, I suddenly realized I could not live without this girl any longer, and there and then asked her to marry me. Her eyes sparkled, she drew a great, deep breath, a smile seemed to engulf her whole being, and she said, 'Oh yes!'

Mind you, it was to be expected, even if the culmination was unplanned and unrehearsed. We had known each other for seven years; we had 'gone thegither' since our later years at school, ever since I spotted this lass with the dark mass of hair, the sparkling green eyes and the warm figure in my father's junior choir at the local village church where he was organist. I walked her home from choir practice, and after that first night we walked many miles, for without cars, with no money, most of our courting consisted of walks to the Grove, beside the river Doon, or cycle runs up into the hills. In due course the village took notice that Janet Morrison and the stationmaster's son were 'gey weel acquaint'.

In time, Glasgow University claimed Janet to study for an MA, while I went to the old Glasgow Vet College. She stayed with her aunt in Paisley and I travelled the forty-five miles to the college each day, but there were stolen moments when we would meet in the Mitchell Library, watching out for 'the Gestapo' – the attendants who prowled around and sternly commanded you to stop talking. Eventually she graduated, and in those halcyon days when there were jobs aplenty she immediately got a post in the Academy at Byneton, and I started as assistant at Mochrum.

Now we had a car between us, and occasionally I could plan my afternoon round to meet her at four o'clock at Byneton. On my one evening off in the week, Friday, we usually went to the ice hockey at Ayr . . . a precious few hours together in our busy lives. We had no money because neither of us was well paid, and we both felt we ought to pay back some of what our parents had given us, for in the forties student grants were non-existent or very small. My mother, starting with six hens, had built up a veritable poultry farm of hens, ducks, turkeys, geese and guinea-fowl, just to see her three sons educated.

We still had no money on that shining day at Heads of Ayr, but we wandered up Ayr High Street wrapped in our own dream world, walking on a pink cloud, looking in furniture shops and deciding what we would have in our own home. (Some of the articles we haven't got yet!) The sun often shines on the Ayrshire coast, but never did it shine more brightly from a magically blue sky as on that glorious day. One week later we bought the ring and all was official. My father thought we were rushing things . . . after seven years! But he was fond of Janet, as was my mother, and they gave their blessing. In a state of extreme trepidation, I approached Mr Morrison and asked for leave to marry his daughter, and to my profound relief he raised no objections. I left with my legs trembling, but my heart singing.

Now something had to be done about the future. I was not overpaid at Mochrum at £10 a week, and although Ian Buchan dropped occasional hints about a future partnership, there was nothing concrete. More important, much as I respected him I felt I could not happily work in partnership with him for the rest of my life. I would always be very much the junior; and, having had a Church upbringing, and at the considerable risk of seeming 'holier than thou', I felt that if I was going to enter into a *life* partnership it should be, if possible, with a more kindred spirit.

So I advertised in the *Veterinary Record*, and – wonder of wonders – in a few days came an offer to come to Bristacombe and discuss a possible partnership there. It was March, one of the busiest months in the vet's year, but Ian gave me a weekend off and, none more Scottish than a Cameron, I set off by train for the foreign land of England. I was met at Bristacombe station by an enormous individual and a very small one – Major Kenneth Davidson and a student, Tom Atkins.

We had a short drive to Chade Lodge, I was shown to my bedroom, and then, to my utter surprise and some embarrassment, this strange new acquaintance dropped to his knees and prayed that we would be guided as to our future. My Scottish reticence was a bit shocked, but this was my first experience of a man who was to mean a very great deal to me, a man to whom prayer was as natural as breathing, a very unusual vet in a not notoriously godly profession . . . a man to whom his Lord was a constant companion and friend.

It was a hectic weekend. Before that night was out (and I had arrived about seven), I had seen several cases and watched two caesareans in sheep, one operation performed on a farmhouse kitchen table, the other on a 'table' of straw bales with a hanging Tilly lamp for light. I was astonished at the dexterity of this large man — and somewhat fearful, for we had never done a caesar at Mochrum. Late at night, Kenneth produced sheets of paper showing the takings and outgoings of the practice for the last three years, and I performed a creditable piece of acting in pretending to understand them, for I had never seen a balance sheet in my life. Before the weekend was over, and in a dazed state, I had agreed to become a partner — an act of sheer audacity, because I possessed barely £100 in all the world. So we talked of bank loans, life policies, insurance brokers and other mysterious and quite unknown matters to me, and in a whirlwind I departed from Kenneth and his wife Susan and headed back north. I was due to start in May – a partner in the practice of Davidson and Cameron.

Janet was delighted at the news, my parents were pleased for me but sorry I was going so far away, and Ian Buchan thought I had fairly landed on my feet. He seemed genuinely sorry to lose me, and perhaps for the first time came out clearly and said I would have had a partnership there in due course.

I lodged with Kenneth and Susan and their three young sons for three months, and I needed that time to adjust to a totally new experience, almost a new culture, and a different kind of farmer who spoke a strange language. For weeks, phone calls needed an interpreter as I could not understand the Devonian dialect, and the Devon farmers found my Scots tongue equally bewildering. The farmers' names for diseases were different from those used in Ayrshire, and every bovine seemed to be 'he', whether male, female or neuter. I remember holding the telephone away from my ear in total astonishment when asked to go and see 'a bullock bad to calve'.

I learned much in those early months, just watching Kenneth at work, for he was a fine vet, a good diagnostician and a magnificent surgeon, beside whom I was a bungling amateur. I also learned that his faith was the mainspring of his life, and while some of his clients pulled his leg and others shared his beliefs, all respected him. Every day before afternoon surgery we would meet, compare notes on cases, read a few verses of the Bible and have a short prayer. In time my embarrassment and awkwardness gave place to a very real admiration, and some of the naturalness of Kenneth's faith became mine. He tried to run his practice as a genuinely Christian concern, right down to the moderate charges for the new, wonder antibiotics for which many vets, having a monopoly of them, were charging extortionate prices. We were very different in personality and background − he was a colonial, born in Kenya, the product of a public school, a former major in the Indian Army, a man of substance, a big man in every way − while I had grown up in a council house, gone to the local school, and was as ordinary as it is possible to be. Yet we were one, bound together by a common bond, not just as vets but as brother Christians.

My brother Fergus came down to Bristacombe to share the long drive north for the wedding, in those days before there were any motorways. A few days later, on 15 August, with two bridesmaids and my twin brothers Graham and Fergus as groomsmen, Janet and I were married in the little village church of

Maryshall, where we had first met and where week by week we had worshipped. I remember little of the wedding; I was in a state of nerves and ignorance as to procedure, not having had a rehearsal or even seen a minister. I just knew I had to say 'I do' at some point, and duly managed to croak the words.

After the reception we took the high road north, spending the first night of our life together at Luss ('Glendarroch' of the famous Scottish soap opera), then on to Morar with its white sands, and finally to beautiful little Plockton, which we had both fallen in love with the previous year when we rented rooms from the Miss Montgomeries, two elderly sisters whose prayers in Gaelic filtered up to our bedrooms each night. That year we had required two rooms – now we were truly one – and the fact of having just one room must have made it plain we were a honeymoon couple; but with the good manners of Highlanders, the sisters made no comment. All too soon we were again heading south to Ayrshire, where the car was loaded to the roof with wedding presents.

We set up house in a four-room flat, which we loved for its beauty and peace. We had more furniture than we had expected, thanks to the generosity of parents and the kindness of friends. Our sitting-room was a bit sparse with one armchair and a tea-chest for the other, but our first home was a place of calm and deep, deep happiness. Janet continued her teaching and gradually I learned the way to all the various farms and holdings, of which latter there were many, for farming had not yet changed from the small family farms to the bigger units. We were still using a number of the time-honoured drugs, with the one great addition of the still-new antibiotics.

I learned much from Kenneth in those early days and gradually my dexterity as a surgeon improved, because from the beginning Ken treated me as an equal and trusted me to get on with the job as if I had been as experienced as he was. The practice was still at the growing stage, far too much work for one but barely enough for two, so, building for the future, I at first took just £6 a week from the takings and we lived on Janet's salary. Kenneth and I had great dreams of branch practices and expansion, and we were sure we would grow. This indeed happened; we soon opened two branch surgeries, but neither of us saw the final fruits of a veterinary hospital – five vets working together and several lay staff and nurses. We worked very hard indeed, and the seed was sown for future growth.

Right from the beginning, Kenneth tried to involve me in the life of his Church, the Church of England. So I taught in the Covenanters, a youth movement which was a Bible class for older teenagers on a Sunday, and a youth club through the week. My initiation into the first club night produced some pain and not a little mirth. It was a cricket night, and I was fielding at mid-on to the smallest boy in the club. He gently hit a ball in my direction, I got down on my knees to casually gather it, and at the last minute it bounced and hit me a whack on the nose, to the delight of the youngsters and the embarrassment of the new leader. Some fielder! I had a swollen nose for a time afterwards, which did not look too good on a newly married man!

As far as teaching was concerned, I was a novice. I had once, when I was a serious sixteen-year-old, taken the tiny tots in the Sunday School at Maryshall when my father couldn't be there. I took the task very seriously, prepared a talk on 'The love of God', and by way of illustration explained to the children, 'You know your mummy loves your daddy – they love you – you love your brothers and sisters, I hope; well, God loves you like that.'

'That's right, Mr Cameron' (Mr! I'd never been addressed like that before), 'my mummy does love my daddy. She sits on his knee!'

Embarrassment of one earnest teenager!

We worshipped at Kenneth's church, but although we did try for a time, we found the

Church of England with its liturgy so very different from the plainness of our Presbyterian Kirk of Scotland that we eventually joined Brookfield Free Church, whose worship was more like home. We were welcomed there by several young couples like ourselves, who, though no longer young, remain friends to this day. Ken was also in great demand as a lay preacher, and one day I walked in the surgery door to hear him say on the phone that he was sorry he couldn't come that particular Sunday, but he was sure his partner would. His partner was horrified, and terrified, having no ambition whatever to climb into a pulpit, but under the coaxing of my persuasive and powerful partner I did eventually go out and take the service, marvelling that a congregation could listen to one of such abysmal ignorance. I had no thoughts then of one day becoming a preacher, but the passing years were to change that and lead eventually from dog to dog-collar – from vet to vestry. Four of us in time formed a group and went out conducting services in North Devon's many picturesque villages, singing as a quartet (how those poor folks must have suffered!) and preaching, and three of that group eventually became full-time ministers.

So Kenneth Davidson not only taught me much as a vet – not only showed me the gladness of walking close to God (something I had first seen in another former major, Ian Thomas the evangelist, of Capernwray Hall, who greatly influenced both Janet and me in our teens and early twenties) – it was Ken who first set my footsteps towards the ministry, though he himself remained a vet. After three years together, he had the opportunity to return to his native Kenya as a vet, and we parted. His place was taken by Bernard Paterson, who had been a student with us, then my assistant, and finally my partner for the rest of my time in practice, and who still works away in glorious North Devon. That is, though, a leap forward in the sequence of this story, so let me get back in line. I owe much to Kenneth, more than I can ever express, and likewise to Bernard, who, though he was a totally different character – quiet, unassuming – but with the same sure faith, took Kenneth's place in every way. I don't believe I ever expressed my thanks to them and my indebtedness to them both, but perhaps if they ever read this they will accept a belated thank-you for our marvellous years together.

By the spring of the year after our marriage, it was clear a baby was on the way. We prepared for its coming with all the joy and anticipation of every young couple. Janet was sometimes far from well ... indeed had a rough time in pregnancy, but she was as uncomplaining as she has always been and buoyed up with the thought of the new life that was at the end of it all. Two days after our wedding anniversary, on 17 August, I ran her to the local maternity hospital and left her there; it was quite out of the question in those days for a father to be present at the birth, even though he was a vet who had delivered many young things and was not likely to faint at a childbirth. I returned from my visits – I had flown round in my excitement – to be met by a very agitated Kenneth, who told me the doctor wanted to see me. With sinking heart I visited the doctor, not knowing what his news would be, but certain it must be bad. The doctor was uneasy, and I've felt to this day he had a right to be uneasy. The baby had been stillborn, which of course still happens from time to time, despite our many advances. But the doctor had allowed Janet to go three weeks over her time, the baby was very large for a first, its heart had been beating fifteen minutes before the birth, but it had been lost in the delivery.

We mourned for our little babe, and comforted one another as best we could, with Janet, as always, doing most of the comforting. The baby was a girl, perfect in every way, and so much the image of her mother that she has been for ever baby Janet. It hurt deeply, and brought me face to face with the question that has been asked of me more than any other in my ministry: the 'why?' of suffering and sorrow. Even today, after more than thirty years, I can never see a little white coffin without a lump in the throat and a sparking behind the eyes. How much harder for my Janet . . . but time does ease the pain. Time also was to bring us four other children, all boys. Neil, Ian and David were all born in England, which fact, as fervent Scots, they have for ever been trying to forget! I did see David's birth and recorded his first cries on tape, threatening to play them over to them when he first brought a girl home! Of course I never did. The baby of the family, Alan, was born in Scotland while I was a divinity student. So we were deprived of our daughter, but have been blessed in four healthy, handsome and strapping sons.

Bristacombe was the scene of several new beginnings, and remains in our hearts always for its beauty, its olde-worlde charm, the warmth of its people . . . and as the place where an apprentice vet became a journeyman, and a journeyman vet became an apprentice preacher.

6

Kennel Capers

'Ow--ooo----ooooo! Ow---ooooo--ooo---oo! Ow---ooo − Wow-wow-wow-oooooooah!'

Thud! My feet hit the bedroom floor.

Bang! An upstairs window was flung open.

'Shut up, you noisy dog, or you'll be sorry!' − my dulcet tones floated over Chade Valley. This was the ritual almost nightly now in our lives. Gone were the days of tranquillity in that delightful little flat at Langleigh Farm, where Janet and I began our married life. The farm was just on the fringe of the town, nestling at the foot of the mighty Torrs, and sheltered as it was in its ring of trees it was a perfect haven of peace, a delight to come home to when the day's work was done and where no hideous cries disturbed the hush and stillness of night. The only sounds were the bleating of sheep grazing the Torrs, or the contented cluck of hens as they strolled about the yard. Periodically farmer Conibear's voice would be raised as he called directions to

100

his dog rounding up the sheep, and in the mornings before breakfast we would hear Mrs Conibear calling the hens to their feed of grain or mash. But these halcyon days lasted an all too brief eighteen months, and life was different now that we had moved to Chade Lodge. The reason for the turn-up in our domestic bliss was that the surgery premises we rented on the High Street, and the house above them, had come on the market, and Kenneth felt he ought to buy the property. This he did, and he, Susan and their family moved to the more commodious house above. Reasoning that if he was prepared to stay above a surgery, we should be willing to live beside the kennels, Kenneth had suggested we move into Chade Lodge, which he had just vacated. We could hardly refuse.

I had always associated the description 'Lodge' with a large property on a Highland moor, much favoured by Cabinet Ministers, American oil tycoons and the like from 12 August onwards for the annual slaughter of grouse, partridge, deer and the almost tame pheasants that abounded in these parts. Alternatively, I had pictured an attractive gatehouse at the entrance to some large estate, olde-worlde in appearance, with roses round the door. The only resemblance Chade Lodge bore to these other Lodges was that it had some roses in the minute plot of front garden with iron railings around it. The property was in fact a rather tatty, far from convenient, jerry-built house of brick and roughcast, erected by the local council for their abattoir superintendent. The rooms were tiny, the lighting was gas, and behind us stretched a mass of buildings, open yards and narrow passageways which had once been the local slaughterhouse but was now rented by us *en bloc* for use as kennels. Above us was a railway line, a spur or off-shoot of the main line, along which daily the giant West Country class locomotives came to let off steam, take on water and generally hang about till their time came to head back to the railway station, there to be linked to their great long line of coaches. Below us, at the foot of the steep-sided valley, was the little township of Chade, composed of new council houses and much older terraced dwellings, but now part of Bristacombe itself. So our days were made hideous by sudden explosions of escaping steam from the monsters above us, though in truth they were magnificent dinosaurs, and over the years we would get grins and waves from the engine driver and his fireman, who could look right into our bedroom windows.

Night brought a cessation of steam explosions, and it was then that some horrible canine, thinking that things had gone a bit quiet, would decide to bay at the moon or recite poetry to his fellow inmates, and rouse us and the dwellers in the valley below – seemingly on the principle that if you couldn't sleep, it was much cheerier to have someone awake with you. So nightly, as Kenneth had done before me, I bellowed at the brutes! He had early made the discovery, later seconded by me, that while a tone of sweet reasonableness was maybe all right for a dog in its home, it availed nothing with a howling hound in kennels. You simply had to shout louder than it. Generally the bloodcurdling threats I uttered had the desired effect as the beast got the message. But the crafty ones would wait till you were nicely tucked up in bed again, about to drop off – and then recommence their nightly song, with others readily joining in the chorus. Then feet had to be shoved into slippers, a dressing-gown or coat thrown on, and with set face and fixed purpose I would have to enter the dark kennels, locate the culprit if possible – not always easy, for very quickly they could look like a class of innocent children when the teacher whirls round to spot the offender. If located, he or she heard my threats uttered at close range; if unlocated, they were all bawled out. If verbal reasoning failed, then one had to try manual persuasion, that terrible thing corporal punishment, now regarded as a grisly relic of man's barbaric past. If all else failed, the dog had to be sedated by injection – and a Mickey Finn slipped into his supper the following night, to avoid disturbing the lieges and being charged with a breach of the peace!

Broadly speaking, there are two types of kennels. There are those purpose-built as kennels, preferably situated miles from anywhere, and run for profit, by sufficient staff, as a board residence. Then there are the kennels which are an extra, an adjunct to a veterinary practice, useful for hospitalizing patients and boarding some dogs, but scarcely paying propositions. Ours were in category two. When first I joined the practice we had a kennelmaid, a girl who was crazy about dogs, and who happily spent the whole day there, cleaning kennels, playing games with the residents, clipping or stripping such dogs as required these forms of hairdressing, and generally keeping a kennel of contented canines. In a separate building were the cats, and these comfort-loving creatures had all the caressing and care a cat could crave. The kennelmaid did all this for a mere pittance. But alas, she left us for another, transferring all the affection so freely lavished on our delightful dogs and charming cats to some benighted male of the human breed! We couldn't replace her. We tried various part-time kennelmaids, at one stage even combining the post of surgery assistant with kennelman, but these experiments proved unsuccessful. We simply could not afford to pay anyone full-time, the kennels barely covering their cost as it was, with feeding, disinfectants, rent – and lozenges for my larynx!

So it came about that in addition to our normal duties, aided and abetted by Janet, Kenneth and I would take week about at feeding, cleaning, exercising the animals, and so forth. The cats were transferred to back premises of the surgery, more escape-proof than their former abode; more than one seemingly innocent feline had done a Colditz on us and 'gone away', making it a trifle awkward when the owner returned. When the mantle of night fell on the scene, the responsibility for keeping the peace was mine. Such was the vehemence with which I verbally assaulted these dogs, daily threatening to come and knock their blocks off, murder them, or generally cause life to be unpleasant for them, that I was sure I heard the words 'Shut up!' from our infant son in almost his first coherent utterance. This indeed was a sobering thought. Suppose he used the phrase to either of his grandparents, or treated the minister to his party piece? I can only hope that I was mistaken, for I'm certain that psychologists would unanimously declare that I had caused irreparable damage to a child's mind. Be that as it may, what is certain is that from a very early age he would sit in his high chair, and when the dogs were giving tongue in their premises would point an accusing finger in their direction and sternly order, 'Quiet, wow-wows!'

But we kept more than dogs at our kennels. In a steeply sloping one-acre field which ran parallel with the drive up to Chade Lodge resided Susan and Veronica, respectively Large White and black-and-white Wessex Saddleback sows. I was already well acquainted with them before we moved into the Lodge. Kenneth had his very new Triumph saloon, while yours truly had the antiquated van initially, so when either Susan or Veronica expressed a wish to visit their mutual husband who dwelt on a farm just outside the town, there was only one vehicle that could be used to transport them. From time to time S. or V., or occasionally S. and V. together, would be coaxed, cajoled and generally heaved into COD 330's interior, something that long-suffering vehicle had experienced many times before as it had often carried pigs of both sexes and all ages and sizes (albeit never the live kind, having in fact formerly been a butcher's van). I will always remember those hair-raising trips with pigs as my companions. No partition separated the driver from the rear of the van, and as there were no windows in the sides, naturally enough my passengers, eager to view the passing scene, would speedily gravitate to the front. Veronica was a good-natured creature, Susan a bit temperamental, so whenever a pig snout appeared over my shoulder to peer out of my side window I greatly trembled for the safety – even the future existence – of my ears: Susan was liable to sample any tasty-looking morsel she came across. We would not have covered any great distance on our trip before half a pig would be leaning over the driver's seat, so that it must have appeared to any onlooker that a pig was driving the van, an impression enhanced by the erratic, swaying course of the little vehicle if both pigs were present and lurching about with the movement of their carriage. I generally tried to make these trips in the early morning or latish evening, and I recall yet one half-awake worker stop dead in his tracks, rub his eyes and shake his head unbelievingly as he stared after a blue van driven by a black pig. Even more startling was the effect on a couple of revellers as they lurched their way homewards late one summer even, and gazed, mouths and eyes wide open as they held one another upright, at what appeared to be a bellowing van driven by an enormous white sow with a black one as a passenger. If that didn't make them hive off with all possible speed to sign the pledge, nothing would, I felt!

When not with their husband, the doughty pair dwelt peaceably enough in their little shed, grazed the field and produced their young, which we sold as weaners. There was little profit in pigs at the time, but they helped pay the rent. They might have been allowed to graze a few years longer had not the nuisance value of their transportation outweighed the profit after a morning adventure. It began with a knock at the door as I was having breakfast. There on the doormat stood one excited little boy, ably supported by a bevy of kindred spirits, of both sexes, in an arc behind him.

'Hey, mister,' announced our visitor, 'there's some little pigs running about on the main road!'

'How many?' I asked – a daft question, as if it mattered, but I'm not at my brightest, unbreakfasted. The spokesman said three, but his attendants quickly corrected him, in numbers varying, as far as I could make out, from one to thirteen. Clearly something had to be done about it, so accompanied by my self-appointed assistants I hurried down the field to the scene of action – readily spotted, since the rest of the gang were all there before me. In a couple of minutes all became clear, though it was to take much longer to correct the situation.

What had happened was that sometime during the night Veronica had felt her time had come to produce another litter. I suspect that she was turfed out of their house by Susan, always the boss, and probably in one of her moods. Now, the field was very steeply sloping indeed, and apparently the only reasonably level, sheltered and seemingly private bed Veronica could find was right under the hedge, which grew, Devon-style, on top of a wall, some ten feet above the main Chade-Bristacombe highway below. There she had given birth, and continued to do so, producing at regular intervals another little black-and-white minstrel. Since sows frequently take some time to deliver the complete litter, clearly the early arrivals felt they couldn't hang about for ever to see how many brothers or sisters they would have but had set about the immediate task of finding food, readily available from any one of the teats neatly arranged on Veronica's undercarriage for that very purpose. The trouble was that with her feet sticking through the hedge, it became a hazardous journey for the newly-born to find the feed trough! The easy way was to walk over mother, but on that already steep gradient her side acted as a shute, propelling her offspring out into the unexplored depths below, where they hung about waiting for something to happen. The craftier members of the litter somehow tip-toed their way along the top of the wall until, finding a teat, they hung on, some of them with their back legs dangling into space. This was the scene which greeted the douce inhabitants of Chade as they proceeded, the adults to work, and the children to school, and which provoked the representatives of the junior brigade to report to me.

It really was a spectacle! Below the wall stood a group of the little minstrels singing a harrowing song in soprano, or perhaps rather more falsetto, voices; above, our brainless sow continued to lie there, producing pigs periodically while, barnacle-like, a few hardy specimens clung tenaciously to her abdominal and thoracic appendages. To some of the onlookers, of whom there were a considerable number, it must have seemed that those piglets clinging to their mother's teats by dint of suction and determination were trying to pull her over the precipice to join the chorus below, while to the uninitiated it might have seemed that the little ones, sticking to their posts of duty, were in fact trying to blow her upwards to safety in the field beyond. Whatever view the public took, I didn't wait to inquire, for the scene was getting out of hand. The din was considerable – squealing pigs pursued by squealing children, the honk of cars seeking to avoid both parties, and the chatter of the ever-increasing crowd, some of whose comments I could make out as I gazed in awe.

'Look at 'em go – oh, there's another gone over!'

'Poor li'l ol' things!'

'Should have been in a house, poor beast!'

'T'aint right, ah tell 'ee. Enough fur the Cruelty man, vur zertain.'

Through it all Veronica lay blissfully on, grunting contentedly, though in time it must surely have penetrated even her thick skull that she was on an endless task. As fast as she produced pigs, these same pigs disappeared. That's what I proceeded to do – disappear fast – before the Cruelty man, the police, the fire brigade or any other body was summoned to the scene. The van was hastily driven down the road, and, assisted by dozens of children having the time of their lives, I tried to round up the now scattered minstrel chorus and pop them in the van. The two remaining 'barnacles' were removed and pushed in front of Veronica's snout; and my poor wife, using these two as bait, proceeded to shoo the lady of the moment to her shed, where she was reunited with her offspring, or most of them. For all I know, some family in the Chade housing estate had roast sucking pig for supper that night, but we still had a fair number, and Veronica seemed well content with her brood and with a job well done. That was the last straw. I felt vets and their wives couldn't be regularly collecting piglets from the public highway, so a few weeks later, with some relief that was nevertheless tinged with regret, we bade farewell to our two sows as they departed for the market. Our pig-farming days were over.

But we had also at the kennels a motley collection of feathered and furred fauna. The former were hens, 200 of them of different breeds, which I kept in the deep-litter system in a large shed. Since a lad, I'd always known hens about the place, and they were a decided source of revenue with a nice tidy profit – if you forgot the hours spent daily in washing eggs. As well as giving me endless pleasure in sitting of an evening watching them, they gave us some extra cash with which to equip our home with what we regarded as luxuries, but what certainly in today's world would be considered necessities. After having electricity installed in the house, the poultry profit provided a brand-new electric cooker to replace the enormous gas monstrosity we had purchased at a saleroom for £5. I recall yet the pleasure the purchase of that new cooker gave us; it was virtually the first new article we'd bought for our home since we'd set up house with £150 between us, and a flat half furnished by wedding gifts. Night by night we'd examine the cooker lest any hint of a scratch should mar its shining surface, stroking it almost as though it was a family pet. Ah me, the simple pleasures of yesterday! Next we managed a fridge; then, with the family growing, a washing-machine; then a real luxury, a tape recorder – all furnished by courtesy of our feathered flock, and all still in use today, very many moons later.

To extend the hours of daylight in their house we installed Tilly lamps set to go out at a particular time, and quite frequently, after a long day in the practice, it would be very dim or even dark when I went round the nest-boxes to collect the eggs. I collected more than eggs one night. Reaching into a dark laying box, I very quickly withdrew my hand with a howl. I'd been well and truly bitten by a rat, either an old one or a sick one, that had been enjoying the comfort of the hay. It slithered out, eyed me malevolently as if I'd bitten it, and slowly disappeared. The wound, in fact, required hospital dressing and the usual tetanus injection. This act of aggression was the opening shot in a war that raged ceaselessly thereafter. Rats produce the same reaction in me as snakes and stoats do – a kind of quiver that starts in the soles of the feet and progresses upwards till the hair finally stands up 'like the quills on the fretful porcupine', as P. G. Wodehouse put it. For other dangerous species like bulls and boars I had a healthy respect, but not this shiver of fear induced by creatures of the night or beasts that seemed to flow rather than walk. So war it was! If our feathered friends gave us endless pleasure and profit, our furred kennel-dwellers produced a smouldering anger and periodic frenzied activity.

There were rats on the railway embankments, and of course the presence of any dog-food brought them into the kennels at night. Going in with a torch, one could spot them speeding up pipes or disappearing down drains. The poultry, with their easily available food and warm, deep bed of moss litter, attracted still more. Of course we tried the Pest Control Officer, but with so many dogs around he could not use poison readily, and there were too many exits to use traps effectively. Clearly, if there was to be any action it had to come from us. Regularly of an evening, father, mother and the two under-fives, Neil and Ian, would sally forth to a rat hunt; our first two offspring, it seemed to me as the months passed, had some terrier blood in them somewhere. We would all don wellington boots, tuck trouser legs into stockings, and wear gloves. I was armed with a large garden fork or spade for digging pur-poses, while the rest of the army sported long sticks or shovels. There was a surprise diver-sion one evening when Mum, who kept her boots in a shed at the back door, eased her feet into them. She suddenly leapt skywards, and to the infinite amusement of our senior boy, Neil, aged four, gave a very passable demonstration of a Zulu war dance, complete with yells. It was only when she succeeded in kicking off her boots and one somewhat dazed rat staggered out that we learnt the reason for the antics. Mercifully she had not been bitten, but ugh! ... even to step on one of the squirming brutes! Then we would proceed in formation to the deep-litter house, and while father dug out the obvious tunnels, mother and children would guard the escape routes. Those brown rats which escaped my weapon were enthusiastically chased by the family with loud yells, shouts and the thump of descending sticks, all to a deafening background of cackles, cries and fluttering from the poultry. Our record kill was thirty-nine in one night. We never completely mastered them, only kept them within bounds, but in the process we probably completely ruined our sons for life, what with yells of 'Shut up!' and 'There he's; hit him!'

But, of course, kennels are the dwelling places of dogs, and our inmates came into one of three groups:

1. Those in for hospitalization, generally following surgery.

2. Boarders from the local populace or visitors.

3. Dogs under sentence of death, and kept by

us for the RSPCA.

Strictly speaking, dogs in this last group should have been kept for only a week, and if unclaimed, destroyed – something I was most reluctant to do, for while occasionally we had a genuine stray, the majority were poor creatures which had simply been turned loose by uncaring owners, quite often when their dog licence fee of seven and sixpence was due. So, because of the good offices of the local RSPCA secretary, a very large, florid, but gentle woman, we came to an arrangement that we would keep these dogs almost indefinitely for virtually the cost of food, while weekly in the local press Mrs Gorman would insert an advertisement: 'Good homes wanted for labrador, sheepdog cross, corgi type', etc. etc. I suspect much of the total cost was met by this generous woman from her own funds, just as after some years she insisted on donating a portable X-ray to us, which proved a considerable boon.

The dogs in group 1, the hospital patients, seldom stayed long enough to become characters or personalities – except one, a lovely boxer bitch called Paula. She had been a boarder on a previous occasion, and I was very surprised to find her in kennels one evening and to be given the message that 'she was in for a spay and would be collected in ten days'. I thought it a crying shame to sterilize such a pedigreed beauty, but dutifully did the deed. In ten days her owner rolled up in his large car to fetch her. We went into the kennels and he asked, 'Why has she a bandage on?'

'Oh, it could come off now really. We just left it on to keep dirt out of the wound.'

'Bandage . . . wound . . . ?' He looked at me, completely flummoxed.

'Yes, it's usual for a few days after surgery,' I replied, equally flummoxed.

'Has she been ill, then?' he inquired.

'We-ell, not ill. Just a bit quiet for a few days. That's usual after an op.'

'Operation for what?' he persisted.

It was becoming increasingly obvious to me that our lines had become crossed, and equally increasingly I feared what would be revealed when the tangle was unravelled.

'The operation you asked for, the spay, the sterilization,' I said guardedly.

He looked at me a long time, at least thirty minutes, I'm sure! Or so it felt before he snapped, 'I said no such thing!' I couldn't really blame him for snapping; I'd have bitten in the circumstances.

'Well, Mr Mooney, I'm very sorry indeed, but the message I received was that Paula was in for a spay and would be collected in ten days. If something is amiss, I can only apologize.'

'I said she was in for a *stay* – and would be collected in ten days.'

He was a well-to-do hotelier and could afford a dozen pedigree boxers, but that was beside the point. Paula was his pride and joy, he'd planned to let her have pups, and we'd ruined his plans. I must say he took it astonishingly well, for she was a really lovely animal. I suppose he might have sued us, but he didn't. It was a genuine telephone-message mistake, and he did have a rather quiet voice. Needless to say, there was no charge for either spay or stay! He even forgave us, and boarded Paula with us again. I suppose he reasoned that we couldn't do any more damage.

Many of the second group, the boarders, were regulars year after year, and sometimes several times a year. Some owners even reserved certain kennels, and the majority of their pets settled in reasonably well to communal life. Many were surrounded by favourite toys or rubber bones from home, and had their own basket and favourite rug. With many came hints that Fifi, or Charles, or Boko, was particularly partial to sweet tea, or a leg of lamb, or a stout at bedtime, and that darling Mimi could never sleep till she'd had her goodnight cuddle. Cat-owners would be even more fussy, as a rule. I remember one owner insisting that her pussy would eat nothing but pancakes, and then only if newly baked. We duly noted all requests, and fed the dogs on biscuits and meat, the cats on meat, fish and milk. To comply with all demands would have required a resident chef! We had one privileged, regular boarder, a pekingese called Chota. Our kennels were really designed for larger dogs, and since most yorky, pom, or peke owners 'couldn't bear to be separated from the little darling', we had few lapdogs to cosset. Chota was an exception. In a weak moment I'd said we would keep him in the house, so in the house it always was, until he recognized it as a second home. I had never been a peke-lover before, largely being put off by peke owners. But with Chota I gained a real admiration for the intelligence, resourcefulness and particularly the courage of the lion dog of Peking. He was a grand wee chap.

One day his owner phoned to say that Chota's right eye had come out of its socket, and what should she do? She was told to bring him right in, and we prepared the surgical kit just in case, though frankly I was skeptical. We had been told at college that if the dog was shaken sufficiently hard by the scruff of the neck, a peke's eyes could, in fact, pop out. But neither in my student or assistantship days had I seen this, nor had I ever met any other student who had. It would be a blood clot, or maybe a bad gash in the cheek at which the poor lady could not bear to look properly – or so I hoped. One glance at Chota as Mrs Kerr walked in the surgery door confirmed that her diagnosis had been spot on. The eye was resting grotesquely on Chota's cheek. Mrs Kerr looked almost on the point of collapse, but assured me a neighbour was driving her home; we sent her off, took the little fellow in, and within minutes had him out of his world of pain, if only for a time. Mrs Kerr had told us before departing that she had been away all morning and had come home to be told by a neighbour that an alsatian had attacked Chota. Then the little fellow had disappeared. It was evident from this account that the eye had been displaced at least five hours before, and the amount of swelling confirmed this. I vaguely recalled that the surgery book had indicated that, if treated in time, it was sometimes possible to replace the eyeball in its socket; we could but try.

As usual, Mrs Drury, our efficient assistant cum secretary, was unflappable, as if eyes lying about were an everyday occurrence. She watched the anaesthetic, and from the other side of the table was ready, as always, to give me whatever instrument I might require. That I didn't yet know. I had, of course, removed a few diseased or badly damaged eyes before, but I confess I quailed before that eye, staring fixedly at me from its resting place on the dog's cheek, as if daring me to touch it while its owner was out for the count. But touch it we did, gently bathing and cleaning. Then, with plenty of antiseptic cream for lubrication, lashings of patience, and firm but gentle pressure, I tried to coax the eyeball back.

'He's coming round,' said Mrs Dru's voice.

'We can't have that; more Pentothal, Mrs D.' She moved to get it.

My normal form of anaesthesia for reasonably short operations was Pentothal (the so-called 'truth drug'), followed by a mask with ether–oxygen mixture to keep the patient at the desired depth of unconsciousness. But to fix a face-mask to a snub-nosed dog was difficult – to one with an eyeball lying on its face, impossible. So more Pentothal was put in a vein. I cannot recall now how long we worked on that eye. To hurry would be to damage it irreparably, yet every instinct was to put the horrible object back in its right place as quickly as possible. Bit by bit it yielded till, with a slight plop, it was back in its socket. It hardly could be described as a beautiful eye as yet, but at least it was an eye again, not a 'thing'. We packed the eyeball around with antibiotic and anaesthetic cream, then sutured upper and lower eyelids together to keep out all light and dirt. In ten days, in fear and trepidation, I removed the sutures and gently prised the eyelids apart — to reveal a squint to beat all others! But the eye was surprisingly clean and clear, and was reacting to light. Clearly one or more of the ocular muscles had been damaged, but I was sure Chota was seeing with that eye — even if all he could see was his tiny snout. Over a period of time the squint improved markedly, and if his two eyes never quite matched again, at least he had two functional ones.

Another regular boarder was Sandy, a handsome Staffordshire bull terrier. Now the Staffordshire can be a tricky customer to handle, because it is very much a one-person dog. Sandy lived for his master, and when master chose to leave him in these kennels Sandy would look at the world with a jaundiced eye, put his chin on his paws, heave an enormous sigh, and indicate that until his master returned he was prepared to put up with this existence, but certainly not to enjoy it. Towards the other dogs he maintained a degree of aloofness, but no aggression. He coexisted, and made it clear that was the way he wanted it. His frequent sojourns with us all passed peacefully, he was absolutely no trouble whatever, and he was a real character. All would have been well permanently, I dare say, had not a party of holidaymakers arrived one Saturday evening with their black cocker spaniel.

They had come on holiday to find their boarding house did not permit dogs, and so hastened to us to plead for boarding space. It was the height of summer, we were very full, but we made room. They were humble folk, and told us that they came from Wolverhampton, and that the dog was called Whisky. He proved to be a Grade A, Category 1 nuisance, a barker with a capital B. Fortunately for everyone's peace of mind, most days his owners took him off our hands to return him in the evenings, when he proceeded to bark incessantly at all and sundry, albeit wagging his tail as if to say, 'No offence, chums.' But it was apparent that Sandy had taken offence. I imagine he had told the new arrival to pipe down, and had been, from the safety of his strong, Sandy-proof kennel, told where to get off by Whisky. Nobody spoke to Sandy like that in any language; it was doubly insulting to his West Country nature to be addressed in the language of Wolverhampton! Sandy morosely brooded, and thought dark thoughts. During morning exercise one day, Sandy had a go at Whisky, who, not imbued with the spirit from which he took his name, fled for dear life. Fortunately the chase was spotted and Sandy restrained in time. But he waited, glaring and muttering threats at this upstart, who – brave as always in his secure kennel – barked back his abuse.

There came a day when Whisky's owners left him behind while they went on a coach trip. All was peaceful in the warmth of a Devon summer afternoon, thought Janet as she pottered in the little garden between rests in a deck-chair, for in a few days our next babe was due. Suddenly the summer calm was shattered by a growl, then a scream, followed by the barking of every dog in the kennels. Hurrying as fast as circumstances would allow, Janet went into the kennels. Somehow, Sandy had escaped from his pen, managed to get into Whisky's and had him pinned to the ground. The poor girl fled for the phone, to be told at the surgery that both vets were miles away in the country. She had it all to sort out herself. Hardly realizing what she was doing, she struck and poked Sandy again and again with the little garden fork still in her hands. She might as well have used a feather duster! The Staffordshire's hour of vengeance had come, he had the spaniel by the throat, and he was not letting go. Almost sobbing with fear and helplessness, the poor girl shouted 'Sandy!' – and, miracle of miracles, where the pain of the fork had failed to move him, the voice of command did. He left the spaniel lying, with a look that suggested 'that was just for starters, look out next time', and walked majestically back to his own abode and lay down as if nothing had happened.

Returning later to the surgery, I was advised by Mrs Drury to proceed with all due haste to the kennels. The battle was over. The spaniel had several wounds, but nothing that ordinary dressings wouldn't heal, while Sandy was sporting several deep puncture wounds. My poor wife had recovered from a state of near collapse, and could now look back and laugh. But it was no laughing matter. Without her presence, there would certainly have been one dead spaniel. As it was, I wondered what I would tell the folks from Wolverhampton when they arrived in a body to take their Whisky out for evening walkies. I told them exactly what had happened, and to my astonishment they were tickled pink. Whisky had never fought any dog before, they said, and when they saw the deep wounds he had seemingly inflicted on that terrible animal, their pleasure increased even more. I did not disabuse them as to Sandy's wounds. Their dog was a hero, head bloodied but unbowed. He was also a non-barker for the remainder of his stay! Sandy bore my wife no grudge; on the contrary, in retrospect he appeared grateful, and I was sure the grunts deep in his throat indicated: 'Sorry about that shemozzle in there; got carried away, what! But I couldn't stand the fellow. Just as well you stopped me when you did.'

Yes, we had our characters amongst our canine guests. There was the young St Bernard who came to be boarded for a fortnight, his front legs resplendent in full-length leather boots, which his own vet had recommended for a tendency to rickets – for, as everyone knows, a St Bernard with rickets would not be much cop carrying his barrel up Mont Blanc to succour some stranded mountaineer. We had another St Bernard, Carlo, who boarded with us for a year, a great, lolloping hunk of good nature. His owners had moved to London and it was a full twelve months before they could find premises suitable to have him with them again. Then there was Boris the borzoi. Like Carlo, he was with us a very long time (I forget now why; something about an owner going overseas), but there the resemblance ended. Carlo was everybody's friend, Boris nobody's. Carlo was one of the gang; Boris would not so demean himself. He was evidently a pre-Revolution borzoi, a real czar, who went about on his own every day from first to last, with his nose in the air. None of your proletarians for Boris! He didn't even sleep beside them, apparently preferring the side of the kennels which was seldom used and where he could keep his own company. I did not like the dog, but I was sorry for him. He reminded me of some European monarch, displaced from his throne and with nowhere to go.

But of all our characters, Cindy was the favourite. She was a gentle brown, black and white mongrel, with hints of spaniel, sheepdog and foxhound blood in her, and maybe a dash of some kind of terrier far back. She came to us as a tiny puppy, one of eight that had been found, with their mother, under a hedge, and rescued by the RSPCA Inspector. The mother made a good job of rearing her large brood, and quite quickly she herself and seven of the puppies had found good homes. One little one was left: Cindy. She grew, appeared regularly in the papers with the others in the 'Good homes wanted' column, but nobody wanted Cindy. She was nobody's child. She saw other waifs come and go, she would amble up to visitors and look up, but always they chose another. I could not understand it, for she was gentle, obedient, loving, with excellent manners, and was, in her own way, quite a character. Then she was taken − at last. She came back to us maybe nine months later. It had not been a good home, she had been turned loose, and in the time away had been thoroughly neglected. She had a beaten, hangdog expression, as had I when I saw her, for clearly she was about to become a mother any day. She produced her pups and, like her mother before her, proved a first-class parent, but in the process lost her figure. No home for Cindy now, I felt sure.

She was given the run of the kennels, for there was no fear of her wandering off. She came and went in and out the gate as she pleased, with her puppies behind her. One day I received an urgent call, dashed out to the car, reversed, and felt a sickening bump. One of her pups had been lying under the car, unknown to me. Cindy came over and licked her dead puppy; then her soulful brown eyes looked up into mine, she put out a paw as if to reassure me, gathered her other offspring around her, and trotted into the kennels to mourn in secret. All her puppies eventually found a niche in some home – only Cindy was left. She was the veritable queen of the kennels and would inspect every new arrival, and welcome it. But she seemed a tragic queen. We continued to let her roam, for she knew no other home and stayed around the yard. We'd had many a desperate chase after escaped dogs when some curious visitor or farmer looking for 'the vetenary' would wander into the yard when dogs were exercising, and forget to shut the gate. But Cindy never wandered. I would not put her down – I could not.

Then one day he came, Prince Charming

himself. He didn't have a white charger; he was dressed fairly roughly; but he was looking for a dog, and clearly, from his talk, he was a genuine dog-lover. He'd lost his last one, and wanted a replacement. His eyes wandered over a collie, a labrador, an alsatian, then stopped at Cindy. His face lit up. 'That's the one,' he said, and as if she knew it, Cindy stood on her hind legs to greet him. The stranger had at last come in from the cold.

The kennels were a bind, often a nuisance, sometimes a heartbreak, but when I saw Cindy go off into the new life with a real master, I thought of the joys we also knew with our dogs. Cindy never came back. She had no need to, not ever again.

7

The Consulting Hour

Every February and March in the town there was much blowing away of cobwebs, washing of bedlinen and splashing about of paint as Bristacombe prepared for its annual invasion of visitors. Being a seaside town with no industry, everything revolved round 'the Season'. Signs offering B. and B. from seven and sixpence to a guinea sprouted everywhere. Hotels that had been shuttered and desolate suddenly came to life, amusement arcades reopened, and in numerous curio-'Present-from-Devon'-shops, proprietors arranged their window displays with great care. Along the sea front and in the main streets where in winter every face was known, there now appeared thousands of strangers conversing with one another in the greatest conglomeration of languages and dialects since the day of Pentecost! The Season was Bristacombe's harvest time. If you didn't make money then – you didn't make money; if tradesmen's bills, including ours, were not settled then — they were not settled till next Season.

I knew that the town and its adjacent caravan sites were filling up, but as I passed our waiting-room for afternoon consulting hour one spring day, I knew without question that the Season was upon us once more, for the room was full, and half the customers seemed to be poodles. The poodle was the in breed of the decade. We had quite a few as permanent residents in the town, but the poodle population multiplied enormously with the coming of summer. I wasn't too fond of the breed — a nice enough and quite intelligent wee dog, but some a bit neurotic, like half the owners! The only dog I'd seen go completely round the bend had been a poodle, after producing a litter of pups. The strain of motherhood seemed to unhinge completely what brain it possessed, and though in a human mother post-natal depression was fairly common, I'd never heard of post-natal hysteria until seeing it in that poodle. The wretched little creature howled incessantly, an unearthly kind of screech that caused the occupants of houses within a hundred yards of the locus to talk of mass evacuation, or poodle-icide! We'd had to keep the dog under morphia, no less, for a week, all other tranquillizers or sedatives proving powerless against that appalling cry.

Sure enough, the first case that day was a white poodle, carried by a glamorous blonde. Though it was a warm day, she was sheathed in a fur coat, her companion dressed in a pink ribbon. I recognized the glamour girl as Tanya or Melinda or some such name, the leading lady of the summer show in the Pavilion. She had been here last year, too. In a voice so refined that I could only comprehend about every fourth word, she gave me to understand that Chi-Chi's blood seemed overheated and she was scratching herself more or less non-stop.

I looked at the dog's skin, then looked again more closely, an unholy joy taking possession of me.

'Where does she sleep?' I asked.

'Well, really she has her own little bed, but you know how it is – she usually cuddles in beside me.'

'I'm afraid she's got fleas.'

The flush started down the lady's visible skin – and that was far down. For all I know, it maybe began at her feet, and gradually engulfed her.

'Fleas! Really! You are most insulting! How dare you suggest such a thing! Where could she possibly get fleas?'

'Oh, from other dogs, or a chair – or her

bed.' I looked heavenwards till the full significance of my words sank in, and when I looked down again, instead of a faint flush was a deep crimson. The lady, it seemed, was not amused, but none the less, fleas it was, as I was able to show her.

'But don't worry,' I purred, 'just give her a shampoo with this. That should do the trick, but you can take this dusting powder too, and use it on her and any place you think they might be hiding.'

The lady was scratching now. Imagination is an amazing thing − and my imagination was working overtime as I pictured her shaking flea powder all round her hotel bedroom, and then dusting herself from head to foot before taking to the blankets that night.

'That will be two pounds, ten shillings, please.'

'Two pounds ten − that is scandalous for a shampoo and powder!'

'Oh no − they only come to ten shillings, with consulting fee. The two pounds is for last year's bill, which has not been paid. Perhaps it was not directed to you?' I smiled serenely.

She paid up unwillingly, then said in a husky voice, and with a languishing look of tender appeal usually reserved for Chi-Chi, 'You won't let this out, will you?'

I assured her our little secret was safe, and

so it has been, until now.

I understood the reason for the tender appeal bit, for the next customer was also from the summer show, and also a poodle owner. She was, I imagined, one of the chorus girls, and came clad in just the bare minimum allowable for appearing in the street. I didn't know what her stage name was, but as soon as she opened her mouth I recognized her place of origin. I grinned and asked, 'What part of Glasgow are you from?'

'Hill Street,' she replied. I told her I had been to the college in Buccleugh Street, which was next to Hill Street. We said 'Fancy that' and 'It's a wee world', 'Just imagine' and 'Would you credit that', then the lady informed me, 'We used tae see the greyhounds goin' in there, so we did, but we never saw ony come oot.' She was right, too. The penalty for being an unsuccessful greyhound was to end up an anatomy specimen in Buccleugh Street!

'I've just had another member of your cast in,' I told her.

'Och, aye — Tanya!' (or it may have been Melinda). 'She's frae Glesca tae.'

'No!'

'Aye!'

'She doesn't sound like it.'

'Maybe no' in here; she can fair pit on the ladi-da, but you should hear her when she's no' pleased — pure Gallagate then! Her richt name's Annie McGonigle. Me, a'm Mary Bell, but a'm jist in the chorus so a don't need a fancy name. Whit wis wrang wi' her dug? She said it wis its high breedin', that the bluid wis ower rich — wis that richt?'

Mindful of my promise, and of professional etiquette, I hastily changed the subject. 'And what's wrong wi' your wee dog?'

'Och it's jist his lugs — they're needin' a guid cleanin' oot.'

I peered in the ears with my auriscope; they were indeed needing 'cleanin' oot'. 'A lot of poodles get ear trouble,' I explained, 'usually just because the hair inside their ears holds the dirt or causes an irritation.' I cleaned them out, and gave her some drops to use on them.

She returned to her former question. 'Wis it really heated bluid wi' Annie?'

Remembering that lady's blush, I could truthfully answer, 'Something like that. Seven and six, please.'

'Ooh, is that a'? You're cheap! The last man a went tae took fifteen bob, so he did. Fancy you kennin' Hill Street. Aye, it's a wee world, i'nt it?'

As a change from poodles, next that day we had a shoe-box, borne carefully in by a little lady of maybe seven, who solemnly handed it to me.

'What's this?' I asked, lifting the lid. Inside was a great mass of cotton wool. Wondering what would pop up, I moved it rather gingerly — kids had all sorts of strange pets; maybe it was a lizard or grass snake. However, it proved to be a squirming mass of naked mice, hundreds of them — or so it seemed, though I suppose the number would be nearer fifteen.

The mouse owner was blinking up at me very earnestly. She smiled and revealed a large gap in her front teeth, through which she lisped, 'Pleath thir, my mummy mouth had baby mouthes, and could you pleath tell me the oneth that will be daddy mouthes and what oneth are mummy mouthes?'

This presented considerable difficulties. First there was the difficulty of picking them up, secondly the problem of marking males and females, and thirdly I didn't know anyway! I replaced the cotton wool.

'You come back in about six weeks and I'll tell you then.' Sexing mice, let alone newly-born ones, was an original request.

The wee hand was clutching a minute purse. 'How many pennieth ith that?' she inquired.

I grinned at her, and handed back the box. 'You keep your pennieth ... eh ... your money; that's all right, my dear.'

The next customer was a boy with a tortoise. 'It's got a sore eye,' he announced.

I peered at the beast. I was willing to believe him, but at the moment its head was inside the shell, and no eye visible. I poked at it and nothing happened. I knocked on the shell; it did not answer my knock. I hadn't at that time treated many tortoises, in fact the last one had been brought, not for treatment, but to be put to sleep. Its owner had rung up in horror to say that her tortoise had just come out of hibernation minus three legs, which had been eaten by a rat, and what was she to do. My wife had advised her to hit it on the head! Apart from the difficulty of such a feat, I'd had to administer a gentle rebuke that you didn't speak to clients that way. The poor creature had been brought in, and we'd chloroformed it and put it out of its misery. I remember initially trying to get its head out – though I hadn't tried hitting it on the skull.

'Look, son,' I said in my most professional manner, 'I think it will be best if you go back to the waiting-room, and my assistant will help me to do this.'

So, summoning Mrs Drury from her desk, I turned to her in the surgery and asked, 'Any ideas on how to make a tortoise stick its head out? What does Major Davidson do?'

For once, that mine of information was stumped. It seemed that Kenneth's and Mrs Drury's lives had been pretty well tortoise-free too, and so far as veterinary husbandry, surgical and medical textbooks were concerned, the tortoise had apparently not been invented when they were compiled. So, left to our own devices, we turned it on its back, tapped its shell with various instruments, and even tried gently to pull its head out with forceps. I was baffled, and picked it up off the table to consider the problem – when lo and behold, its legs came out, and its head. It seemed legs and head worked together. So we ended up with Mrs Drury contriving to hold the creature and pull on its legs at the same time, to keep the head from slipping back out of sight, while I had a look at the eye. It was a nasty conjunctivitis. With difficulty I managed to direct some eye ointment on to the general area of the eye, summoned the boy back, gave him the ointment and told him to insert some twice a day, as if it was the easiest thing in the world.

'You know, of course, how to get the head out?' It seemed he did not. 'You a tortoise-keeper, and don't know that! Well, you have to pull its legs out and you'll find its head comes too, OK? Get your wee sister or somebody to hold it up for you.'

'Right!' he replied, and departed, clutching his baffling beast.

Poodle Number 3 appeared, led in by a little man wearing a bonnet, preceded by a woman of vast proportions, wearing blue hair, matching the colour the dog had been dyed for the time being. When the small man took his bonnet off I half expected he'd have the same shade of blue, but being bald, I suppose that would have been difficult.

'Our little dog has developed a large black lump on its head. Come, Charles, show the gentleman.'

Charles obligingly lifted the dog on to the table. Charles's principal function in life was clearly that of dog-handler, daily trotting behind his wife as if he too were on a leash. Every year we had examples of this syndrome where dog had apparently displaced man in a wife's affections, and making the cry for women's liberation appear ridiculous. In fact, witnessing this sickening spectacle several times, I had felt that someone ought to put in a public plea for male lib.

'Would you care to show me the lump?' I asked the lady, for nothing was very obvious through the hair.

'Charles, show the veterinary doctor the lump.'

At the command, Charles leapt into action, scrabbled about among the hair, and pointed. I wondered if Charles was naturally dumb, or only when his wife was present to speak for both of them.

'When did you notice this?' I asked.

'Only this morning. It was horrible then, and has grown since,' said the Speaker.

'And it will go on growing too!' I said.

'Oh, dearie me,' she wailed in a high soprano – surprising really, for with her build I'd have thought she was more a contralto, if not actually a baritone. She wrung her hands, and I gazed fascinated, for this action was often referred to in melodramas, but seldom actually seen. It produced quite a clink and jingle as her many bangles, rings and trinkets met head on. 'Can nothing be done?' she bayed.

'Oh, yes, quite easily. I expect you were walking on the Torrs yesterday?'

'Oh, you wonderful man! How did you guess?' She gazed at me in wonderment, and for one awful moment I thought she was about to embrace me, so I backed away hurriedly and picked up a pair of forceps. I dare say it was all right for her to embrace Charles, if she ever did, for he only came up to her shoulder, but since I was as tall as Charles's owner, I feared for my ribs in such a bear hug.

'Now, don't worry if your dog gives a little

yelp. I'm about to pull the lump out' – and before she could protest at this cruel act, I did it, and held it up for her to see.

'It's a tick ... very common around here, especially on the Torrs. They fasten on to sheep, dogs, or any animal, and suck its blood, and so grow quite dramatically – something like a vampire,' I smiled. I held it up in front of her and said, 'If you look carefully, you can probably see its legs moving.'

She gave a yowl, and pushing Charles effortlessly aside proceeded to kiss and cuddle 'mama's poor darling little baa-lamb', who, it appeared, had been a 'brave little dinkums'. Indeed, a dog had to be something special to preserve a vet's admiration, with owners like Charles's missus around. Charles was commanded to pay up, which he did. He replaced his bonnet and, wearily trailing the dog's lead, followed his lady. Clutching her 'clever little poppet' to her vast bosom, she sailed forth like a battle cruiser. It was a frightening spectacle, enough to turn any discerning male permanently against matrimony.

There followed in rapid succession three Bristacombites. The first had a female cat to neuter, and was advised to bring it back on operation day, Wednesday, actually the next day. The second carried a basset hound with a haematoma (blood blister) in its ear, a condition common in long-eared dogs, prize fighters and front-row forwards in a rugby scrum, and inclined to produce a cauliflower ear. The basset's owner was also advised to return on the morrow. The third was yet another poodle, this time with entropion, a condition found frequently in poodles, where the eyelids tend to turn inwards so that their eyelashes constantly irritate the eyes and produce infection. Whatever else we said about the breed, we had to admit they were good vet's dogs, boosting the income considerably. If only they could pick their owners, I thought there might be some hope for the species! The entropion was also scheduled for the next day. Since we already had a bitch and two other cats booked in for spays, clearly either Kenneth or I would spend most of the next day in theatre.

That seemed to be the lot, and I was just taking off my white coat, preparatory to starting the afternoon visits, when the door burst open and the blue poodle owner and little Charles bearing the dog arrived again in a state of near hysteria. Dinkums, it appeared, had suddenly gone round the bend. They'd returned to their nearby boarding house, and the lady had proceeded forthwith to reward her brave little dog with a slap-up feed, when poppet, or baa-lamb, or whoever he was, had quite suddenly rushed round the room, yelping, pawing his mouth, rolling over, jumping up, and generally giving every sign of having flipped his lid. The battle cruiser seemed about to do likewise, or explode any minute, so I called to Mrs Drury to take her into the waiting-room and calm her.

'Sit on her, if you need to, but keep her out of the surgery,' I whispered. Mrs Drury, who was about a third the size of Charles's helpmeet, gave me a pained look which I took to mean that the odds were hardly fair – a bantamweight taking on a heavy. 'You can cope,' I assured her with a smile, as she led the sobbing lady by the arm, like a tug with a liner in tow.

'Now, Mr . . . er . . . Charles; let's have a look at your dog!'

I prised open the poppet's mouth, then reached for the forceps again, stronger ones this time. I'd guessed what I would find, the description being fairly typical of the trouble.

'Hold him tightly,' I said.

The little man did this with great gusto, gripping the dog by the scruff of the neck in a manner I'm sure his lady would not have liked at all, and which caused the dog to yelp loudly. Charles seemed to be enjoying it too. I only hoped Mrs Drury was sitting firmly on the lady next door. I fancy if she'd appeared and seen her man getting down to things, and doing what he'd clearly wanted to do for some time to his rival for the lady's favours, there might have been another instant haematoma! A quick yank, and I drew out the forceps with a chop bone in their jaws. It had been lodged firmly across the dog's hard palate, and had produced the same sort of effect as raspberry seeds or nuts under a person's false teeth — only more so.

'Strewth!' exclaimed Charles, the only word he uttered during our entire acquaintanceship.

'Take that with you,' I said, 'and tell your wife from me never to give the dog chop bones, chicken bones or any others which can splinter or wedge across the dog's mouth. Tell her, while you're at it, that the dog's much too fat, and is in danger of a heart attack at any time!'

Charles departed, bonnet purposefully stuck on his head, shoulders back, dog yanked along on the lead. I hoped he would lay on thick what I'd said. That way he'd maybe get a bit more himself at the feeding-trough. He was clearly a real man again — at any rate as far as the waiting-room. Yes, good vet's dogs, poodles!

8

The Volks from Away

'Hello! Is thack the veterererinary . . . (click) . . . surgeon?'

'Yes – Cameron here.' I was trying to place the voice, with its odd clipped pronunciation and background of clicks.

'This is Mr Badger.' Ah, I had it now. Mr Badger had considerable trouble with his dentures, which at times stuck out like a boxer's gum-shield, and when he made a speech of any length they slid up and down, clicking like castanets. He must have had these teeth for forty years.

'What can I do for you, Mr Badger?'

'I do nock know if you can do anythink.'

'As bad as that, eh? Well, what does the trouble seem to be?'

'I very much fear I have foot . . . (click) . . . and mouth disease.'

'You have foot and mouth, do you say?' I knew about the mouth . . . the foot was a new development.

'Well, so far I seem to have escaped, but one of my cackle, my Shorthorn, ackchually, has contracked it.'

'What makes you think it's foot and mouth?'

'I do nock think – I know, Mr Cameron. The signs are exackly ... (click, click) ... as the book describes.' He paused, as if gathering his verbal resources to have a run at the next bit. 'She is lame, and blowing bubbles.'

'Blowing bubbles, eh?'

'Yes, bick ones too, and has clearly acuke discomfort ... (click, click) ... in the mouth and foot.'

Mr Badger was always very correct in his speech, but judging by the number of clicks and longish pauses, he was probably blowing a few bubbles himself.

'Any other animals affected?' I inquired.

'No-o-o ... jusk the cow. Do I phone the police or the Minister of Agriculture?'

I could just picture the Minister of Agriculture in some lofty Whitehall office trying to make sense of a cow blowing bubbles in Devon, reported by a man with shoogly teeth.

'Don't phone anybody! I'll be out to see her within the hour. It may not be as bad as you fear.'

'Thank you, Mr Cameron, I know you mean

well, but I fear it is a for . . . for . . . forlorn hope.'

I could see Mr Badger sitting at his phone, one hand gripping the instrument firmly, the other at the ready as a tooth-catcher or manipulator. Mr Badger was a solemn little man who wore at all times a hat so firmly planted on his head that one felt it was part of his anatomy, while across his round little abdomen hung an enormous watch-chain. He blinked at the world through horn-rimmed spectacles, and generally gave the impression of having just returned from a funeral. His Anthony Eden hat, if now somewhat green with age, was undoubtedly his distinguishing feature. What a cigar was to Winston Churchill, an umbrella to Neville Chamberlain, or a pipe to Harold Wilson, so a hat was to Edwin Badger. He was one of the large contingent in the area who were described by the Devonians as 'the volks from away'. 'Away' was a delightfully vague term denoting Somerset, Scotland or Swaziland. If you weren't from North Devon, you were from 'away'. This band of immigrants was a mixed bag. Some were officers from one of the three Services who had sunk their demob payment in a farm, and who for the most part were doing well; they were keen, intelligent, genned-up on their new life and willing to learn. We had farmers who had come from other parts of the country, and almost without exception they had proved outstanding. Although Devon was exceedingly beautiful and its land fertile, some of the farming methods were fairly primitive, and with the modern methods of the incomers allied to Devon's rich soil they very soon forged ahead. But there were others of humbler lineage from 'away'. By and large, these were 'volks' who had longed for a little place in the country, and in the glories of sunny Devon, with its gentle people and slower pace of life, they were enjoying a more leisurely, if at times uncertain, existence.

Mr Badger was of this latter breed. He was a retired greengrocer from London, who had apparently cherished a secret desire to settle down in the country and own his personal little piece of 'England's green and pleasant land'. With great daring he had taken the plunge, retired early and bought about fifteen acres. His smallholding was at Martincombe, that district of patchwork fields stretching up the steep surrounding hills, famed for its warm climate and early strawberries, and with a honeycomb of lanes leading to the various cottages and little farms which perched so precariously on ledges and outcrops that one felt that any sleepwalker stepping out of his front door would disappear into the abyss, and be gathered up, in whole or in part, hundreds of feet below.

I had only been at the Badger residence once before, and it had struck me on that occasion that while Mr Badger was very likely a first-class greengrocer, with every brussels sprout accounted for each night, he was not in personality exactly a ray of sunshine; though maybe an expert on cauliflowers, his knowledge of cattle was, if not nil, very nearly so.

He was consulting his famous watch when I arrived – probably, I thought, a parting gift from the Allied Society of Costermongers and Greengrocers, or some such worthy body. Beside him stood Mrs Badger, whom I had not met before. She might have been his twin, being exactly the same size and shape, possessed of a matching pair of spectacles and abdominal bulge. Only the watch-chain, and of course the hat, distinguished the male Badger from his mate, with perhaps a suggestion in Mrs Badger's expression that she had come from an even more tragic funeral than her man. They were a cheerful pair! . . . But then, I suppose if you have spent a lifetime receiving complaints from an unfeeling public that one orange was bad, an apple had a worm in it, and a lovely juicy lettuce had harboured an even juicier slug, you are entitled to feel that life is a bit on the grim side.

'Well, then, let's see the Shorthorn,' I said in

my cheeriest manner, endeavouring to spread a little sunshine around the sorrowing Badgers. They led me silently to their tiny shippen, which only held four cows. There was the cow, drooling saliva, and every now and then smacking her lips and blowing a bubble. She seemed to be standing firmly enough on all four feet, so I suggested he turn her loose and let me see her walk. Sure enough, she had a slight limp. Examination of the offending foot disclosed a stone lodged between her clits.

'That's all that was wrong with her foot, Mr Badger. Now for the mouth.' Grabbing her by the nose, I swung her head round, looked in the mouth, felt the tongue, and palpated the submaxillary glands of the throat. Then I announced in my spreading-joy-around tone, 'Nothing to worry about. No ulceration in foot or mouth. She has wooden tongue, due to a germ called *Actinobacillus lignieresi*, affecting the tongue and soft tissues around. I'll give her an injection, and leave you a bottle to give her a dose every day. In ten days or so, she'll be as sound as a bell.'

'But her sympcoms are so like foo . . . (click) . . . and mouth disease,' he said despondently. I think he was genuinely disappointed and had been looking forward to writing to some greengrocer friend, saying: 'Dear Jack (or Bill, or Bert), I'm afraid I've got bad news to report . . .'

'Well, Mr Badger, a lot of diseases have similar symptoms. If you look at a medical dictionary, you can imagine you have any number of things wrong with you, and rush off to make your Will.'

Over the ritual hand-washing in the kitchen, I inquired, 'How was the lambing this year?'

'Quite good,' he replied lugubriously (it would have been an education to find him on a bad day, I thought). 'We had ten twins, but the trouble is the ewes will keep lambing at night. However,' he added, some excitement coming into his voice and transforming his expression from deep solemnity to a kind of sombre dead-pan look, 'I'm having no more lambings at night. Next year they will all lamb through the day.'

'Good for you!' I congratulated him. 'What's the secret?'

He looked at me rather pityingly, as if I should have known by now. 'Why, I'll only put the ram out with the ewes through the day this autumn, then all the lambs are bound to arrive by day. It's so simple, really!'

I tittered, then hastily changed it to a fit of coughing, for he was absolutely serious. Hastily, before I exploded, I bade them goodbye, then laughed non-stop for about three miles of my journey. A childless couple, they fondly imagined they had discovered a secret that had remained hidden from sheep-breeders since the first sheep walked the earth. If Mr Badger announced to his neighbours his master plan, as I'd no doubt he would, I could imagine the comments in 'The Fox and Grapes' and 'The Jolly Huntsman' for the next few months as the locals discussed 'the plan o' that yur zhopkeeper from away'.

I was dreading the next call, for a very odd reason. The Old Mill was one of my favourite farms, a delightful spot I'd marked out in my pipe dreams as the little farm I'd buy one day when the finances would allow it. The Horne family who lived there were very friendly, always welcoming me like some long-lost brother, and no matter the hour of my arrival, by day or night, miraculously the coffee was ready waiting. The farm only covered forty acres, but Mr and Mrs Horne, having come to that haven of peace to escape the city rat race, were somehow making it pay, with their herd of Guernseys and intensive pig-farming. There was nothing terrifying about the case I'd to see; merely a cow with bursitis of the hock joint. It was my other patient who worried me. Some two weeks previously, when I'd been cleaning a cow, I'd noticed that Uncle, who lived with the family, had been anything but his usual bouncy self – he resembled, in fact, a half-shut knife as he draped himself over a cow.

'What's the trouble with you, Uncle?' I inquired. 'You're not as cheery as usual.'

He groaned and spread himself even more listlessly on the cow. 'It's my water. This gravel in it is murder, and the blasted doctors can't seem to do anything. They don't look at you, just write a prescription and say, "Here! Try this!" ' He looked at me piteously. He was a little terrier of a man, and moaning was foreign to his nature. He went on, 'Could you not give me something?'

'Oh, sure,' I replied in a moment of bravado – one up on the medics – which I soon realized was playing with fire. 'We've got the very pill for you.' We had, in fact, an excellent diuretic which flushed out the kidneys like a hose! We had used it successfully on numerous dogs, and had even had success with stones in the kidneys, the drug appearing sometimes to dissolve or break up the calculi.

'Give me some to try,' he pleaded, and – foolishly – I did. I warned him that if anything went wrong he must contact his doctor and stop the pills right away, and left him. I'd been a worried man since, and had even scanned the obituary notices, fearful of finding his name. But he was still there, looking as grey as before, walking straddle-legged, and doubled up over the cow I'd come to see. I was sorry to find him like that, but relieved to find him there at all. Casually I asked, 'How did you get on with the pills?'

'Tremendous,' he said, 'they worked marvellously. The only trouble was that they brought such lumps of stone down, it took me about an hour to pass each one. I tell you, you could have put them in a rockery. Look!' – he rummaged in a waistcoat pocket – 'did you ever see anything like these?'

I goggled, and gulped 'Never!', then added hastily, 'I think you'd better stop these pills, and get to your doctor and ask for an X-ray.'

'Ach, doctors!' he snorted, condemning the whole medical profession in two words. I talked to him for a time, managed to persuade him to do as I suggested, relieved him of the remainder of my pills, and went on my way, considerably shaken by the jagged calculi the old man had passed.

As it happened, my next call was actually to a doctor's farm. Dr White was an easy-going, friendly soul, with a limitless fund of stories. He had retired relatively young from a busy Midlands practice and, with his Irish wife, kept about the muckiest farm in the area. It was quite a feat to walk across their yard without having a wellington sucked off in the slime! I was constantly surprised at the cases to which I was called, many being akin to conditions in man, but it seemed that the doctor, having hung up his stethoscope, so to speak, was determined never to take it down again. He used to peer over my shoulder at whatever beast I was treating, and give me some racy anecdotes about comparable cases he'd had. Today I was setting a broken tibia in a calf, and he enlivened the proceedings by a tale of a former patient whose leg had been put in plaster by some orthopaedic surgeon in Birmingham. Later, examining the leg, set with several layers of Gypsona, the doctor ran his finger between the leg and the top of the plaster and explained that the said surgeon in Birmingham had put the plaster on too tightly. 'Leg went gangrenous,' said the Doc, puffing at his pipe as if gangrene was no worse than chicken-pox, 'and of course he lost the leg.'

A visit to Blackhill was apt to be a long-drawn-out affair, since Mrs White generally had a piece of paper with a list of patients to be seen 'when you're here anyway'. I don't know how she did as a doctor's wife, but clearly she was right at home in the role of farmer, and constantly wore an old pair of corduroys which were so stiff with dirt that I'm sure at night they stood upright in her bedroom like a suit of armour. But she was a cheerful soul, and today had lined up about a dozen cows for pregnancy diagnosis. Again the doctor accompanied me, and told me a long, involved tale of a Polish soldier who had married an English girl during the war. They had come to him when the wife was pregnant, and Dr White had worked out the date the baby was due. At five minutes past midnight some months later, the doctor had been roused from slumber to hear the Pole say in accusing tones, 'Dr White! You told me my wife would a baby have on July twenty-first. It is now five minutes past that, and no baby there is. What are you going to do about it?'

The thought crossed my mind, as I continued my PD's, that what with Badger's cure for night lambings, and the Pole's insistence that if a doctor said a day he should keep to it, sex education had been badly neglected in our land. I was spared any further 'Revelations of a Midlands Doctor' by Mrs White coming with a message that I was to go with all speed to Major Biggleswade's farm, where four heifers had been found dead and some others were very bad. Hastily washing my arms, I leapt into my jacket and my car, and put my foot down. Four dead – what could it be? Staggers, possibly . . . bloat, unlikely . . . what? The yearlings had apparently died without a struggle, as if poleaxed. A further half-dozen were staggering about, or were down, twitching and groaning.

There was a fair old hiatus, those awful few moments when the vet is surrounded by a sea of anxious faces, waiting for some word of hope. Major Biggleswade, another of our 'from away' people, was a first-class farmer, who had but recently moved from a small farm to a large one, indeed one of the best in the district. He tended to get a bit red in the face when agitated, and he had every reason to be bright red now. Four fine, fat, Devon yearlings was a considerable loss — another six would be catastrophic. At such a time the old grey matter is strained to the limit, as one attempts to recall, and mentally tick off, all the differential diagnostic features. Botulism . . . anthrax . . . magnesium deficiency . . . lightning stroke or electrocution . . . There was just nothing to be seen externally. It could only be a poison of some sort, I thought, and my heart, already pretty low, went right down into my boots, for the world of poisons — apart from reasonably obvious ones like bracken or lead — was a maze. The toxicology book was a most discouraging thing to read because most of the poisons had similar symptoms, most resulted in death, and in the vast majority of instances the book mournfully recorded that treatment was unavailing and a positive diagnosis could only be made on post-mortem. I didn't think the Major's blood pressure would stand up to me saying to him, 'I'll be able to tell you what it was when they're all dead!'

Something had to be done. I looked in the mouths of all the dead beasts, and in the fourth

I found something — a twig with some chewed-up leaves on it. Animal dead without a struggle — sometimes twigs still in mouth . . . far back in the limbo of forgotten things, something stirred.

'Show me where they were grazing,' I said, for all the sick beasts had been brought into the barn. Major Biggleswade took me round to a little paddock, and there in a corner was what I sought — a pile of hedge clippings. I poked about in it, brought out some twigs, and held them up.

'There's the trouble!'

'Hedge clippings?' he asked in bewilderment. 'Surely these don't kill.'

'This kind do; they're yew clippings, absolutely lethal. Beasts can die in five minutes, some still with leaves in their mouths.'

The poor fellow sat down on a large stone and put his head in his hands. Not for nothing was he a major. He had been at El Alamein, fought his way up Italy, and later in Germany. Within moments he was in command again. 'Can anything be done?' he asked.

I was frantically trying to recollect the few paragraphs in our course that had dealt with yew poisoning. My memories were not comforting.

'Look, Major, it's no good building up your hopes. Yew is nearly always fatal, and a quick killer. Our only chance is to get that yew out of them as quickly as possible. As far as I can recollect, the books advise a rumenotomy, but by the time we'd opened up one of your beasts and taken the yew out of the stomach, I reckon the others would be dead. What I do know is that yew kills by direct action on the heart, so let's have a go with heart stimulants.'

We injected the six survivors with adrenaline, then poured all the purgatives I had in my car over the poor beasts' throats – linseed oil, epsom salts, a bloat mixture with turpentine in it: everything remotely resembling a purge, proven and unproven, went over to try to shift that yew quickly, but I feared it was a hopeless business. I stayed a while, then went home, ostensibly for a meal but in reality to look up the poisons book. It was cheerful! It seemed that yew was invariably fatal, but a case had been recorded in 1859 when somebody had saved a beast. As an added item of interest, the author further informed us that yew poisoning also occurred in man, but only in lunatics! I've often ridiculed the reports in newspapers that 'doctors were fighting to save' somebody or other. Whenever somebody is ill, it appears that doctors don't simply treat, they battle for the patient's life. We did actually fight for these beasts' lives, almost hourly keeping them going with stimulants, in the hope that our various charges of dynamite would work in time. Two more died, four survived . . . just . . . and had diarrhoea for about a fortnight. But they lived.

So, in the ever-changing kaleidoscope that made up our lives, I had spent an afternoon with 'the volks from away'. I had begun with a serious disease that wasn't; I had learnt the great secret of day-time lambings; I had learnt how not to treat humans for renal calculi, and how not to predict a delivery date; and I had learnt how to face crisis and loss with dignity, as Major Biggleswade had done.

The men of Devon were, and are, a delightful, friendly race. Their rich, rolling tongue is music in the ear. But in the main, critical as it may seem, the farming standards in Devon thirty years ago were poor and primitive, and their improvement is certainly due, in part, to 'the volks from away'. Of that I'm 'sartin sure, m'dears'!

9

Never!

'Crowbars,' wrote Jimmy, and I could see by the blot he had really stabbed the word out with his pen; then to make sure I'd grasped the horror of it all he had written it again. 'Crowbars! He actually used crowbars at a calving – I ask you!'

I sat back and tried to imagine the scene, and before me came a dreadful picture of a vet, probably with a horrible sadistic leer on his face, actually levering a calf from a cow in the way you might scoop the yolk from a boiled egg with a spoon. That couldn't be right, I thought – right in any sense. If the man had done that, either he had a dash of Frankenstein in his heritage, or he had gone round the bend; I'd heard of such things, especially when clients didn't pay their bills and drug firms were getting decidedly shirty about 'your outstanding account with us, to which we referred one month ago'. I shook my head to rid myself of the nightmarish pictures. Jimmy had been a pal at the old Vet College, and while I had remained doucely in my native Ayrshire as an assistant, Jimmy had departed for the warmer clime of Somerset, there to learn the trade – and, I've no doubt, cause a flutter in a few feminine hearts, for there's no doubt he was a real charmer, was Jimmy. We didn't correspond very often, but out of the blue came this racy letter from him, most of which, in the manner of assistants in every profession from time immemorial, had been devoted to slanging his boss in carefully chosen, selective but definitely vitriolic terms, reaching his most outright condemnation with the reference to crowbars. No, I couldn't imagine quite, at that stage of my experience, how crowbars could ever be necessary in calving a poor beast, but there and then, as Jimmy had already clearly decided, I vowed with all the confidence of the inexperienced that there would never be a time when I would need to use such force. Never! Never! On that I was quite clear.

But times change, and the stage of seeing everything as black or white tends to pass in the arena of bitter experience. The passing years have a habit of making us swallow our words as we realize how much we still don't know, and Jimmy's reference to crowbars came vividly back to me some years later.

I was in bed, tucked up with hot-water bottles, having alternated the previous day between penicillin pills, throat lozenges and a cough bottle. I had flu, and none of your forty-eight-hour varieties either! In fact as I lay sweating it out, it came to me that maybe I should have made my Will, but since my life insurance was already being used as cover for the cost of my partnership in the practice of Davidson and Cameron, there didn't seem much point in a Will. I would either have to get better, or (as seemed more likely) quietly decease, and hope there would be enough somewhere for the funeral. While in this cheerful frame of mind, the phone rang.

'Yes,' I croaked, hoping it would be a wrong number, a forlorn hope at one o'clock in the morning.

'Parkhurst, Higher Shelfin, here. Is that the vet'nary?' inquired a voice.

'Yes,' I croaked again.

'Is that you, Mr Cameron?' asked the voice, doubtfully.

'Yes,' I repeated. It seemed my laryngeal mechanism had got a bit jammed somehow; probably stuck up with cough bottle.

'We've a cow bad to calve. She's been at it for hours now and nothing's happening. Can you come?'

'Sure you aren't hurrying her?' I gasped, my

larynx springing into action at the thought of leaving this warm bed.

'No, calf's coming all right, but it's very big,' said Mr Parkhurst.

I groaned. Bernard, who had succeeded Kenneth in the practice after the latter departed for Kenya, was not yet a partner, and was in any case away visiting his parents for the weekend. I groaned again.

'What's that? I can't hear you proper, like. Seems to be a bad line.'

'I'm on my way,' I assured him, and crawled slowly out of bed.

It was only when I staggered out to the car that I realized how weak I was. My muscles ached, my legs had been replaced by jelly, and the wind and rain that cold January night cut right through to the bone. I was not, on any count, looking forward to this. Mr Parkhurst was a first-class farmer, one who knew his onions, who seldom if ever panicked, and if he said the cow was 'bad to calve' I was sure he would be right. He was also a very particular farmer, set a high standard, and expected the same. I did not think he would readily overlook failure, and I groaned again. Who'd be a vet?

The fine modern cowshed was warm after the night air, warm and aromatic with that lovely mixture of smells that pervades a byre — hay, silage, cattle cake, the animals themselves

— a smell that always made it feel good to be a vet, working with living things. But not that night; the magic failed to work its spell, for I couldn't get over my own wretchedness and the shivers were coming continuously as I struggled into my calving-coat. Soaping the arm — at least the bucket of water was warm — I examined the patient. Farmer Parkhurst was quite right: the calf was coming normally. It was also large, very large, and big, roomy and strong as the Friesian was, she was not going to deliver this calf unaided. I got the calving-chains on and tried a bit of traction. I had about as much strength as a newborn kitten!

'Can you give a bit of a pull here?'

'I can't,' said Mr Parkhurst, 'I'm only a week out of hospital after a hernia. But Andrew can lend a hand.' I said I was sorry about his operation, groaned inwardly and looked at Andrew, all in the one go. Andrew was a big lad, the oldest of the Parkhurst boys, but he was only fifteen. Andrew and I pulled on the chains, the cow bellowed and strained, but the calf came not an inch.

'All we need is a strong pull here. Can you get any helpers?' I asked.

'Not at this time of night,' he replied, shaking his head.

'Then we're in trouble,' I said. 'This calf is going to take some shifting; you daren't pull,

I've got the flu and that leaves one fit man, Andrew.'

(Here let me insert an explanation. I have often noticed a look of horror come over the face of the layman when I describe a calving. I have seen the word 'barbaric' form in the mind, as they think of maybe six men pulling on ropes or calving-chains to deliver a calf. In defence of the veterinary profession vis-à-vis the medical, I would explain that the vet cannot, as with a human mother, arrange a half-ton cow in the optimum position for delivery: the calf may weigh anything up to a hundredweight; almost invariably the cow lies down on her side and the vet has perforce to lie on his side, stomach or even back, and with an arm that numbs rapidly, try to manipulate the calf. All this by way of explanation of what's to come! If someone says, 'The obvious answer is a caesarean section,' I can only reply that in those days we were not so expert in cattle or so ready to whip out a knife, and at two a.m. on a winter morning a caesar, with no assistance available, was just not on — so there!)

I looked around our company. What could we do? To wait for morning and more muscle power was to have an exhausted mother and probably a dead calf. There was no drug that could safely be given to increase these contractions. That cow had already given all she'd got, and even our brief attempts to assist her had visibly tired her. It had to be . . . could think of nothing else. It was a case for crowbars . . . of a sort. I explained to Mr Parkhurst and Andrew what I felt had to be done. Father looked about as happy as I was feeling, which was wretched with a capital W — and not only physically, but mentally, for I was about to break one of my 'nevers'.

'But is it safe?' asked the owner.

'No,' I had to reply, 'but while I've never done it, it has been done, and unless you can produce six strong men we haven't a hope of delivering that calf. Come on, Mr Parkhurst,' I said with an attempt at flippancy I was far from feeling, 'if you and I were fit, we'd not be beaten, but we're just a couple of crocks tonight.'

'Reckon you're right at that,' he agreed with a hint of a smile. I had never actually known him to let himself go and laugh, his dour, deadpan countenance always masking his feelings. You never knew where you were with this man — except out, I was sure, if you failed.

'Now then, Andrew,' I explained to the son, 'you're the important one here tonight. Do exactly as I say. When I say "stop", you stop at once. When I say "steady", I mean an inch at a time. Can you handle it?'

There was a flicker of eagerness on the boy's

face, but he immediately got rid of it. I thought as I looked from father to son that I had seldom seen such a pair of dour Devonians. I don't know why, but they reminded me of Scrooge, the bad Scrooge at the beginning of Dickens's *Christmas Carol*, only they were more full and fair of face than the old miser. I suppose my subconscious was recalling to me the reluctance of all the Parkhursts to pay their bills – or maybe I was delirious! Stop dreaming, I chided myself, and get on with it.

'Well then, lad, let's have it,' I said.

Soon a roar was heard as the tractor was started, the byre door flung open to admit a blast of freezing air and choking diesel fumes as the boy reversed his mechanical steed right up to the door, and through it. The door was wide, the cow was right opposite it, which saved a bit of shifting around, and operation Broken Vow was about to commence. The leg calving-chains were fixed together to the tractor towbar, and when I repeated, 'An inch at a time, mind you,' young Andrew nodded and did just that, while I, with my hand inside the cow, felt for progress and tried to guide the direction of pull. I felt the legs budge and move up into position, yelled 'Stop!', and at once the tractor stopped.

'Now for the tricky bit, the head,' I shouted over the tractor's roar. As with the legs, now the head chain alone was linked to the drawbar, and I nodded. I glanced at Mr. Parkhurst and thought he'd be back in hospital shortly at this rate, for his chin was almost tripping him. To say he didn't like it was fractionally an understatement! But Andrew was inching forward, and I soon had other things on my mind than Parkhurst's long face, as I tried to guide a very broad face into the mouth of the uterus and up into the vagina. It was coming, a minute fraction at a time. The cow, poor beast, bellowed as the pain really gripped her, and now that the head was coming, she strained with might and main. Feverishly I tried to assist the extra large forehead or poll into the passage, and as finally all was in position bellowed, 'Whoa, there!' Fortunately, young Andrew got the gist of what 'Whoa' meant, and stopped dead. I really take my hat off to that fifteen-year-old lad. He drove the tractor like a seasoned expert − literally, as I had asked, inch by inch. We were well on the way now; another pull on the legs, then the final pull on the head, until to the immense relief of the cow, its owner and its midwife, the calf's head was free, its eyes blinking at me, its tongue sticking out of the side of its mouth. Its whole attitude, I thought, was one of disgust and outrage at the indignity of the whole affair, and as it smelt the diesel fumes and felt the icy blast coming in the door, I'm sure it said,

'What a dickens of a way to arrive — and what a place, noisy, smelly, wet!' In short, it felt as I had felt when I left my hot-water bottles: that life would be a far better thing if one could stay in this warm bed. But it wasn't going to get the chance now — no fear. Having come so far, the battle was won, and the tractor–Friesian combination soon did the rest. The calf came with a rush, hitting me with such force in the stomach as I tried to catch it that I was deposited unceremoniously on the seat of my pants in the dung channel. But what did that matter. I was pretty wet by now anyway, what did anything matter, we'd done it! We had an enormous bull calf, looking to my wearied eyes already half grown, and there now followed a period of mutual congratulations. The cow, which, astonishingly, had remained standing through all that traction, was already, as with all mothers, putting the pain of the past behind her as she licked her large son; old man Parkhurst was actually congratulating me — I couldn't believe it — while I, my hand inside the cow to make sure there was no damage, said, 'Well done, Andrew! Great driving, lad!' at which the boy, forgetting for a moment the code of the Parkhursts, actually smiled.

As I made my weary way homeward, I reflected on the events just past. I shuddered to think what might have happened if the driver's foot had slipped on the clutch, but otherwise I was not too morose at having broken one of my self-imposed commands. A 'never' had gone for a burton, but in retrospect it seemed to me that a steady, controlled pull had been much more effective, and quicker, than six pairs of hands tugging at ropes. Jimmy's boss had known what he was about when he used a crowbar, calving-ropes attached, as a lever, no doubt against the concrete lip of the dung channel.

Flu or not, I was out early next day, fearful lest something had overtaken my patient. I needn't have worried. She was lying down, chewing the cud, having evidently had a hearty breakfast, which was more than I'd had. Parkhurst senior was with me, and as he looked at the beast and at me, he observed, 'She's looking better than you are, Mr Cameron!' I thought wryly that wouldn't be hard. Clearly we need worry no more about the patient. In fact, my only concern now was what farmer Parkhurst would deduct from the calving fee for diesel and use of tractor!

The trouble with one 'never' going down the drain is that others are sure to follow. It's a bit like an alcoholic; the first drink is one too many and opens the floodgates. Accompanied by two students, one a coloured lad from Nigeria and the other a Scot, I was right out at the fringe of the practice on the moor. Here several veterinary practices met, all roughly the same distance from home, so in each case the various farmers would compare notes as to how their own vet did the job. One of my moorland clients was Hockridge, and a rougher establishment would be hard to imagine. It was really a ranch he ran out on the moor, his buildings filthy and primitive even by Devon standards. What the dwelling-house was like inside I cannot say, for I never was in it, but since Hockridge was a bachelor, only washed about every three days, and shaved maybe once a fortnight, I could well imagine what his house was like. The reason for the visit was the annual tuberculin test and I anticipated a long-drawn-out affair, for Hockridge's young stock roamed freely 363 days of the year, the other two days being when they came in for the TB test. They were as wild as mountain deer, and this year, having heard that he had added some twenty Galloways to his stock, I knew there would be high jinks, for even your half-domesticated Galloway can 'kick a fly off your bunnet'.

We heard them before we saw them — a series of bellows, whistles, shouts and curses floated over the moor to us. Rounding a bend I saw Hockridge with some of his pals and neighbours, most of them mounted on ponies, with much hallooing from the riders, slowly guiding a motley collection of steers and heifers of many colours and breeds towards a temporary paddock he had made from five-bar gates tied together. This was the corral, but whether it was OK (as in the Western film) remained to be seen. All that was certain was that we had a fight on our hands. The idea was that one by one the animals would be driven into a home-made crush, which at the front was simply a gate, and behind had a plank of wood which was lowered into place when the animal had entered. There was no yoke for the neck, and the crush side from which I had to operate was just a few planks, the other side being the gable end of the cowshed.

As the two students and I dressed for the fray, the Scots lad, astonished, said, 'I've never seen anything as slap-happy as this,' while the Nigerian lad observed, 'It is rather primitive, is it not?' They had come to 'see practice' in its various forms, with pictures in their minds gleaned from the latest textbooks on hygiene and animal husbandry – of up-to-date crushes, gathering and shedding pens, a concrete yard which could be hosed afterwards, and a little niche for the vet beside the crush where, in safety and some degree of comfort, he could do his job. Instead, before them stretched a sea of sweating bovine backs, their owners kicking and plunging about, while outside the stockade a group of men with sticks and curses sought to prevent the beasts leaning on their home-made restraining wall. Since the two lads were going to assist me with finding the ear marks and noting down the identification individually, they realized that they had to enter the arena. Over the wall we went, and I heard one of them mutter, 'Now I know what the Christians felt like, facing the Roman lions.' Still in one piece, but having accumulated a few kicks and much dirt on our various persons, we reached our point of operations.

'Let's try and do the Galloways first while they are still packed in,' I bellowed at Hockridge, who nodded. But between the concept of any great plan and its fulfilment, there is many a snag. So it was to prove. The only way to get a beast into the crush was for one of the men in the bunch to take its tail, and with the assistance of others, manhandle it to where we awaited it. The more manhandling that went on inside, the more the beasts pressed on the restraining five-bar gates, the result being that those helpers outside cursed those inside, while these sweating, dung-covered figures cursed back. Since most of the words were in broad Devonian – and some of them new to me – and with the snorts and roars all around, fortunately all was not understood by my two lads, the Nigerian merely observing, 'I think they are swearing quite a lot!' He sure hit the target; in fact if all that was said and shouted that afternoon was written down, this chronicle would be ten times as long.

We did get some Galloways tested, till there was an interruption in the flow; one black beast simply took off like a rocket, almost straight up in the air, and jumped the gates. In ten seconds flat it was over the hill and out of sight. The guardians of the gates were divided in their opinion. Some mounted ponies to recapture the fugitive, while the rest bawled at them to come back. But the damage was done, for in no time at all the rest of the beasts had cottoned on, pressed against the gates and were off. Soon all that was to be seen of the various actors in the drama was one vet, two students, and a few tested bullocks which had passed through into the farm courtyard. We sat down to wait, and eventually the cowboys and their scattered herd came back. They had all but reached the pen when the same Galloway steer kicked upwards again like an Olympic high-jumper and was off at a fast rate of knots.

'Let it go,' I bawled, 'and bring the rest.'

It would have taken John Wayne and James Stewart, with maybe some help from the Magnificent Seven (provided it was on one of their top-form days), to get that one back.

'What will you do?' inquired the Scots student.

'Nothing,' I replied. 'They'll never get that one.'

'But what if it should have TB and infect the rest?' asked the dark lad.

'Then that will maybe teach farmer Hockridge to get a proper pen.'

Thus another 'never' went out the window: never to leave a job incomplete. Eventually, wearily, we got the last beast tested, and we headed for the nearest tap to remove some of the dirt. It was then that Hockridge played his ace, informing me there was a bullock bad to calve in the shippen, whither he led us, opened the door and stood back. I gaped, then said, 'How long has she been like this?'

'Reckon about two days, since she started, like.'

Lying in front of us, on a bed of filth, was a heifer having her first calf. She was lying on her side, but stretched full out, so that her chain (incongruously the one secure beast was chained) was all but throttling her. The heifer was far through, and protruding from her were the head and fore-limbs of her calf. Two days, I thought — by the smell, more like two weeks. This was a typical piece of Hockridge neglect. I whirled round on him, demanding, 'Why did you not call us before?' to which he replied, again typically, 'Reckoned since you was comin' anyways, might as well wait and get the visit paid by the government, like.'

I thought of the lecturer who had told us that we would probably have to educate some of our clients. I wonder where he would have begun with Hockridge.

'Look,' I said, 'there's one of three things we can do here. One: shoot the cow. Two: do an embryotomy and cut the calf up into bits. Three: try to calve it. I'd suggest to shoot her would be a kindness.'

'Nor, she be out of a good 'un an' I'd like to save her,' he answered. Clearly this was to be his milk cow, since every other hoofed creature was out on the moor.

'Right then!' I glared at him. 'Plenty of hot water, soap, towel, and quickly.'

'Ain't no hot water in house.'

'Then boil some – plenty.'

We waited, already tired, dirty, dishevelled. There was no offer of tea – we were out in the wilds. I looked at the two students, both silent, both experiencing for the first time how crude their future calling could sometimes be.

'You know,' I said with an attempt at cheerfulness, 'the first vet I saw practice with used to say: "You may not see much practice, but you will see life." You've been in my lady's chamber, to treat her darling little King Charles spaniel, since you've been here. Now you're getting about as rough a glimpse of practice as you could imagine, and you're going to be seeing worse yet before we leave.'

Eventually Hockridge came back with two buckets of warm water. We all washed in one, I sent him for his tractor, told him what we were going to do, then pumped the contents of the other bucket, now containing liberal quantities of antiseptic and soap, into the cow's uterus, and we began. Hockridge wasn't as good a driver as young Andrew Parkhurst had been, but he wasn't bad. The calf came a bit. We paused while more water was fetched for lubrication purposes, because all the uterine fluid had long gone from that little heifer. I reckoned she'd had about enough pain; she was past helping us with contractions, so I gave her a spinal injection, which would take away most of the suffering. Eventually one foul calf was removed and the uterus pumped out with more antiseptic, and while one student inserted pessaries, the other gave her penicillin. I left him half a dozen bottles of protein hydrolysate to put some nourishment into the poor creature. Then, telling Hockridge I would be back tomorrow to see her, we were off. His mouth actually fell open when I said I was coming. The government wouldn't pay for that visit, nor for the calving. He opened his mouth to say something, but it was lost as I revved the car and drove away. My two students were very quiet on the way home. I knew what was going through their minds. First, thankfulness that they would be off on the morrow and therefore not need to attend another trip to the moorman and his bullocks to read the results of the test in three days' time. The other thought was of the horror they had seen, and of the tales they would tell to incredulous fellow students.

'Tractors. He actually uses *tractors* for a calving!'

In fact, I never needed to use a tractor again, but I had not quite done with sacrificing my sacred cows; I was glad the students had gone by then, though sorry they did not see Hockridge's heifer – for she recovered, astonishingly, and he paid a whopping bill! That was the only way I knew to educate this client.

My last 'never' to disappear left me with a red face. Jim Glover, whose shop was just across from our surgery, breezed in one teatime and said, 'Alex. Could you spare a minute to look at my old bitch? There's something not right about her.'

I nipped over the way and saw Jim's whippet, which was wandering about aimlessly, her back slightly arched. I took her temperature and noticed there was a slight uterine discharge.

Then I palpated her abdomen, and asked Jim if she'd ever had pups. Her abdomen was certainly enlarged a bit.

'No.'

'When was she last in season?'

'I can't remember; ages ago. She's so old I think she's stopped.'

'Well, Jim,' I said quite confidently, 'she's got a condition called pyometra, very common in maiden bitches. Her womb is swollen, but not too big, and some discharge is coming away. It might mean a hysterectomy, but we'll try some tablets first, at her age.'

'Right, Alex,' said Jim, and came over for the tablets.

The next morning at nine a.m., Jim walked in again in his usual jovial manner and reported.

'Alex. I thought you'd like to know that the whippet had a pup through the night. Will she still need that operation, do you think?'

'Er, no, Jim . . . I think the womb will be OK now.'

I heard an echo over the years from the old Vet College: 'When you are asked by an examiner for the causes of enlargement of the abdomen in a bitch, along with enlarged liver, enlarged spleen, dropsy, pyometra and the rest, never forget the commonest cause of all, pregnancy.'

I had mentally noted that, chalked up a 'never forget' in my mind and lo! after these years I'd forgotten. Bang had gone another 'never'.

Henceforward I decided that the only safe thing with 'never' was simply *never* to say or even think 'never'!

10

Surprises of a Caesar

I came out of the shop, turned left, and started to make my way back to the surgery. I'd been to the barber's shop for a much-needed haircut, for what with lambings, calvings, tuberculin tests and all the rush of the spring work, I'd had little time for any 'short back and sides'. However, a glance in the mirror that morning had startled me to the point of realizing that if I didn't have it done soon, I'd either need to go round the various hairdressers and ask for an estimate, or let somebody have a go with sheep shears. I had an operation scheduled for four o'clock, but until then I was free. So after our post-lunch conference and time of fellowship, I left Bernard, my new partner, to cope with afternoon consulting time and any subsequent calls, and wandered along to my hairdresser.

Barbers' shops are great places for brushing up on the local news, so it was with my knowledge much increased and thatch much diminished that I started back along the street. For a vet, or for that matter a doctor, to walk along the main street of a small town is fatal. It always seems on these walkabouts that half the population have been waiting for this very opportunity, and they converge from every direction to engage in conversation about the weather, the football team, the new vicar – all part of the softening-up process before coming to the nub of the matter; some free advice about their pets. I listened to a sad story of a goldfish, a positively harrowing tale of a cat's encounter with a terrier and subsequent injuries, and was then hailed for the third time with a 'Hello, Mr Cameron; the very man I wanted to see.' I found myself pinned to a shop window by a large individual whom I didn't know from Adam but who evidently knew me, and with an arm spread out on the window front on either side of me, escape was difficult. I tried to follow a complicated story delivered in a loud voice, in broad Devonshire dialect, about some kind of fit his dog took, 'only it isn't really a fit, if you know what I mean'. I think we were at the point in the story where the dog was lying twitching on the kitchen floor, when I became aware that I wasn't hearing my captor any more. His mouth kept opening and closing, but not a word came to me. For one nasty moment I thought I'd gone stone deaf, till I realized that I couldn't make him out because of the greatly increased background noise of engines revving, cars tooting and drivers shouting, a din that was increasing in volume by the minute. I wondered what was causing the traffic jam and incurring the travelling public's wrath, till a vague uneasiness took possession of me and, ducking under my warder's arm with a 'Better bring him along to the surgery, Mr . . . er,' I took off and hared for our premises, passing on the way a policeman obviously heading for the heart of the storm, which, as I had feared, was the footpath and main street outside our surgery.

These things, as everyone knows, are of course all a matter of cause and effect. The initial cause in this instance was that outside our door was parked Bernard's car, a perfectly proper and safe place to leave it. However, in front of Bernard's Ford was a client's Land-Rover, while in front of that again was a car and trailer with my four o'clock patient arriving. Opposite the three cars was parked a butcher's van, thus considerably narrowing the space through which other vehicles could proceed, but all would have been well had not a large touring coach tried to negotiate the gap, thought better of it, and just sat there, waiting for something to happen. Around this convoy of vehicles quite a little crowd had gathered, including many of the bus tourists, watching a farmer emerge from our front door propelling a sheep, followed by Bernard with a snowy white lamb tucked under each arm. The situation was further confused by my four o'clock farmer trying to direct *his* sheep in through the door, while the onlookers watched with great interest, even clicking their cameras, convinced that this was one of the tourist attractions of Devon.

Now, had it not been that the Easter weekend was early this year, there would not have been so many cars and coaches about, getting themselves intermingled with our lambing season. This could be regarded as one cause, yet from another viewpoint, had not my client arrived with his sheep at the very moment another was departing with sheep and lambs, there would have been nothing to see, the coach would probably have managed to squeeze through, and there would have been no crowd of spectators. Or yet again, if the client of the first part – he whose lambs Bernard was depositing in the Land-Rover beside their bleating mother – had phoned to make an appointment, this clash of comings and goings could have been averted, but being one of the easy-going Tuckers he had just – typically – arrived unannounced. Or – pursuing our quest for the cause of chaos even further – had we not, as a partnership, acquired something of a reputation for our sheep work, and particularly our caesarean operations, nobody would have been there at all. As I observed earlier, the whole schemozzle was simple really, when you came to think of it; merely the operation of the law of cause and effect. The cause? ... a departing caesar patient had met up with an arriving one, and (together with two white lambs) this had gathered a crowd and stopped a coach. The effect? ... bedlam, a queue of cars all along the street, hooters going full blast, drivers ditto, police striding to the scene, and myself galloping into the surgery and arriving in a state of near collapse. Surprising what such a little thing could cause – but then the surprises of a caesar were many and varied. In this instance order was quickly restored by the policeman (who fortunately was our close friend Johnny) simply driving Bernard's car up a side street opposite, which let out the Land-Rover, enabled the coach to move on and the whole log-jam to drift by.

Many vets had been doing the odd caesar for years, but Kenneth had pioneered it in our area. The thing had been talked about, and we had farmers arriving from many miles away for 'the Major's operation' because their own vet didn't do it or believe in it. These men would pay cash for services rendered and depart, remaining true to their own man for everything else. Kenneth was now practising in his native Kenya, but, like Elijah's mantle of old descending on the young prophet, his reputation had passed to Bernard and me, and each year our caesars grew in number. So the second surprising thing about the caesar was the number we carried out, sometimes six a day, plus, of course, all our other spring work. A sheep would arrive in a van, in the boot of a car or on its back seat with the cushions removed; occasionally it might have the luxury of a trailer to itself. We did caesars for a variety of very good reasons — for example, where a very large lamb was just too big for a little hogg having her first lambing; or where there was a prolapse of the vagina, a common occurrence which rendered normal lambing difficult, if not brutal.

Principally, though, we did caesars in such volume because of a condition known as ringwomb, and surprise of surprises, there wasn't any such condition, said the pundits. When Kenneth had first written to the *Veterinary Record* of the condition he had been answered in strong terms by one of the best-known vets in the country, who firmly declared that after many years in practice he had never come across 'this so-called ringwomb', and suggested that if the sheep were left alone, they would lamb normally. He said, in effect, that Kenneth was rushing his fences, and his 'ringwomb' was merely a stage maybe twenty-four hours before full term and a normal birth. Letters flowed in week after week taking sides in the debate and suggesting all manner of remedies, most of which we'd tried without success. What we described as ringwomb was a condition where a ewe came into labour normally, at full term, but where the os (the mouth of the uterus) simply did not open, or open enough, to allow steerage way for the oncoming lamb. Examination of these ewes revealed a hard ring, the os, either completely closed or only slightly open, and no matter how long we'd left the ewe, the condition had persisted. I'd seen ewes in labour for days, and die with the womb still closed, the 'ring' remaining firm. We'd thought it was a hormone deficiency, but none of the oestrogens or sex hormones had proved successful. Someone had reported success with spinal anaesthesia – the idea being, I suppose, that this removed pain and allowed relaxation of the muscles – but it hadn't worked for us. Since Hoare's *Veterinary Therapeutics* informed us that 'in functional constriction of the cervix uteri, extract of belladonna freely applied might overcome the spasm and allow delivery to take place', we'd tried belladonna, with little result. In fact, short of 'eye of newt, skin of frog, web of spider and cow parsley gathered at dead of night, the whole to be compounded and mixed when the moon was full', we'd had a go at most things. So in the end Kenneth had started doing caesars, and all we knew, despite the pundits, was that for a condition that apparently didn't exist we saw an astonishingly large amount of it in Devon, in any breed of sheep but principally in the native Devon Closewools. Each year, we were saving the lives of very many ewes and lambs by means of this operation. It had almost become a kind of status symbol with the farming community, with farmers comparing notes at the weekly market about how many 'of them thar operations us's 'ad'. I rather fancied that the ewes who'd had it were themselves a bit uppish with their girlfriends who'd lambed normally, and probably showed off their operation scars to the wondering gaze of the common throng.

The whole phenomenon of the increase in caesarean sections was surprising, but it would never have taken place if it had not made sound economic sense; that this was a fact was due to Kenneth's business acumen, his skill and his character.

To convince a farmer, be he Devonian or Dalesman, Lancastrian or Lincolnshire, from Caithness in the north-east to Cornwall in the south-west – you had to show him that he was making money, or at least saving it. This

Kenneth did. Considering the time and skill involved, his charges were low; compared with human medicine, they were ludicrous. For a successful caesar with live lambs and a live mother afterwards, he charged three guineas. If the lambs were born dead, but the ewe survived to breed another year or be fattened for slaughter, it cost two guineas. If the whole thing was a dead loss, the charge would be about £1, which barely covered the cost of drugs, anaesthetic, nylon, catgut, etc. Since a mother and two lambs was valued at £20, clearly there was profit in it. Even if the lambs were dead, at two guineas the ewe was still saving brass. If there was a risk of total loss, well, there would be that anyway if she was left alone, slaughter in that state bringing at most £2. Clearly, reasoned the farming community, there was money in it, and the news caused a stirring of interest akin to a miniature gold rush in men who would never previously have dreamed of taking a mere sheep to a vet.

The second factor was that Major Kenneth Davidson was a superb surgeon, his big, beefy hands being remarkably swift and dexterous, in full control of his task. Compared with him I was at first a ham-fisted bungler, but I learnt much from watching and assisting him at work. Perhaps I never matched him, for he was a born surgeon while I was a vet who did surgery out of necessity, preferring diagnosis and medical treatment to knife work; yet in time apparently it was said that 'the Scottish vet'nary be all right, nigh as good's Major'. Bernard, however, having seen much practice with us as a student and then succeeding Kenneth in the practice, was accepted from the beginning as having been well trained.

At first everything was carried out on the farm, sometimes on the kitchen table, more often on bales of straw in a draughty barn by the light of a Tilly lamp, or in an even more exposed corner of a hayshed where the lambing pens were sited so that one worked with an audience enthusiastically bleating either in praise or criticism. In those early days, too, the operation was carried out under a general anaesthetic, using chloral hydrate intravenously. While results were encouraging, losses were heavier than we wanted, because with dirt or spiders' webs festooning the walls of the shed and straw getting into the wound, a wide selection of bugs abounded to cause sepsis. Also, with a drug like chloral hydrate the lambs were born anaesthetized, and if weakly (and usually they were in the early days before farmers were educated to send for us in time) they didn't come out of the anaesthetic. Results improved markedly when we had the patient brought into our surgery, where we had light, warm water in abundance, aseptic conditions and all drugs and instruments to hand. They further improved – dramatically – when we did it all under local anaesthetic, so that lambs were bleating within minutes of being delivered, thus providing mother with a further incentive to recover. In time we rarely lost a ewe, and as the ewes were brought to us increasingly early as the years passed, death in the lambs was also cut to negligible proportions. A persuasive reason for bringing the sheep to us was that the scale of charges I mentioned could operate, with no visit or call-out fee being necessary, 'and missus could do shopping or 'ave a hair-do, like, wile yow be 'aving 'er belly cut'.

But if the profit motive and the Major's surgical skill were two important factors in the surprise soaring of caesar statistics, there was a third factor no less important. The farmers knew Kenneth Davidson was to be trusted. Some shared, some admired, some laughed at his unashamed Christian principles (' 'ee be verry religious, like'), all recognized and respected his sincerity, and even those who never went near church or chapel (and most Devon farmers worshipped periodically) acknowledged that 'the Major be a good man, a right good un; you can trust 'ee'.

The surprises of the caesar did not end with

its popularity and growth, its acceptance by the farming community or the scepticism of many critics in the profession. Day by day, things happened, the folklore increased – and my four o'clock appointment that day was no exception. Mrs Drury, our extremely efficient secretary and general assistant, had asked if her younger sister, who planned to be a nurse, could come and see an operation. The client that day, farmer Hawkins of Pilton Grove, was having his first case, so he arrived with his two strapping sons to see the job, while Johnny, our friendly 'bobby', having cleared the High Street, thought he might relax briefly and view the proceedings. We also had a student seeing practice with us, as we invariably had in the spring. To complete the party, Jim Glover, our ebullient butcher from across the road, was there. Jim had quite a history. He had been a real Casanova and a plausible rogue until recently, when just sitting in church he had been converted – 'gone religious', they said – and it showed, to the extent that he now stayed with his own wife instead of somebody else's, came home sober and paid his debts, all to the great astonishment of his former associates. Jim had taken to coming in regularly for a chat, so his presence that afternoon meant we had quite an audience for theatre.

Now, at this point in the proceedings I think

I should warn, as television announcers do from time to time, that 'in what follows there may be certain scenes that could upset some viewers', so if you are one of the faint-hearted you might be as well to skip a couple of pages!

The ewe having been ushered into the Operations Room in the midst of all this concourse, and the spectators having positioned themselves around, I took what was the first step, soaped my arm and examined her *per vaginam* to ascertain if she did in fact require surgery, or if the lamb could be delivered in normal fashion. This examination is not painful, but uncomfortable; just as the patient tenses himself, grips the arms of the chair tightly and fears the worst when the dentist says 'Open wide', and produces a strangled groan when the offending molar is tapped, so the ewe gave a slight grunt – when there was an almighty clatter, and I looked round to see the would-be nurse out cold. I hadn't done a thing; no knife had gleamed in the overhanging arc lamp; no blood had dripped to the ground, so I thought the girl's reaction boded ill for her nursing career. (In fact she did in time become an excellent nurse.) Mrs Drury, with perhaps just the suggestion of a flush colouring her cheeks, whether of embarrassment, sisterly concern or sisterly condemnation I know not, supervised the carrying of the body into our waiting-room cum office, where it was laid on a couch to recover. Bernard was to be at the desk writing for a time before going out on a case, and he promised to stay till the girl came round and make sure she didn't stagger outside with deathly countenance, or rush screaming up the street; so all then trooped back to the theatre.

I hadn't liked what I'd felt. The cervix of the uterus was tightly closed all right, but it felt dry, and there was a distinct aroma, which was not Chanel No. 5, as I withdrew my hand.

'You've got a dead lamb or lambs here, Mr Hawkins. This operation won't be easy, which is a pity, since it's your first. You could get a couple of pounds for her if you sent her into the slaughterhouse as a casualty, and with dead lambs there's a fair chance of losing her if I operate. It's up to you. What do you want?'

'What would you advise?' He was a well-spoken, well-educated man, by no means poor, perhaps socially a cut above most of our clients, and maybe a trifle superior in manner.

'Well, she's a young ewe, and as ninety per cent of caesars lamb normally next time it might be worth the risk, but it will be trickier than usual. You must decide. Surely she must have been showing signs of lambing for some time?'

'Yes, she's been paddling about a bit for a few days, but nothing to show. We're here now anyway, so go ahead,' a statement which I'm sure he was soon to regret. I think curiosity more than anything decided him. Neighbours had seen a caesar – he hadn't.

So the ewe was lifted on to the table, on her back, hind legs lightly restrained by tapes, while the farmer stood at the sheep's head and held the fore-legs. Then the team swung into the established routine, Mrs Drury on one side of the patient, myself on the other.

It's always difficult for a narrator to decide how much detail should be put into his narrative, but just in case any reader finds himself on some lonely island with a pregnant ewe requiring assistance, it might be as well to sketch in the main steps! First, the soft wool of the sheep's underbelly is plucked, then the remainder is soaped and shaved, and swabbed with antiseptic. Using a very short, fine needle, the skin is anaesthetized, then the muscles beneath, and finally, with a longer needle, right down to the peritoneum. All the sheep should feel is the first prick, and that was so in this case. Next, the operation cloths were clipped in position, leaving only the area for incision visible. I was conscious of six pairs of eyes watching closely.

Preliminaries over, we were ready to commence. Mrs Drury clapped a scalpel into my hand from our tray of sterilized instruments, and with one bold stroke the skin was incised. The sheep didn't feel a thing, but judging from the indrawn breaths I heard, others did – particularly when blood welled up, to be immediately swabbed by my assistant, allowing a clear view of the little bleeding vessels, which were clamped, but not before we lost one of our spectators. With a muttered 'Alex, I couldn't do that for a pension,' our butcher was off. Evidently Jim didn't go in for black puddings, or a wee drop of blood wouldn't have worried him! I next cut the muscles, then, carefully, the shining sheet of the peritoneum, looking for all the world like fine plastic. A loop of bowel popped up into the wound, which it had no right to do, and it was speedily put in its place. There beneath was the uterus, and gently one horn of its V-shape was brought through the incision to the exterior. A healthy uterus with a living lamb in it was always, to me, a thing of beauty, and normally I thrilled at this moment, seeing there the wonderfully soft yet strong organ the Creator had designed, with its intricate array of blood vessels to feed the developing embryo and supply its every need. But not today! This uterus was far from a pretty sight. It was doughy to the touch, puffy, oedematous and a dirty greyish colour instead of a healthy pink. I was vaguely aware of a voice behind me saying rather faintly, 'I'd better be off before the sergeant comes looking for me.' I cut into the horn of the exposed womb, and at that point one of the strapping, six-foot Hawkins boys departed, muttering, 'It's getting a bit hot in here.' He looked a trifle grey, I thought. I don't know about the heat in the room, but there was certainly a stench. 'Paddling about for a few days', farmer Hawkins had said. That lamb smelt as if it had been dead for weeks, and as I removed it and threw it into the lamb basket, with no pretence or excuse son number two departed for the door at the double. Reaching round to the other horn of the V, I removed a second lamb, also putrid. Farmer Hawkins, whose forebears had no doubt sailed the seas with the men of Devon under Raleigh, Drake, Frobisher and the original Hawkins, now felt a sudden concern as to the well-being of his family. 'I'd better see these boys are all right,' he explained as he hurriedly left us. I thought it was like the ten little niggers; soon there'd be none.

The vet student had taken farmer Hawkins's place at the sheep's head. I thought him strangely silent, and, glancing up, saw beads of sweat on a decidedly pale forehead. I was sweating too, but for a different reason; that unhealthy uterus was the very dickens to suture, as the stitches kept tearing away. It was hard work.

'Perhaps you'd just check on Mrs Drury's sister and our clients,' I suggested to the lad. It was his first caesar and he couldn't have picked a worse one. It was decidedly nasty, with the smell of decay heavy in the air. Now Mrs Drury and I were left alone. Fortunately the sheep was lying still, but I knew she'd leap to its head if it struggled. I also knew that she would not leave the room – I'd be more likely to yield first!

'Not very nice, Mrs Dru, is it? It'll be touch and go with this one.'

'One of the worst we've had,' was all she said, snipping away at catgut as I completed the second row of inversion sutures in the uterus and tucked it back inside the abdomen. The rest was routine – nylon continuous sutures for peritoneum, then muscles, and finally my favourite mattress stitch for the skin. Then the whole area was thoroughly cleansed, and dusted with sulphonamide. Without my asking, she handed the loaded syringe of penicillin (the farmer would give the ewe an injection each day for a week), and asked, 'Phenergan?'

'Yes, the first danger here will be shock.' She knew my drill and drugs of choice. 'Some pituitrin, too, I think. It's a risk, but the sooner she's pushing out that muck, the better. I only hope the sutures hold.'

So it was done, the sheep lifted down – a

very exhausted, ill sheep – and as I removed my gown and started scrubbing away the smell of death from my hands, my assistant was already at work disinfecting the table, gathering and cleaning instruments, and putting them into the sterilizer with fresh operation cloths and swabs. You never knew when they would be needed again. Feeling a bit fresher, I sallied forth to find the departed spectators and saw a horrible sight. The two Hawkins sons were sitting on the stairs leading to the upstairs flat, and they were green! It wasn't clear whether they were at the stage of sickness where they feared they would die, or at the next stage where they feared they would not die. Father was leaning against the outer door, and, though pale, he at least looked human. Our student was OK and making animated conversation with Mrs Drury's sister, who still seemed happy to lie on the couch. She got short shrift from her older sister. 'You still here? It's time you got up from there and did some work. Come and help me clean up next door.' That was enough. The sister was better and out of the door, hot-foot for home. Mrs Drury smiled, 'I thought that would get her up.'

The ewe was gently carried out to its trailer, followed by its green and white owners. I gave father some words of instruction on follow-up procedure and he was gone. The ewe recovered

– so did all the human casualties.

It was just as well Mrs Drury had sterilized everything, for at eight o'clock that night Humphrey Yeo of Wayside, probably our biggest sheep-farmer, phoned to say he was on his way with two for caesars. I groaned, because I was on duty that night. Our student had been invited out for a meal and Mrs Drury did not work in the evenings. It was a bit late to get baby-sitters, so, as we had done many times before, Janet and I picked up our two sleeping infants, aged three and one, putting Ian into a carrycot and carrying Neil, and headed for the surgery, there to await our patients. The carrycot was plonked down on a bench with its one-year-old blissfully asleep, while Neil, yawning prodigiously, sat swinging his legs from the same bench. He couldn't sleep; he had a job to do. So, with my wife assisting, we did two more caesars. We worked well together, and she knew the routine by now – swab, swab, clamp, hand this, hand that.

Now the lambs are delivered, twins, and three-year-old Neil leaps to his task. His is the job of clearing the nose and mouth of mucous, rubbing the lambs' chests with straw to dry them and get the breathing going. If not successful, operations are suspended while father does mouth-to-mouth respiration – who said the medics thought of it first! – and in forty-five minutes the whole task is over, and one ewe and Neil's two lambs are carried out to the trailer . . . lambs born as hundreds around the area had been born, lives saved in the fashion that Julius Caesar, Queen Elizabeth II and countless others had been delivered. Another forty-five minutes and we had another little ewe with a very large lamb, a caesar having been performed in this case because the lamb's horns were so far developed that they were preventing passage through the vagina, a quite common occurrence in the Exmoor Horn hogg. These two had been a sheer delight to perform and one felt a sense of achievement, seeing two happy mothers, three healthy lambs and one satisfied farmer depart into the night; it provided a needed corrective after the seventy-minutes' struggle with death of the afternoon.

Well, the day was over, and as we gathered up instruments together I could steal a kiss from my present assistant, something that could not be done with the other, for either she or Janet, and probably both, would have up and dotted me one. Yes, there was something to be said for a husband and wife partnership, not to mention some early training for the family.

On the stroke of ten, we entered our living-room, just as the phone was ringing. It was Alf Spicer.

'Mr Cameron, uz's got a sheep right bad to

lamb. Uz hears tell as how you'm got an operation that can save the lamb; be that right?'

'That's right, Alf, bring it in.'

Normally I didn't do caesars after ten o'clock, reasoning that they could wait till morning, but it was just ten now, our student was back, and I had him volunteer to come and assist. Out for tea, indeed, when other folk were working – where was the dedication in young vets nowadays! So the children were deposited in their beds once more, and after a cup of tea, Ian the student and I set out for positively the last caesar of the day, leaving instructions with Janet that if anyone called, there was Black Death in the town, or the 'vet'nary' had suspected rabies – anything to stall till morning. We delivered Alf's Border Leicester ewe of triplets, to his immense delight. I think he thought the operation was responsible for manufacturing an extra lamb. He was happy, student Ian was happy because he had seen a good caesar and he'd done his first suturing and injections. Me, I was asleep two minutes after hitting the pillow – a sure sign of the Black Death!

Our chronicle of the surprises of a caesar would not be complete without one more instance. Caesars were not confined to sheep. In fact, caesars were becoming so numerous that I felt Bristacombe was becoming more Roman than British. I did a few in cattle, one in a sow, which was rather like squeezing one's Christmas presents out of the Christmas stocking, one by one. I did a few in cats and of course, next most common to sheep, in dogs. One of these was a valuable Yorkshire terrier. By now Mrs Drury had left us to be simply a wife and mother, and after a young man, Brian, and a girl, Jill, had been with us for short periods, our new secretary was a lass called Ann Brooks. She had had thoughts of becoming a nurse, but instead became an animal nurse and our general factotum. She was a bonny girl who'd been in Sunday School when first I knew her. She was a first-class assistant, and had just proved it yet again in the case of the little yorky's caesar. Mother was all right, but we were having considerable trouble in getting her offspring going as they had been born anaesthetized. I remember Ann and I were down on our knees beside mother and young, working like mad on them, when Bernard walked in. I glanced up and saw him pause as if he'd been struck. Looking at mother and pups, I said, 'Lovely sight, isn't it, Bernard?'

'Beautiful,' he replied, looking at Ann.

'You feel you just want to cuddle them,' said Ann as she caressed a pup.

'Rather,' said Bernard.

'We're having a job getting them going. Could you lend a hand?'

There was no response. Bernard had a dazed look about him.

'Bernard!' I thundered, 'would you mind getting down here and work on saving these pups?'

'Eh?'

'These pups, Bernard, artificial respiration!'

'Oh, er, rather, I'm sure that's the right thing to do.'

'Then do it. Give Ann a hand with her pup.'

He was on his knees in a flash, his face wreathed in smiles as he knelt beside her.

After a time, I said, 'I think I can safely leave you two to cope now.'

'Rather!' said Bernard. 'I mean, we'll manage.'

And so they have, as man and wife, for many years. Yes, a caesar can produce many surprises, like target practice for Cupid, whose arrow, fired over a Yorkshire terrier and its puppies, unerringly found its mark that golden day.

11

The Good, the Bad and the Ugly

I was looking forward to the day. I had a full round to occupy me, and no cases to strike terror into the heart, so far as I could see. I had no colts to cut, whole herds to de-horn or cows to calve. It promised to be a day of relaxed working, meandering through the Devon countryside instead of the usual rush. Furthermore, I had my new little Austin van to break in; having started with an antiquated Morris van, followed by two new, but very much post-war, utilitarian Ford Populars, this was the best car I had yet owned, and the thrill of its newness had not yet worn off. Moreover, I was to be travelling in some gorgeous countryside, away up on the high plateau above the sea which here and there cut into the land, forming coves, usually with a cluster of houses beside them that were very much in demand for holiday homes. The cases, then, were easy, the day perfect, and to add cream to the cake, my first call was to a new client. What more could a country vet desire?

As I drove down to Hillcroft, I thought that although it might be all right for an olde-worlde, summertime-only residence, as a permanent home it left a lot to be desired. I had been to it once before when the former owner lived there, and I remember thinking initially it was the place the writer of the song 'Let the rest of the world go by' must have had in mind. It was, as the song described, 'a sweet little nest somewhere in the west', it was un-doubtedly 'a place known to God alone' be-cause it could be seen only from directly above, and for anyone desirous of letting the rest of the world go by, this was spot on. The entrance was unmarked, just a gate into a field, along which one drove till motor transport could proceed no further, for it was as if one had suddenly come to the edge of the world. From there, far below down the steep hillside, Hillcroft could be seen. It comprised a thatched cottage and a few farm buildings, several with their roofs falling in. If you didn't need running water, electricity, easy access or even a standard toilet, then Hillcroft might serve, but as a place to farm and earn a living it was tough going.

The new owners had spotted me descending the hill, carrying what I thought I might need.

They had asked me to come and inspect their livestock, give it all the once-over and advise them on a few points, and they welcomed me as they might some long-lost uncle bearing tidings of good fortune. I thought it likely I was the first human being they had seen for some time. I was ushered into the sitting-room and there regaled with coffee right away.

'You must excuse us not being very straight and tidy, but we haven't had time to get all the things we want, and well' . . . she paused . . . 'we thought it more important to get some animals than a lot of furniture.' I thought they both, Mr and Mrs Robens, looked ridiculously young, the dew of innocence still upon them, and somehow very vulnerable in this big old world – and in the farming world too, which had its share of sharks swimming around looking for easy prey. They were clearly just married, their furniture was sparse and saleroom, and since I knew all about that, I had a kind of fellow feeling and couldn't help but warm to their eager, fresh enthusiasm and general goodwill to all mankind.

'We only moved in last week. In fact it may not seem like it' (*ma pauvre innocente*, I thought), 'but we were just married on Mayday.' It was then 20 May, so I asked them how they were settling in.

'All right,' said the young husband, 'but we've

only seen two people since we arrived, and, well, coming from London, we're finding it a bit strange.'

'Never mind,' I tried to console them, 'you'll get to know a few folks in time. Mind you, you're going to have to slog pretty hard for a while to get this farm into shape. It's been neglected for years.'

'We know that,' the young fellow nodded, 'that's how we were able to buy it. It was so much cheaper than anything else on the market.'

'Well, I wish you success,' I said, reading between the lines and realizing that they had probably sunk every penny they had, and a whacking overdraft or mortgage besides, into their dream home. 'How did you come to get in touch with me, and how can I help you?'

'That's easy,' piped up the young wife. 'We asked the postman the first time he came . . . he's one of the two people who've been down. Well, we asked the postman about vets, and he told us different names, but he said you were a Scotsman, and we know how good Scots engineers and doctors are. Besides, well, the name Croft sounded Scottish and we thought that was a sign we should ask you to be our vet. But you're, well' (they may not have piped water, I thought, but with the number of 'wells' the wife used, they'd never run dry . . . strange the corny thoughts that come to you when a born talker is going on), 'well, you're different from what we thought.'

'Sorry to disappoint you,' I grinned. 'Tell me, what did you think?'

'We thought you might be older, and be big and broad, and maybe even wear a kilt.'

'A kilt in Devon?' I laughed. 'With the breezes whipping in from the Channel? As for the rest, well' (I was using it now), 'I'm big and lean instead.'

'Oh, but we're not at all disappointed,' she rushed on, 'we like you and I'm sure you will be very good.'

'That remains to be seen. Thanks for the coffee; now for some work. What do you want me to do?'

'We want you to look at all our animals and see if they are healthy, and . . . well, we want you to tell us which of our cows are going to have a calf, and when to send for the . . . man that brings the bull.' She blushed.

'You mean the artificial inseminator, AI for short. Right, we'll see the cows first.'

'We don't know very much, but I've been studying this book' (her husband waved a slim volume entitled *Farming Made Easy*), 'and we listen to "The Archers".'

'My hat,' I thought, 'innocents abroad!'

'But before you do anything, we, well, we . . .

210

how much do you charge, and how soon do we, well, have to pay you? We could give you something today, but it might not be enough.'

That was the first time anybody had offered me money before I'd done a job, I thought. I liked them all the more!

'We send out our statements monthly, but let's forget about payment for a while until we see how you are getting on. If you need advice, you can ring me any time if you think I can help. We don't charge for phone advice.'

I could see the young fellow sigh as if a great weight had been taken from his shoulders concerning payment, and with that we headed in procession to their little cowshed, Mr clutching *Farming Made Easy*, and Mrs a large blank notebook and pencil. In the cowshed, which was the only building, apart from the dwelling-house, whose roof was intact, were eight Channel Islanders, a mixture of Guernsey and Jersey. I looked them over. They'd had somebody honest buy that group for them, or else 'The Archers' or the omniscient book were better than I thought. They looked excellent beasts, and I said so. I had to inspect them one by one, it seemed, though clearly they were in the pink of condition, so for the sake of doing something I took all their pulses and temperatures, which were duly noted in the wife's large book under the appropriate name of the ani-

211

mal. Then I had a quick listen at eight chests, felt eight udders and eight dewy noses.

'Sound in wind and limb,' I pronounced cheerfully. 'Now for some PDs. Could you possibly bring me a bucket of water, soap and a towel?'

'Certainly,' said Mr Robens, and departed at the double.

'He'll soon draw some from the well,' explained the wife.

I couldn't believe it, in this day and age.

'You really have to get water from a well?' I asked incredulously.

'For the present, yes. We plan to collect rainwater in barrels, and when we can afford it we're going to install a pump. It's all very exciting.'

As I looked at her flushed young face and saw the eagerness of this city-bred couple, my faith in mankind was restored somewhat. The age of the pioneer was not quite past, and I hoped they would make out and weather the first hard few years. By now the water had arrived. I soaped and lathered my arm, and inserted it in the rectum of the first cow, conscious that every move I made was being closely studied. From cow number 1 to cow number 2, and I was proceeding with number 3 when Mrs Robens asked, 'Why are you doing that?'

'I want to be able to tell you which cows are

in calf, which are not, and how far on the pregnant ones are.'

Her face cleared. 'Oh, I see; it's just like an enema before an operation, you are doing.'

'Pardon?' I queried, not following the drift of her thought.

'I had an operation once, and I had an enema before it, but your way is much quicker and not so messy.' I stared in bewilderment, as she asked, 'But why do they need an enema before a pregnancy test?'

'I'm not really giving them an enema, Mrs Robens, it's just that you can't put your arm in a cow's rectum without getting it dirty!'

That settled, I turned again to the patiently waiting number 3. I was busy palpating the uterus when the voice came back at me again.

'But why do you need to, well, do that, and get your arm dirty? What's it for?'

'To find out if the cow is in calf or not. You can mark the first two down as not in calf.'

I could see two puzzled faces staring at me. Very slowly Mrs Robens laid down her book. I could not think what I'd said or done, but clearly their faith in Scots vets in general and this one in particular was shaken.

'But . . . but . . . you're in the wrong place,' she expostulated, while her husband blushed crimson. Then she went on, doubtfully, 'Or are cows different from people?'

I could see I had been taking too much for granted. They couldn't have heard the episode from 'The Archers' dealing with pregnancy tests. I really had to turn away from these two intent young faces to avoid doubling up in mirth. I gulped a few times, and then explained: 'The only way I can tell how far on in calf any cow may be is to examine the womb through the rectal wall. I don't go through it,' I hastened to add, before they conjured up pictures of holes poked through rectal walls. 'The womb lies below the rectum and, like feeling through stiff paper, I can examine it and tell roughly how far on a pregnancy is. I can't really tell below ten weeks, though some vets claim they can, but after that I can give a fair estimate. Mind you, it's not by any means a hundred per cent accurate, but it's a reasonable guide.'

They still looked suspicious that I might either be doing irreparable damage to their cows or having them on, so I picked up Mrs Robens's book and her pencil and proceeded to draw the relative positions of rectum and uterus. I then turned back to the long-suffering cow number 3 and said, 'Put this one down at about fourteen weeks. You can work out the approximate date of calving later.'

So we proceeded along the line. Four were in calf, the furthest on being seven months. From the cowshed we went on to a ruinous shed, in which reposed two large white sows. I didn't bother with temperatures, etc., there. They were clearly as right as rain, and equally clearly very heavy in pig. Next we cursorily inspected the sheep – six ewes – which they had carefully penned for my arrival. I looked at their feet and mouths. They were old ewes, but they might get a couple of breeding seasons from them. I explained about foot rot, about inoculations for a variety of diseases in sheep and lambs, and promised to speak to Bill Haley along the road to see if they could run their ewes with his ram. I thought a ram with only six wives would feel distinctly cheated and grossly insulted, when all his pals had about ten times that number.

I was just turning away from the sheep pen, when I remembered. 'Oh, yes, a word about pine.'

'We've got it,' said the wife enthusiastically.

'Eh?' I said. 'Who told you about pine?'

'Oh, everybody knows about pine and what it does,' she exulted.

I couldn't see anything to be so chirpy about in having pine, and felt that somehow our lines were crossed again.

'Show me the pine,' I demanded, peering more closely at the sheep.

'It's in the house. We keep it in the kitchen.'

'In the kitchen?'

'Yes, I've six of it.'

'Six, in the kitchen? Isn't it a bit crowded?'

'Well, the kitchen is rather small, but they only take up a little corner on a shelf,' she said, as if that made everything clear.

'I think we must be talking about different things,' I suggested: 'Pine to me is a disease – really a deficiency . . . in sheep. What is it to you?'

'Oh, I thought you meant the disinfectant which was recommended to us as fine and strong.'

That settled, I explained that pine in sheep is a disease where the sheep simply pine or waste away, and that it is the result of a deficiency of cobalt in the bloodstream, which deficiency in turn comes from the ground. I went on to explain that you could dress the ground, which was not always easy, or wholly satisfactory; the better way, certainly for the owners of six ewes, was to give the sheep, individually, a supply of cobalt.

'It's not absolutely certain that it is cobalt alone that is missing, since it has been shown that iron also, if deficient, can cause the condition. There's very little pine in Devon, but along this plateau, it occurs. I've some pellets in the car – they're called "bullets" in this case – so if you come along with me, Mr Robens,

I'll let you have a supply. You can also borrow my gun for shooting them over the sheep's throats, which might save you a scratch or two. Oh, by the way, pine also occurs in cattle, so I'd dose them as well.'

Mrs Robens had been busy scribbling all this down, obviously as an appendix to *Farming Made Easy*. I could imagine them both at night, side by side on the couch, swotting it all up.

'Now come and meet Jeremy,' said the little woman. 'He's in the orchard.'

The only Jeremy I knew about was the local MP, but this Jeremy was a donkey.

'We inherited him with the farm,' burbled Mrs Robens, 'and, well, we thought he would be very useful for pulling the milk up to the hill top on some kind of sledge, when our little tractor sticks.'

I duly admired Jeremy, and reflected that either his former owner was an ardent Liberal and had called his donkey after his MP, or else he was of another party and had meant a donkey's name as a constant insult to the Liberals.

I thought by now I had seen everything and said I'd better be on my way, but they insisted I come and drink more coffee and talk about their general strategy. While the coffee was being prepared, Mr Robens and I talked, with

Mrs Robens frequently hopping through from the kitchen to hear the discussion.

'I think you've made a good beginning,' I said, sincerely, 'but you will have to decide whether you are going to specialize or diversify.'

'Oh! Ah!' exclaimed the two in unison. I reflected that an awful lot must be missing from their textbook and 'The Archers'!

'What I mean is that on a small farm you have either to choose one thing, and gear all your planning to that – say, your Channel Islanders – or you can decide to have several different sources of income. In your position, and on this farm where your only crops will be grass and hay, I'd say, diversify – don't put all your eggs in one basket. I'd right away repair the roof of that old barn and get some hens in there in deep litter, and when you can afford it, I'd buy one or two beef animals, young beasts, which you can fatten up. That would give you milk, beef, eggs and pig weaners to sell, so you will always have the till ticking over.' I leapt to my feet. 'I really must be on my way.'

Accompanied by the young fellow and cheered on my way by fervent thanks from his wife, I reached the car, gave him the mineral bullets and gun, and was off. My ego had been considerably boosted because they had hung on every word I'd said, whereas in Ayrshire I was more often than not told by the farmer what he wanted, like issuing instructions to the plumber to fix a new washer on a tap.

My next call was to another 'townie' couple, who had been clients for several years now. I stopped the car at the top of their road as I always did, and gazed at one of the loveliest little bays I know – Forest Bay – which looked exactly as it sounded. At the foot the sea, surging ceaselessly in to the shore, met the forest, whose feet were almost in the waves, and whose trees covered all the visible land around, presenting a scene of great beauty and an atmosphere of timelessness. I felt I must get a photograph, for that day the sea was a deep, deep blue, contrasting with the softer blue of the sky and the various shades of green of the forest. Below, on a little knoll above the beach, stood the old manor house, looking, as always, perfect in that setting, as if it had grown up naturally with the trees. Only one thing marred the scene. Just above the tree-line, and indeed cutting into the forest itself, was a great gash of turned-up earth, a strip completely devoid of vegetation. Here stood a pig farm, a large one now, owned and run by the Ingravilles, the tenants of the Manor. I nosed the car down towards the piggery, saw no one about, and drove on down to the house.

I remembered my first visit there and my

introduction to Mr Ingraville, clearly not his original name, for he was Polish and had been a cavalry officer when the Nazis invaded his homeland. His wife – well, I don't know what she had been, though an actress was hinted at, and certainly I never saw so much make-up on one face at any given time of day or night: layers of it, scrapeable with a knife! The other member of the Ingraville entourage was Cleopatra, a pet pig, who ran about the house like a dog. They were charming – very – in manner, yet I always got the feeling that the whole thing was a great charade.

Today's call should be easy, for they wanted to discuss scouring in their piglets and how we could prevent it. I rang the bell and walked into the lovely old house, which now had a distinctly aromatic odour of pig about it. To my surprise, instead of the normal gushing welcome I was met by an obviously angry female face and a distinctly morose male one. Clearly there had been conflict, with one another or with a third party. It proved to be the latter in the person of a poor, lean, rather shifty-eyed and distinctly odoriferous man, nervously twisting his cap in his hands. I recognized him as their pigman.

'Ah, here's the vet; we'll see now if you're telling the truth,' thundered Madam Ingraville. 'Come, Leopold,' she called over her shoulder, and her husband duly trotted to her side. 'You come too, Walters,' ordered the prima donna, and all three leapt into their Land-Rover — well, the lady rather flopped in, having no longer a leaping figure. Like a little dog, I followed on in my Austin, wondering what calamitous event had occurred. I thought probably a pig had lost a tooth, or something similar, remembering how they had called me out over twenty miles one evening to see a pig with a cut ear, the cut proving so minute that all it needed was a dab of Vaseline. But I was wrong in this instance, as speedily became plain, for there, lying in the yard at the foot of a wall, was their boar, the father of the herd, and it was plain to see he would father no more pigs. He was very dead. I looked at the body; nothing was obvious externally to help in diagnosis.

'Has he been ill?' I asked.

'No, he has not,' came the raging reply, 'he has been killed — by him!' And she pointed dramatically at the wretched Walters. Lady Macbeth couldn't have done it better. Mr Ingraville meantime was spluttering in Polish, of which language I knew not a word, but I could make a very fair guess at what he was saying; just to make it clear, he ended with an explosive, 'Blast you, you murderer!'

'I tell you, I did nothing, sir. I just found him

lying here,' said poor Walters.

'Pshaw – a likely story. He was quite all right an hour ago,' said Mrs Ingraville.

'We've seen you kick the boar, you wretched asass . . . asass . . . killer,' came Mr Ingraville, on cue with his line.

It was a rather nasty situation, and while I didn't go overboard for either Ingraville, neither did I think very highly of Walters. It was clear I was going to have to arbitrate in the affair, to be the detective who was to ferret out the truth. So from a veterinary surgeon who had come to discuss scouring pigs, I was changed in a moment to the pathologist in a homicide . . . or rather a pigicide. I hadn't come prepared to do a post-mortem, but I had a few scalpels in my bag, so got to work. I found the cause of death, too, to my great surprise and relief, though I doubted if it was going to help to restore normal relations and general bonhomie between the warring factions. The boar had bled to death from an internal haemorrhage in the abdomen. It could conceivably have been a kick, it could have been a fall. I could see no trace of an aneurism, and I was pretty sure in my own mind that somebody or something had landed the poor old boar a hefty thump. I explained this to the watching threesome, and immediately Mrs Ingraville went into her pointing routine with quite a long speech, the gist of which was that they would sue Walters for damages, and he was to be gone and never darken their pighouse door again. The wretched man, as white as a sheet, protested his innocence once more, turned on his heel and went. He was back in two ticks, having forgotten his bicycle and lunch-tin.

'He shan't get away with this. We will definitely prosecute,' said my lady. I pointed out that no one, certainly not I, could say for certain that a kick had done this; there were no boot nails embedded in the skin, or traces of shoe leather on the abdominal area, such as there would certainly be in the annals of detection, and they should consult carefully with their lawyer before they embarked on a voyage with a somewhat suspect chart. I was invited down to the Manor, but since they were both seething and seemed likely to be so for some time, and having no particular desire to witness the dash of a cavalry officer or listen to the soliloquies of a tragic queen, I left them, and proceeded to the next call and happier things.

Near Forest Bay, at the mouth of a little river, stood a large, imposing country house, which was owned and run by the Church of England as a retreat, a conference centre, a refuge of peace, a haven to which came those in need of instruction, or rest and renewal of body, mind and spirit. Attached to it was a farm, with, amongst other things, a herd of Guernseys. In fact the whole setup bore some resemblance to a kibbutz. Kenneth, himself a lay reader of the Church of England, was on the committee of the Centre, so we offered our professional services free, only charging for drugs supplied.

I started off very suspicious of the whole thing. It was not that my Scottish upbringing made me resent giving anything free – it was more my Presbyterian background that made me then suspicious of anything non-Presbyterian. If the Roman Catholic Church was on the road to perdition, then the Anglican Church, especially the High Church, wasn't far behind! But that Centre opened my eyes, for there I met numbers of people, clergy and laity, who were always jumping up and down in their liturgy, who burnt candles . . . even incense . . . and who bowed to the altar – all things that were utterly alien to me; yet amongst those folks, so very different from me in the expression of their faith, were men and women who were truly saintly. It was not a 'halo round the head' kind of saintliness, it was certainly not a sickly or weak thing . . . it was as if these people, from every walk of life, had learned a great secret, discovered a truth long sought . . . and found abundant wealth. They were gentle folks, and in contact with them, some of the sharp corners of my square Presbyterian position were smoothed over. The person I saw most was Ursula (Bernard could never get her name right and called her 'Hiroshima'). Ursula was in charge of the cattle and was not unlike her Guernseys, a sort of golden glow surrounding her, as if a light was burning within. But she was far from other-worldly, was an expert with cattle, and, slim little thing though she was, could tackle heavy tasks. She also had probably the cleanest, most sterile cowshed and dairy in Devon. The task for the day was simply to wash out a cow, that is, to insert a metal catheter into the womb and pump in some antiseptic solution, to clear up the lingering metritis or inflammation. But veterinary practice is full of surprises, and one often hears the words, 'Oh, when you're here anyway, would you look at such-and-such?'

The such-and-such on this occasion was a cow with an enormous lump, about the dimension of a size 3 football I used to kick as a laddie. It was one of those cases that looks much worse than it is, though I don't suppose the bearer of the lump would agree. The lump was on the chest wall, just behind the shoulder, and was in fact an abscess, probably caused by a horn-poke from another cow. This one was ripe for the knife, so having obtained an old bucket from Ursula, and advising her to stand well back and hold her nose, I lanced it, to let an enormous quantity of pus drain into the bucket. The hole was made big enough to allow complete drainage, and before I had finished Ursula was busy with the disinfectant in her cowshed. No form of poison had a chance with that girl around!

By now, my gastric juices were straining at their leash to get at some food, so having duly supplied this at a café, I went on. I had an appointment with an RSPCA inspector at two-thirty. I met him at the farm, which I didn't know . . . it wasn't one of mine, for that would have complicated matters. There we inspected three dogs, all collies, while their surly owner looked on in silence. They were in a deplorable condition, and it made my temper rise. All were thin to the point of emaciation, two had deep, toxic, weeping wounds, which hadn't happened yesterday. The third was an old dog, partially blind, its eyes covered over with matter and its body a mass of bedsores. I saw the little shed which was their home, with its earthen, foul, stinking floor . . . no wonder there were bedsores!

'Why did you not have these wounds treated, and what caused them?' I asked.

'Reckon they wuz caused by them barbed-wire fences. I did put some tar on them, like, an' left it to nature. She be the best healer.'

Stockholm tar treatment, once, and leave it to nature. Mind you, he was a wild man, and probably carried out his philosophy on himself, but he was for the high jump this time. The RSPCA were definitely pushing this case, and I was there merely to be 'an expert witness' in court. The dogs were taken into the Society's care, pending a decision as to their future. It was an ugly business. These dogs had served him well as sheepdogs, but, like all too many hill farmers' dogs – even sometimes shepherds' dogs – they were simply flung some food and shut in a dark corner. Yet I'm certain, with the loyalty of their kind, they would have defended him with their lives. Yes, an ugly affair.

The next call wouldn't take long, I thought. Further along to the next village, and now at the furthest point of the practice, perhaps twenty-eight miles from home, I had simply to give a dog its distemper inoculation. I found the house with difficulty, and was conducted to an upstairs flat by the landlady. I thought I was back with the dogs again, because that room stank of a mixture of cooking, stale tobacco smoke, spirits and just plain dirt. A figure rose from a couch as I entered, the landlady having simply, and without apology, thrown open the door.

'Mr Leighton-Jones?' I asked.

'Flight-Lieutenant Leighton-Jones, old boy,'

came the correction.

The room was very dim, with drawn curtains, and as he switched on the light I saw a swaying form, clutching a glass in one hand and a cigarette in the other; but what instantly drew my eyes was his face. I had seen burned faces before, but none quite so dreadful as this one, which looked as if the surgeon who had done the skin-grafting had been tackling his first case.

'I'm sorry,' I said, 'I didn't know you were in the RAF.'

'Not any more, old chap . . . not any more . . . hic . . . when you're no more use to them, you're O-U-T . . . *out* . . . damn them!' he cursed.

'Were you Fighter or Bomber Command?' I inquired.

'Fighter . . . old Spitfires . . . I was one of the Few, as they called us . . . till I bought this,' he said, lifting his chin to reveal even more scarring on his neck. 'A Messerschmitt 109 got me on my tail. Pretty, isn't it . . . well, say something, damn you!' and he thrust his face close to mine. He reeked of gin, and his eyes had the bloodshot look of the heavy drinker.

I drew back involuntarily, and said simply, 'I'm very sorry.'

'Sorry! That's all we get now, sorry, sorry, sorry. What good's sorry? Can that cure you, give you a new face, huh? What woman would look at you with a face like that?' he pointed. 'And it's sex that makes the world go round.'

'I'd always heard it was love,' I said.

'Love!' He spat it out. 'No such thing, only sex!'

'Were you married when you were shot down?' I asked.

'Still am. Got a wife somewhere, but no job, no prospects . . . and this!'

I was about to ask where his wife was, but he forestalled me.

'I left her. Can't ask a woman to live with this.' Again he thrust his face into mine. 'But I get by; there's compensations,' holding up the bottle, 'and others.' He winked incongruously.

I thought it was time I did what I'd come to. do, so I said, 'You asked us to inoculate a puppy. Where is he, or is it she?'

'It's a bitch, and a blasted good one, so don't you go messing it up with your inoculations.' He opened a door to reveal a bedroom, with a recumbent female form, out cold, and from the room came bounding a lovely Irish setter.

'Trouble with women is they can't hold their drink,' he muttered.

The dog was all over him, licking his hand, pulling at his jacket, licking that scarred face. I found the scene in those sordid surroundings at one and the same time indescribably ugly and infinitely moving.

The injection was soon over, and the dog, after an initial yelp, bounced and rolled all over the place.

'She really is a beauty,' I enthused. Setters were amongst my favourites.

'Course she is, didn't I tell you? Now I suppose you want to be paid?'

'If you care to, or we'll send a bill.'

'No, get it over with. I'll give you a cheque,' which, after a bit of searching for his cheque-book, he did.

He got up and lurched towards me, and grasped my jacket lapels. He had a point to make, it seemed, and I was his prisoner.

'By the way, what do they call you . . . vet . . . vet . . . vet'nary surgeon, what were you with in the last show, eh? Bet it was something safe, like the Pay Corps – or no,' he paused and laughed as at some huge joke, 'it would be the Medical Corps. Half of that lot were blasted vets, I always said.'

I told him I had been too young to join up at the outbreak of war, and by the time I was that age, it was well on the way to being won; and as a vet student, I was deferred.

He sneered, gave me the full flavour of his aromatic breath, and muttered, clutching my lapels firmly, 'Knew what you were doing, eh, didn't you?'

I counted ten, laid down my case, disengaged myself from his clutch and said, 'Flight-Lieutenant, it so happened I wanted to be a vet. I am truly sorry for what you have suffered,' I held up my hand, 'though I know you don't want pity. We all in Britain owe you fellows a tremendous lot ... and we know it. But I didn't think any Battle of Britain pilot would let any Nazi fighter down him for life. If you're not a phoney, get up and fight, sir, and as for love, just look into your dog's eyes. Maybe somewhere there's another pair of eyes that still look like that, for you. Good-day to you.'

And I left him, open-mouthed, swaying on his feet. It was unfair, I thought as I left, that I who had suffered nothing should preach at someone who'd been through the hell men make of their world. It was ugly, as all cruelty is ugly – the cruelty of war, the cruelty of what it could do to people's lives – but I consoled myself with the thought of that Irish setter, to whom its master was the fairest thing on earth.

I turned the car's nose towards home with an unpleasant taste in my mouth, thinking of the callousness of that shepherd towards his dogs, and the senselessness of war that could produce scars that reached right down into a man's very spirit. Yes, an ugly afternoon, and it was not quite finished, for I had one call still to make.

Mr Pike would probably have come bottom of my list of favourite clients. He was an incomer from the north, though the locals would soon overlook that, but he was a swaggering, coarse braggart of a man who knew all the answers, and proceeded to demonstrate it by making an unholy mess of what had been a good farm. If I'd been asked whether I'd like to spend time on a desert island with Mr Pike or a rattlesnake, it would have been a close vote. Rumour had it that he was now in Queer Street financially, and he owed us quite a bit. I was going to his farm to treat a cow, but I knew I'd have to talk about his account, and this I always detested. As I pulled into his yard he was bellowing at a lad carrying a bucket, and he wasn't choosing his words as he let the boy, one of his sons, know what he thought of him. He greeted me with a glare and a nod, and strode towards his byre, with me following. Not a word was spoken till he stopped at an Ayrshire cow, gave her a slap, and growled, 'Felon . . . a bad un.'

I examined the cow's udder, having learnt that 'felon' was one of the many names for mastitis. One of the cow's quarters was as hard as a board, a summer mastitis caused by a bug named *Corynebacterium pyogenes*.

'When did she calve?' I asked.

' 'bout week ago.'

'And I bet she had this when she calved.'

He glared at me, and muttered, 'Aye.'

'What have you done for her?' I queried.

'Stripped out a lot o' muck – stinkin', it were, put in some o' your penicillin and rubbed her bag with mustard.'

I nodded and said, 'I'm afraid, Mr Pike, it wouldn't matter what you did, you wouldn't clear that. She's lost that quarter. It's called summer mastitis, what she's got. She picked it up when she was dry, and unless the beast is really ill with it, and some are, very, you wouldn't notice it. We recommend that when you're drying off a cow at the end of a lactation, you fill the udder with penicillin, then seal off the teats with something like collodion. It isn't a hundred per cent, but it's as good as we know . . . that, and inoculation against it, which isn't a hundred per cent either. I'm afraid there's nothing I can do for that quarter, but she can go through life on three wheels.'

'Typical of you fellows; nowt I can do for it, then a whackin' great account.'

'Uh . . . huh . . . well, about your account, Mr Pike, we haven't had a penny for three years. I'm afraid I'll need to ask you to let us have something on account now.'

His face cleared like a summer storm passing. In so far as it was possible for Pike to become all sweetness and light, he did. He even attempted a smile, but since it was so long since he'd used the smile muscles, it came out as a kind of twisted leer.

'I know, Mr Cameron, but things have been hard lately. I'll let you have it within a fortnight.'

I looked at him suspiciously, but short of digging in my heels and saying, 'Pay now,' I didn't see what I could do, so left it at that. He even shut the car door for me as I got in, and signalled goodbye. I should have been warned!

So I turned the car homeward. It had not been a hard day; in fact in terms of numbers of visits done or difficult cases, it had been a very easy round. But in types of visit, the day had ranged from the sunshine start with those two innocent pioneers and the visit to Ursula and her Guernseys, to the encounters with the Ingravilles and Pike, the unpleasantness of the cruelty case, and the representative of the RAF . . . ex! Though few in number the visits had covered almost the whole animal spectrum, from donkey to dog. In retrospect the day had deteriorated in quality, going from good, to bad, to ugly, and as if in keeping with my mood as I drove home, I saw great black clouds massing out over the Channel. We were in for a downpour, I thought; how quickly a day can change, and one's moods and emotions. I reflected that this had, in fact, been a day typical of veterinary practice – and of life. Oh well, just time for a bite of food before evening surgery.

In practice, each case history is either a complete story, or a continuing saga. For the most part, that day of the good, the bad and the ugly, as I had mentally dubbed it, was a serial story, and produced repercussions which shook our practice and affected several lives. Take the ugly. The hill farmer was tried for his cruelty, had the book thrown at him, his old dog was put to sleep – a kindness, that – and his other two found worthier masters. My other dog client, the Flight-Lieutenant ... well, his cheque bounced, and on enquiring for him a week later I found he had gone, taking his setter with him. I wondered, was it just possible he was looking again for eyes that had once shone with love for him, and maybe could again? Or was it, as seemed most likely, a drift to some other flat, some other companion, and daily dependence on the bottle? I would never know.

Pike did a moonlight flitting two weeks after my visit, taking stock and possessions with him, and leaving only his debts and no for-warding address. The Ingravilles fought their case against their pigman but, largely because I could not categorically say that death *had* come from a kick but merely that the injury *could have* come from such a blow, they lost. In Scotland I reckon it would have been 'Not Proven'. Costs were awarded against them, and some weeks later Mr Ingraville was declared bankrupt, his sole assets being one shotgun, the majority of his possessions meantime having been safely passed to his wife's name. I never saw them, or Pike, again – or their money. It was a real blow to the solar plexus to lose two large amounts. There was a certain amount of wailing and gnashing of teeth as we sought to meet our monthly drug bills, because we were at the time in one of the many financial recessions we'd experienced since 1945.

Ursula continued in her own competent way, while the Robens – well! I was wakened one morning about six-thirty by the insistent ringing of the phone. Milk fever, I thought, as I reached for it. The voice at the other end was plaintive, even accusing, and the gist of the message was that the cow I had said was seven months in calf had been due by Mrs Robens's calculations to calve that night, and, well, they had sat up all night, and it hadn't calved.

I groaned and smiled at one and the same time – which is not as easy as it sounds – and explained: 'Mrs Robens, I told you that our tests were not a hundred per cent accurate, certainly not to the day, and even if they were, cows – like people – can be ten days before or after the nine months and that is still normal.' Quite a speech for the time of day, I thought!

The client wasn't satisfied, and asked, 'But how will we know if she's calving?'

I groaned again, this time without the smile. 'Where is the cow?' I asked.

'In its shed.'

'Is it standing with its back arched, or paddling about uncomfortably on its feet, is it groaning, grunting or making any other noise, and has it any water or other discharge coming away?' – a ten-second lecture on calving.

'Well – no.'

'What is she doing?'

'Lying down and chewing her cud.'

'Then, lassie, you go and do the same – well, lie down anyway!'

The little woman phoned a week later (at a respectable time) and, breathless with excitement, informed me that Belinda had calved, everything was fine, but, well, they had missed it, for having kept watch for a week, they'd gone to bed that night, exhausted.

'And she did it all herself, Mr Cameron! Isn't Nature wonderful?'

'It surely is,' I agreed.

Well, animal nature anyway. I wasn't so sure about the human variety, but I hoped that this refreshing twosome would be spared the harsher side of things for a time, and the morning dew of their innocence would linger a while. It helped to offset the Pikes of this world!

12

Monkey Tricks

I had done it! I had actually bowled an off-break. The first time I'd been a bit doubtful, thinking maybe the ball had hit a bit of dirt or something, but two in a row surely couldn't be luck. I saw myself as the Jim Laker of our Monday night team; far better to use the head and by sheer skill trap a batsman than rush up with a full head of steam, as was my wont, and find my fastest ball despatched for four. So in a state approaching bliss, I prepared to bowl a third spinner in the portion of yard at the kennels ideal for such practice, when Janet's voice summoned me back to reality. I remember there was a note of urgency in it that perfect late summer evening as she called, 'Visit, darling. Mr Trevelyan is on the phone and he seems very upset. He wants to speak to you.'

So with a sigh I threw down the ball, dreams of glory banished for the moment as I

239

picked up the phone.

'Alex?' (in Devon they always sounded the 'x' in my name instead of the more usual Scots abbreviation of 'Alec'). 'This is Charlie Trevelyan.'

He sounded strained, not at all the usual cheerful greeting of our local zoo owner and administrator, whose TV appearances with some of his pets had endeared him to millions of children. He went on, 'You know that escaped monkey . . .' His voice actually broke. 'Could you come up right away? I'd appreciate it.'

'Why, sure, Charlie, but what's up?'

'Look, I'd rather not talk on the phone; I'll see you soon.'

I went to my car in some perplexity. What could have upset Charlie so? I had seen him fight his way through some pretty tough times and overcome many disappointments as he sought to establish his zoo, until it became, I believe, the biggest private one in Britain. I knew all about the escaped monkey, too – who didn't? The saga had begun several weeks back when Charlie, well pleased with life because it had been a profitable season at the zoo, walked out after breakfast for his morning rounds. Suddenly he was pulled up dead in his tracks. There were monkeys on the roof, and the realization hit him that the only person who kept monkeys hereabouts was himself. He bellowed, 'Irene!' and his head girl came at the gallop. She was a bonny, blonde, gentle girl, passionately fond of animals and expert with them.

'Irene! There's monkeys on the roof!'

'I know, Mr Trevelyan, I was just coming to tell you. It's the Dead End Kids.'

Breathing fire and slaughter, Charlie with his head girl headed for the Dead End Kids' enclosure, Charlie roaring, 'Who did it? Who let them out?'

In fact he found that the crafty 'kids' had let themselves out. The lock of the enclosure had become corroded with the sea air, and the rest the monkeys did for themselves. The 'kids' were rhesus monkeys, one of the smallest, most common, most popular and certainly most mischievous of all the macaques. Many a visitor had required placating after an arm had reached out and removed his spectacles, pulled his child's hair or stolen an ice lolly. The daily cleaning of their pen was a comedy turn, for invariably one of the bunch would steal a mop or throw a bucket of water over the attendant – and now eight of these bundles of trouble were free amidst an unsuspecting public, only one of their number remaining blissfully asleep through it all, and no doubt cursing herself later that she'd missed all the fun. Three were recaptured that day, leaving five at large, in the midst of the holiday season! Of course the police had to be notified, the local paper gave wide coverage to the 'great escape', and the media kept the world informed of developments. Anyone seeing the escapees was asked to contact the zoo and for days it was inundated with calls, not one of which proved accurate. It seemed as if every dog or cat crossing a road had become a rhesus monkey, and sightings were reported from far and near. After three days a further three monkeys were captured just a mile from their home, leaving two still 'gone away'. A lady in the town found herself confronted by one of them in her hall one day. The monkey fled upstairs and went into the bathroom, whereupon the lady shut the door on it and phoned the zoo. Charlie and Irene arrived with net and box, and opened the bathroom door in time to see the monkey coolly unlatch the window and escape. However, its freedom was shortlived as it was caught the same day in a garden shed at the same house. One left to catch, but that one was to cause many heart flutterings, produce a considerable furore, and generally become a legend. Never had Bristacombe gained so much publicity, rivalling for a time Loch Ness and its famous beast! Stories abounded of the antics of this rhesus; some were no doubt apocryphal, but others had a grain of truth in them, for he was at large for weeks, enjoying to the full his freedom in this best of all worlds and living it up as only a rhesus can!

A courting couple seated on a park bench had heard a rustle in a rhododendron bush behind them, imagined they had a Peeping Tom, and, while the girl remained demurely on the seat, her gallant swain edged his way into the bush, to come face to face with a character from a Tarzan film. Which was the more startled is hard to say. Both gave a yowl, both leapt in the air, as did the waiting maiden, while the monkey made his escape via the trees around. The gallant lover emerged with blanched countenance and made for safety on the bench beside his girl, where they clutched one another tightly − till the ridiculous nature of their pose struck them and they headed for the girl's home. Their story had by now grown − the brave young blade had saved his girl from attack and driven off what was possibly a gorilla! Imagination is a wonderful thing; imagination in the cause of love is a source of even more whopping tales than fishing!

Most sightings of the creature had been in one area of the town just up from our surgery, a couple of streets of terrace houses some four storeys high. The monkey, of course, found plentiful scraps of food in dustbins, but in houses so perfectly endowed with drainpipes the rhesus soon discovered that it was easy to obtain tastier bites. One little girl went to the kitchen on some errand, in time to see the rear end of the creature disappearing through the tiny top window. Her parents had refused to believe her story and impressed upon her the advisability of always telling the truth. Another woman, a guest-house owner, having seen her guests to bed, was enjoying the luxury of a long soak in her bath when she got the feeling that she was no longer alone; sure enough, there at the window was a wrinkled face and two beady eyes surveying her with interest, three storeys up. Whether the monkey was male or female she knew not – but, causing a miniature tidal wave, she had leapt for a bath towel, with a yell that startled all her guests.

I liked the story of the little lad who had gone into the kitchen to find the monkey sitting on the table eating a banana. He rushed to the living-room and announced: 'There's a monkey on the table,' to be told not to be ridiculous. Shortly afterwards the mother had cause to go to the kitchen, and the crash of her fainting on the floor fetched her husband at the double. The monkey had by now escaped. 'I told you there was a monkey here,' Junior protested, and earned himself a hearty clout on the ear, as if he somehow had been the cause of the mother's condition. There was a state of unease around Montpellier Terrace and adjacent streets, but all efforts by Charlie and his staff to capture the errant one had been in vain. By the time they reached a sighting, the Dead End Kid was probably in another kitchen, and the uneasiness grew. A warm, well-fed monkey was probably harmless, but this one had been at large for weeks now, the nights were getting chill, and who could say what might happen?

There was one final happening, the truth of which I cannot verify, but it's a good story anyway. It concerned Billy Biddlecombe. Now the town of Bristacombe had few real drunks, but Billy was one of them, a regular soak, unless his wife kept him under restraint. On this occasion he was on his own as his wife was staying the night at South Molton with her mother, so Billy had a night out with the boys. Returning late, he fell into bed, placing the remains of a bottle of Scotch on the bedside table for night-time emergencies. Wakening late in the night, just as dawn was streaking the sky with pink fingers, Billy had felt in need of a thirst-quencher. He reached out a hand and failed to make contact with a bottle. He groped about, muttering to himself, until he became aware of other mutterings in the bedroom. His bleary eyes searched the room in vain till finally he beheld, in the dim light, a hairy creature clutching a bottle and observing him from the top of the wardrobe. Billy stared in sheer mortal terror, his eyes, it may be presumed, growing larger by the minute (though of course no one was present to confirm this), till in the grip of the horrors he dived under the bedclothes, where he remained until his wife found him at eleven a.m. that day. The veracity of this story could not be confirmed since Mrs Biddlecombe could make nothing of her husband's utterances, Billy himself was convinced he had progressed beyond pink elephants to hairy monsters, and the monkey wasn't telling. The only certainty was that a half-bottle of whisky was found on the top of the wardrobe, and Billy never touched another drink for the rest of the year. But while the monkey might have wrought some moral benefits on the likes of Billy Biddlecombe, it was clear that something had to be done, and soon, for the physical safety of others, particularly children in their prams. Nowadays, of course, a knockout dart would probably have been fired at the fugitive, but they were unknown then, and his daylight appearances were so fleeting that he eluded every effort at capture. That was the state of the saga of the Bristacombe monkey when I got into my car that night and drove the mile up to the zoo. Charlie was waiting for me at the gate, very agitated indeed. He grasped my arm and filled me in with a rush of words.

'We got a phone call tonight saying the rhesus was on a roof. He had been down on to the terrace and had stolen a baby's bottle from its pram. Everybody was up in arms, so I knew what had to be!'

Charlie went on to tell me how he had spotted the errant one on the roof, and had taken careful aim with his .22 rifle, steadying himself with his arm on a wall. He mustn't miss; at all costs he mustn't only wound, for then the monkey would have been really dangerous. It must have been a terrible moment for Charlie, for if ever a man loved animals, had patience with them and made allowances for them, it was this man. He didn't miss. The little animal came cascading down the roof and its reluctant executioner had to turn away, his hands over his ears so as not to hear the thud of its fall.

I was still mystified about why I had been called by the time I reached Charlie's living-room, though desperately sorry for him. There lay the little creature beside the sack into which it had been thrown after its death. I looked at it in pity, and with interest. I had often read in Western epics of some bad lad having a hole neatly drilled between his eyes. Here I witnessed it for the first time; the hole was exactly that. I looked again.

'Charlie! He's still alive!'

I looked round at the poor man, who could only nod. Tears were coursing down his cheeks.

'Yes, Alex!' he managed to say at last. 'I want you to save him.'

I examined the monkey; it was deeply unconscious. A superficial examination failed to detect any broken ribs, but only an X-ray would show that, and who knew what internal injuries there might be — besides a bullet through the brain.

I took Charlie by the arm, made him sit down on a couch, and sat beside him.

'Now look, Charlie! You know I'm just about as fond of animals as you are, but it would take a brain surgeon to save him, and there are no vet brain surgeons. Besides, no human surgeon would attempt anything without sophisticated tests, and possibly the nearest place for that might be London. The only reason I can think of that he's not dead is that, at the angle you shot him, the bullet must have travelled upwards and missed any vital centre — but Charlie, there's only one hole. The bullet is still in there. I can't save him.'

'Well, will you let him take his chance, as long as he doesn't suffer?' he pleaded.

Who could refuse? 'All right, we'll have a go, but you know, boy, that the chances are about a thousand to one.'

Charlie nodded.

I gave the little creature, clinging so tenuously to life, a shot of morphine, sufficient to ensure he would remain unconscious, sat with the Trevelyans for a time and watched my patient. The breathing was coming easy and regular, not laboured. I was satisfied he would be out for the night.

Next morning early, the phone rang. The message was not unexpected.

'Alex, he's gone. We sat up with him; he didn't suffer.'

I hesitated; it's not easy to tell an animal-lover this: 'It's best, Charlie, best for him and for you.' Then, trying desperately to find some word to cheer, I said, 'Remember what the poet said? — "One crowded hour of glorious life is worth an age without a name."'

He'd had his hour. He had known, for a time, the glory of freedom.

13

To Die or Let Live

Leaving the car in the private parking space of The Willows, I quietly opened the fine wrought-iron gate which, like everything at The Willows, betokened excellent taste and the money to indulge it. I climbed the first few steps that led to the garden path, as I had done often before, but today, before proceeding any further, I paused and sat down on the garden wall. It was quiet there, and I felt badly in need of a few moments by myself to control my emotions before going on to the next case. Glancing over my shoulder, I could just see the roof of the house, and towering above it, the rocky knoll at whose feet it nestled. Safe in the knowledge that my presence was as yet undetected, I gave myself up to the luxury of a rest and reflection.

It was a glorious summer day, and in the garden behind me bees droned and buzzed as they inspected the many flowers for nectar, while in the shrubs and trees blackbirds sang, sparrows chirruped and chaffinches chattered. In front and far below me were the glorious and much-photographed sands of Mortecombe, stretching three miles into the distance, the far end barely visible in the heat haze of that blazing August day. On the sands, as always on such a day, were hundreds of people, but so vast was the beach and its attendant dunes that there seemed plenty of space for everyone.

I could see little figures dotted everywhere, soaking up the sun and acquiring a West Country tan (you could always tell the newcomers by their white faces), but also up and down the beach many football or cricket matches were in progress. Mostly it was cricket, because at that time a Test Match was on many miles away; from dozens of radios the voices of John Arlott or Brian Johnston would be giving a ball-by-ball commentary on the fight for the Ashes, inspiring the beach contestants to emulate, or identify with, a Compton or Cowdrey, a Statham or Laker. Parked here and there on the vast beach were little vans, each with a queue beside it, seeking the cool draught of an orange squash, or a temporary respite from the heat in an ice-cream or lolly. In the sea figures leapt and splashed, and I'm sure shouted and screamed, but up here all the noises of men were drowned by the crash and thunder of the

251

ocean, whose majestic, foaming, curling break-
ers plunged beachwards, bearing surfers on
their backs or swamping rubber-dinghies. Over
all stretched an azure blue sky, merging blue-
grey with the sea at the distant horizon. It was
a typical summer scene of joy, gladness, relaxation or the thrill of adventure – yet I felt none
of these today as I watched, for I could not
forget Silver. As if my thought had been their
cue, at that moment a line of ponies came over
the brow of the gently sloping hill which
formed a perfect backcloth for the long expanse
of golden sand, washed ceaselessly by the dying
foam of the waves as the great green combers
reared far out to launch themselves at the shore.
Silver should have been along with these ponies. Two weeks ago he had been with them,
someone on his back, probably a child experiencing the thrill of a first riding lesson, for
Silver was quiet, gentle, trustworthy, ideal for
beginners – and just two streets away from
The Willows, Silver was dying in the loose-box
where I'd left him.

It had been perhaps ten days ago that John
Wilkinson, owner of the stables, had called me.
Silver had been brought in with the other
ponies to be groomed and made ready for
another day's toil over the dunes, and up the
hill and fields beyond. But something was
clearly wrong with the little grey pony that

morning. He walked stiffly, dragging behind the others, and stood in his box listless, head down, pained-looking. Silver had a temperature and I set out to discover why.

'He was all right yesterday, and when we put them out to grass last night,' said his owner, as I listened to Silver's chest with my stethoscope. His lungs were clear, though his respirations were faster than normal. He had no nasal discharge, no obvious abscesses, just that stiff, 'don't want to move' look. What was it? I ran my hands over neck, back and limbs − nothing. It was only when I ducked under his head at the feeding trough that I found it, and as soon as I touched his brisket (the pad of muscle and fat at the front of the chest), he whinnied and reared. The wound there was not big, but already it was a dirty, almost black, colour. I didn't like it, for I knew what had caused that wound, or was at any rate ninety-nine per cent certain − an adder. Every summer we had adder bites. Every summer I'd treated cattle and sheep, but principally dogs, and all had recovered uneventfully. I'd never seen one in a horse, and by the look of it that wound had happened the night before, probably just after he'd been turned out to grass and had lain down for a roll and a delicious scratching of the back to get all the itchiness and stiffness out of him. He must have lain on the snake, because the viper seldom bites unless molested. This was one of the many occasions when I wished that our patients could talk, just to be sure of the details. So here we had a bite, or, from the look of it, several bites, some fifteen hours ago — a long time for the venom to be circulating in the bloodstream. I cut open the black, diseased area, drained out the discharge already puffing out the whole brisket, washed and syringed with antiseptic, and used antibiotics both locally and parenterally, plus a few other drugs which had always sufficed before. We did not stock snake venom antidote; in fact it was doubtful if there was a hospital then in the whole area which had any, but I'd never found it necessary.

Every day, sometimes twice a day, I'd seen Silver. He'd had every drug I could think of, and also those suggested by the vet I'd called to give a second opinion. The stable girls had bathed, cleaned and poulticed that wound, which daily grew bigger. They'd stayed on in the evenings to talk to the little pony, sponged down his fevered, sweating body, worked on him ceaselessly and caressed him lovingly. We fought very hard, and so did Silver, but it was a losing battle; in an incredibly short time the whole brisket — skin, fat, muscle — just rotted away and sloughed off. Today Silver was down. He could not get up and he would never get up. I had not injected him today, for there was no point; the battle was lost. I'd merely stroked the little beast's neck, pulled his mane and said, 'You've fought hard, boy, but we must take you away from all this pain now.' But I couldn't! As I looked at those trusting, soulful brown eyes – I couldn't do it! I chickened out! Somebody else must do it. I think John Wilkinson understood when he saw me rise from the little animal. He hadn't questioned it when I asked him to phone the RSPCA inspector and get him to come with his humane killer.

It all came back to me as I sat there on the garden wall of The Willows. Even now the inspector would be on his way; perhaps already he'd arrived, and soon there would be a merciful release. I blamed myself for not finishing the job, and puzzled again if there was more I could have done; one always did. These moments communing with Nature didn't take away the disappointment, but they brought some healing and put things in perspective. The tides would still ebb and flow, birds would still sing, and up in these dunes a few adders would still lurk for the unwary like the gentle Silver, for the ceaseless war in Nature of creature upon creature, and the constant fight to counteract the evil, would still be ours to win or lose.

At last I went on up to the villa, one of

several in that lofty place. I'm sure the gardens were a blaze of glory – they always were at The Willows – but they were passed unnoticed that afternoon. I rang the front-door bell and Miss Plumtree and a horde of dogs answered the call. I knew that there were, in fact, eight dogs, all cocker spaniels. I wasn't too clear about the number of Plumtree sisters. There were three I'd met at their fine house with its magnificent view, while others were vaguely alluded to, but the number of dogs was always eight. The sisters were aged anything from fifty to seventy-five; it was impossible to say, for they dressed, wore their hair and conversed in a way that was pure Victoriana. The furniture of the house and the jungle of pot plants in every room all spoke of a bygone age. Clearly the sisters had been well endowed by father Plumtree, long since deceased, but despite their wealth they always seemed to me rather forlorn, left behind like driftwood on the beach when the tide has ebbed, and a little bemused by this strange modern world. They were called Emily, Letitia and Victoria, and in the way they fluttered around, fussed, became flustered, yet always remained completely courteous, I thought I could see Miss Marple, Agatha Christie's famous detective with the kindly manner but air of bewilderment. Well, not in *all* the sisters. Victoria was the exception, and Victoria was addressing me now.

'You will take tea?' she inquired, though really it was more a command than an inquiry. One always 'took tea' with the Plumtrees. With others you had tea, drank tea, or enjoyed a cuppa – at The Willows one took tea.

'And how are you, Mr Cameron?' asked Miss Letitia.

'Very well, thank you.'

'And Mrs Cameron, and your two dear little boys?'

'Thriving, thank you.'

'How is your garden?' ventured Miss Emily timidly. She was clearly lowest in the pecking order of the Plumtree girls, and though they employed a gardener, Miss Emily was never happier than when out there. It was her great love in life, and I thought likely her place of escape from older sister Victoria. That worthy had been well named: I'm certain that papa Plumtree, on first beholding this latest arrival, had taken one look at the square jaw, wide forehead with a furrow even then on the infant brow, and had pronounced unhesitatingly, 'Victoria.'

'Oh well, my garden is nothing compared with yours,' I answered Miss Emily, 'but it's coming on.'

By now afternoon tea had arrived, brought by some inferior minion from the kitchen, and I knew from the past that polite conversation was the order of the day till this afternoon ritual had been observed. It was positively *infra dig.* to discuss the purpose of one's visit till tea had been taken.

'Isn't this a terrible world we're living in?' said Letitia.

Thinking of Silver, I agreed heartily, 'Terrible.'

'These strikes – I'd sack the lot of them!' pronounced Victoria.

'Oh, ah . . . yes,' I grunted, picturing the toughest shop steward quailing before this redoubtable lady.

'And that man Attlee. It beats me how dear Winston can possibly stand him,' she went on.

I am a strictly non-political animal, certainly in public, but I was moved to say, 'Oh, I don't know, Miss Plumtree. He did a lot during the war, and he and Mr Churchill seemed to work well together then.'

'But he's such a *little* man . . . and as for the rest of his gang . . .' She left it unsaid, but I had a picture of Messrs Wilson, Dalton, Bevan and their colleagues with masks on their faces and bags marked 'Swag' on their backs. I hastily changed the subject.

'These are lovely scones, Miss Plumtree. Who's the baking expert?'

'Our Mrs Buxton does most of it, but these

are actually Emily's.'

Little Emily looked abashed, embarrassed but also pleased. I fancy nobody ever took notice of poor Miss Emily. The meal proceeded to its leisurely close, the trays were removed, then Miss Victoria leaned back to issue the order of the day.

'It's little Rupert. We want you to take him away and put him to sleep.'

I gasped! 'But he's only a baby. It's only months since I gave him his distemper inoculation.' I looked at Rupert lying peacefully on a couch. 'What on earth's wrong with him?'

'His ears are too long for a cocker; they get in his food and this will certainly lead to ear canker. Also he's had one or two little cysts between his toes. I'm afraid he's from a weakly strain.'

'But, Miss Plumtree, ear canker and interdigital cysts are nothing, and can be easily treated. You can't put a dog down for that.' Attempting to be flippant, I added, 'It's like putting Mr Attlee down because he's too small!'

'And a very good thing too.' Clearly I'd said the wrong thing. She went on, 'But it's a totally different matter. Rupert is our dog and our responsibility. Mr Attlee is a man, and can presumably look after himself, or have a wife do it for him.' The implication of the last phrase was that there were some women foolish or irresponsible enough to do anything.

I really was seething. Over the past year or two I'd destroyed three or four dogs, two at least for no very good reason; but this was getting ridiculous, indeed criminal. Long ears! These dogs were highly pedigreed, the sisters were apparently genuinely fond of them, and presumably vice versa. I had protested before, and had been overruled and informed that if I would not do it, they'd get Mr Dick. That gentleman kept a pet shop, and I knew he used strychnine for his destructions. I couldn't have that.

'Look, Miss Plumtree,' I argued, 'Rupert has his whole life before him. If you find him . . . ah . . . imperfect, I could easily find him a very good home.'

'No, Mr Cameron, we wouldn't dream of him going to someone else and not knowing if he was happy. I'm a Christian Scientist and I know that our little doggies have a better life waiting for them on the other side. My sisters and I have talked it over' (I knew who'd done the talking!) 'and have decided this is much the best thing, best for Rupert. If you cannot do it, I'm sure Mr Dick will.'

It was blackmail. At least with my method,

the dog didn't know a thing. With strychnine it was agony, if only briefly. It was also monstrous that these old ladies, who'd lived a completely sheltered existence, who had never had to move out into the wider world to earn a living, should decide for a trusting animal whether it should die or be allowed to live. Suddenly, as I looked at them, they seemed rather sinister and terrible, no longer the Miss Marple detective — but the murderers. But then, if you believed that a canine Valhalla was just around the corner, I suppose you could sleep not only with a clear conscience, but with a smile of bliss. Did Christian Scientists believe that? I must check.

So Rupert accompanied me to the car. I knew in a few weeks I would be summoned to Epivax his successor, and keep up the required number of eight. The little black dog frisked and frolicked all the way to the surgery, eagerly studying the passing scene. With our specially concentrated Euthatal, all he knew was the prick of a needle, in five seconds blissful sleep. In thirty seconds he was dead. The death sentence had been passed and carried out. I felt a bit sick.

There was another dog tied up in our back premises, also a spaniel, but this time a large dun-and-white one with brown splotches on her, and the most gentle face and tender eyes you ever saw.

'What's that one in for, Mrs Drury?' I asked.

'To be put down.'

'What! Why?'

'I'm not sure why. She's not young, she has a small mammary tumour, but I think they've just got tired of her.'

'Who were her owners?'

'I didn't know them. They were strangers to me, just paid cash and left.'

'Well, Mrs Dru, I'm not doing it. I'll take her home.'

So the dog became part of the Cameron household. The name Lass seemed to suit her, and she soon readily answered to it. She proved herself to be a lovely, quiet, soft creature, gentle with the children, beloved by them, and the most obedient member of the family! The tumour was tiny, benign, harmless. One day I'd remove it, but there was no hurry. I don't know if Lass had any thoughts of the delights of some future life, but she most certainly enjoyed her remaining time in this one. She was one of those where the decision was to let live, to the delight of all concerned.

At nine that evening the phone rang. Janet and I looked at the clock, then at each other, and both said, 'Parkhurst.' This was his regular time for ringing. Though very well-off, he was always after free advice — almost weekly.

'Bristacombe 250, Mr Cameron speaking.'

'Good-evening, Mr Cameron. Parkhurst, Shirwell Ford, here.' (He was a cousin of the one who figured in 'Never!'.)

'Good-evening, Mr Parkhurst.' I glanced wearily at Janet. We had to go through the whole ritual every time, as at The Willows, but without the scones!

'Fine weather we're having, Mr Cameron.'

'It certainly is.'

'Perhaps a trifle dry for the root crops, wouldn't you say?'

'You could be right.'

'I expect you have a lot of visitors about in town?'

'Thousands of them.'

'You'll be kept busy, then.'

'Yes.'

'Oh, Mr Cameron . . .' (now we were getting to the request, though he always managed to make it sound like an afterthought or intrusion into our polite conversation) '. . . I wonder if you could just slip over tonight and do a little job for us. Sister has an old cat she thinks it would be better to put to sleep.'

'Why? Is it ill, or in pain?'

'No, just old. Its hair has got a bit matted, and it smells rather.'

'I'm sorry. I won't be over tonight, Mr Parkhurst.'

'You won't?'

'No.'

'Why is that?'

'Well, Mr Parkhurst, my partner's on holiday, it's been a long, hard day, it is not an urgent case, and it can very well wait till morning.'

Steel in his voice now! 'Sister would like it done tonight.'

'Well, now, if you care to jump in your car and bring it here, I'll oblige, though matted hair is common in old cats and can be cut off or combed out. Besides, I was on your farm just the other day, and no mention was made of it then. Surely it hasn't grown old in a matter of days?'

Long pause . . . I guessed what was coming. Still very polite . . .

'Oh, Mr Cameron, brother and I were talking one night and we thought it might be an advantage to have two veterinary surgeons, from different practices. If you don't feel you can come tonight, I might have to ring someone else.'

He'd come this blackmail once before and had insisted I turn out quite late one evening to see a lame ram, which he admitted had been lame for nearly a week but which definitely needed treatment that evening. Not wanting to antagonize a client, I had successively bitten my lip, gnashed my teeth, frothed at the mouth, and gone. But not tonight. I'd had enough killing for one day. So, equally politely, I replied, 'Well, now, Mr Parkhurst, that might be a very good idea and then you could ring your other vet alternate Fridays for advice. Yes, a good idea! But if you do decide you still want my services, you can give me a ring in the morning or bring the cat in tomorrow, for it's getting a bit late to come tonight. Good-night to you!'

I slammed down the phone in great glee. I'd wanted to do that for a long time to old Parkhurst . . . the man who paid his bills to us once a year and then asked for discount . . . the man who kept his bills to a minimum by regular free advice by phone . . . the farmer who usually didn't want you to call unless you were passing anyway, so that he wouldn't have to pay a visit fee, but who expected instant service when he clapped his hands. Yes, I'd enjoyed that. There was a lot of the unregenerate in me yet!

Parkhurst was at the surgery next morning, cat-basket in one hand, a jar of cream as a peace offering in the other. I looked at the old cat. Its hair was matted, but that didn't matter, being merely an indication that it couldn't clean itself properly any more. But it was thin to the point of emaciation, it had few teeth left, its head was down. Life held nothing for it now. The decision to die or let live was, in this case, easy, and the carrying out of the decision painless, indeed a kindness. The old man departed with his now empty basket, and for the first time I felt sorry for him. He had plenty of money, an excellent farm, first-class herds of sheep and cattle. He was a man respected for his knowledge of the local breeds and a judge at local shows – in short, a successful man, yet somehow as he limped towards his car that morning, an empty cat-basket in his hand, he seemed curiously forlorn; even, strange to relate, somehow vulnerable.

Perhaps this curious experience was but fancy, as unreal as dreams that fade in the full light of day. Maybe it was for me, in an odd sort of way, future events casting their shadows before them; but somehow, just momentarily, I pictured Parkhurst as an old man in a hospital bed, with no close family of his own and, respected as he was, a man with few real friends. I wondered, would there be for him, as for the cat, a merciful release?

Maybe these were the first musings on experiences that would come to me in years ahead; I cannot say. As a vet, I took hundreds of lives; I had a licence to kill, yet I never enjoyed it, and would certainly never wish such a weight to be put on any man in relation to human life. In some cases, I have to confess, at the time I would more cheerfully have taken the owner's life (as with Miss Victoria Plumtree) when a trusting animal was just put out of the way for no good reason. But for others – like Silver and the cat – I knew that, repugnant though it was, to hasten death was an act of mercy and kindness.

I have since then, over many years and almost weekly, stood beside a bed and watched someone fight a brave but losing battle, and I've pondered deeply. It is my view that in such cases, assuming everything is being done to ease the patient's suffering, to take life would be, very often, to deprive a husband or wife of experiences and moments that are very precious and forged only in the fires of suffering, shared together. But there are other cases where I've wondered . . . I have gone into an enormous ward of geriatric patients, the beds close together, scarcely allowing passage between them, beds containing people who have lost all awareness of surroundings and all control of their actions; I have seen folks lose all dignity, privacy, individuality, and become increasingly distressing for their loved ones to behold week by week. Cabbages! That's how society has labelled such poor beings. I know all the arguments against any form of euthanasia, at any time, and respect deeply the views of all who hold them. I have the highest regard for the sanctity of human life, and a deep love of old folks. As a minister of the Gospel, I have no doubts of the reality of that other world, nor of our basic belief that man is an eternal spirit. I know all the questions regarding any form of euthanasia – I give no answers. I only know that many times I've come away from a scene of extreme weakness or debility, and with indignation and concern have said to myself, 'I wouldn't treat a dog like that!' I have, conscious (oh, so conscious) of my own helplessness, wondered what He, who was and is far from helpless, and whose hands in Galilee were tender to soothe and to save, would do in our day, in a ward of folks weary, longing, sighing, yes! and asking to be released to 'go home' – and I've heard an echo as of old, saying, 'Blessed are the merciful – for they shall obtain mercy.'

14

Instant Results

The buzzer in the telephone switchboard was going as I went in the surgery door: extension 2 — that was from our house. Mrs Drury, that model of all the virtues in a vet's secretary cum assistant cum anaesthetist cum bookkeeper cum receptionist, was already coping.

'I'll give him the message, Mrs Cameron.' She answered my raised eyebrows. 'Your wife on the phone. Just after you left, a call came in from Hopkins, the Grange. A cow with a stroke.'

'A stroke, eh?' I pondered. 'Know who these folk are, Mrs Dru?'

'No, Mr Cameron, they're new clients; a small farm out Fardley way. Mrs Cameron said they sounded very upset on the phone.'

I glanced at the other case-list for the day so far. There would be plenty more before night, so I initialled those I was off to, leaving Bernard to pick up the rest.

Fardley was one of these little out-of-the-way places that abound in Devon and are part of its charm. I felt my spirits rise as I drove along and a song came to my lips. (One of our students seeing practice had once reported to his wife in wonderment, 'He sings as he drives!') It was a gorgeous May morning, fields were greening up with early summer freshness, trees were bursting into leaf, birds were skimming merrily in front of the little Austin van as she cruised along the famous sunken Devon lanes. They weren't really sunken. It was simply that generations of farmers had built dykes, then covered them with earth, and on top planted a hedge, thus making high walls which were excellent windbreaks from the cold nor'-easterlies or wet westerlies for sheep and out-wintered cattle. These were the high hedges that had driven my old teacher Sandy Gray to distraction on his honeymoon years ago in Devon, when he snorted, 'Glorious Devon, if you could see anything over these hedges!' — a sentiment that many had echoed since. But it was glorious Devon that morning, with the high banks a mass of yellow primroses. Yes, it was good to be alive, to be free, to be a country vet on such a day, so why not sing a stave or two! I had been through Fardley before, a tiny hamlet tucked away off the main roads, just a cluster of houses and little farms, and a sign marked 'Post Office' pointing vaguely in the direction of a small thatched house. Roses were already in bloom on the walls, lupins and peonies making splashes of colour in the borders, as I walked up the path and entered.

I had apparently been observed, for there behind a tiny counter was a little old lady with rosy cheeks, eyes creased with wrinkles which I suspected had been produced more by smiles than tears, and a gentleness and serenity about her. She greeted me with a hearty 'Good-morning' and equally heartily I agreed it was, and asked if she could direct me to the Grange.

She looked at me over her spectacles. 'Oh, you'll be the veterinary! Now would you be Mr Cameron or the young vet?' I said I was both; both Mr Cameron and young.

'Yes, you do look young,' she said a little doubtfully. 'I thought you must be the assistant.' She went on: 'You'll have come about Grizelda?'

'Grizelda? Who might she be?'

'She's Mr and Mrs Hopkins's Guernsey cow – a darling creature, as gentle as a lamb, and so are the Hopkins. We're all Chapel, you know,' she added, as if somehow this explained everything. I nodded, 'Me too,' not to be out-done. (I had early discovered that as far as the Christian religion went, in England you were either Church or Chapel, the latter designation

271

covering Baptist, Methodist, Congregational, Independent Missions, Pentecostal and a few others – in fact virtually everything that was non-C. of E.) She was a delightful little body, twittering like a perky chaffinch, but finally she recalled that I had asked for directions.

'You just go over the ford and take the first lane on the left, and that's the Grange. I do hope you can help Grizelda.'

So I left my little pippin of a postal officer, thinking there was bound to be customer satisfaction there at all times. I found the Grange, left the car in the lane and pushed open a gate, to be greeted by a huge man and a tiny little woman, who had obviously been awaiting my coming with anxiety.

'Good-morning to you,' I called.

'And to you, sir,' they replied with old-world charm – I almost expected the lady to curtsey.

'You found us all right, then,' boomed the man in a voice that reminded me of a stop on the organ marked 'Basso Profundo'.

'Yes, I found you,' I responded, thinking this was rather obvious; I went on to explain that the lady in the Post Office had directed me.

'That would be Miss Browne with an "e" at the end,' explained the little wife. 'She's Chapel, like us; we're mostly Chapel here-abouts; it's Grizelda,' she added. I wasn't sure whether that lady was also Chapel, but thought it was about time I saw her. First, however, Mr Hopkins had to explain.

'We've mostly had Mr Warman before' (Warman was the opposition – a deadly and not always very ethical rival), 'but you're just as near, and we heard you were Scottish and the Scottish were very good with cattle.' I thought wryly that we used to have a great name for stealing English cattle – but hoped I would live up to their expectations; nevertheless, a cow with a stroke could mean anything from a cerebral haemorrhage to a tumour on the brain.

Eventually I was allowed to see Grizelda, little Mrs Hopkins bounding on in front and throwing open the door of a loose-box. In one corner was a calf some twenty-four hours old, while on a deep bed of spotlessly clean straw lay Grizelda, deeply unconscious. I tested her eye and ear reflexes, took her temperature and pulse, my every move being watched intently. I felt I must go through the motions and justify their faith in Scots vets – but one glance would have told the most raw recruit to the veterinary profession, even if he hadn't the initial advantage of a Scots pedigree, what was what. I had been astonished since coming to Devon at the many who had not seen a condition that was a daily occurrence back in Ayrshire, and in most dairying districts of Britain.

'Never had aught like this before,' boomed

Mr Hopkins, as if divining my thought.

'Can you do anything?' earnestly entreated his little wife.

'Yes, Mrs Hopkins, I think I can soon put Grizelda right. Could you just bring me a bucket of water, not too hot, soap and a towel?'

She departed at the double while I got out my flutter-valve, calcium bottles, tin of needles, bottle of iodine and a swab. Then, having put one of the calcium bottles in the bucket to bring the contents to around blood heat, I clipped the hair over about an inch of mammary vein, swabbed with iodine, and said to my client, 'Now! I hope a spot of blood doesn't worry you?'

'Nay, lad,' boomed farmer Hopkins, 'seen plenty of that in the first war.'

'Right then, you hold that,' I said, giving him the calcium bottle with flutter-valve attachment to hold, preparatory to gravity feed into the bloodstream. 'When I tell you, turn the bottle upside down and let me have the end of the tube.'

I stuck the large-bore needle into the mammary vein, and out spurted some rich, dark blood. I called for the tube, when there was an almighty crash, and I turned to see one client flat out on the floor and the calcium pouring from the tube (miraculously the bottle hadn't broken), while blood still flowed from Grizelda.

My assistant who had seen plenty of blood had, like not a few others, fainted. His wife was hovering over him, so I hovered over my patient, inserted the nozzle into the needle, and soon the life-giving calcium was gurgling merrily into Grizelda. One bottle in, I turned to the human casualty and suggested to his wife (who was buzzing around like an agitated humming-bird) that she should get her husband a cup of water and also mop his brow with a cold cloth to bring him round. I didn't know if that would help, but a glance assured me he would be OK, and it gave her something to do. Then the second bottle of calcium borogluconate was injected subcutaneously and in about fifteen minutes Grizelda was sitting up, looking around her, as was Mr Hopkins.

It was a close thing who would recover first, but Mr Hopkins made it by a short head. He gazed at his Guernsey in wonderment, while Mrs Hopkins looked at her man in concern. Then both looked at me and said, 'It's a miracle; you've given us back our Grizelda,' and with that the lady of the hour lurched to her feet unsteadily and headed for her calf who was giving tongue from one corner, while farmer Hopkins, on equally rubbery legs, staggered up from the other. They were like two punch-drunk boxers who'd had about enough. Little Mrs Hopkins was ecstatic, and hopped about betwixt one and the other, enthusing, 'My, sir, it's just like the Bible — Lazarus being raised from the dead, or being born over again!'

I didn't know whether she was referring to her husband or Grizelda, though I fancied the latter, and agreed it was a good description. Over the inevitable cup of tea, which I waited to drink to make sure the old man was all right (one was offered tea at virtually every call in North Devon), I explained the phenomenon to them.

'Your cow had milk fever, Mr Hopkins. In the old days they thought it was a germ in the milk that caused it, so it got the name, and they used to inject a weak solution of iodine into the udder — mighty uncomfortable, but now and then it saved a cow's life. It was certainly better than the older cure of whisky, which never yet saved a cow with milk fever, but I suppose by the time the cow had had a drink, and the farmer and the vet a few each, they were all past caring anyway when the poor beast died. By and by somebody on the Continent found that you didn't need iodine, that water would do; then somebody again found that to pump the udder up with air was even better. But all these were shots in the dark. When they worked, it was simply because they stopped the udder producing milk, which allowed the level of calcium in the cow's blood to rise again, but of course the udder was often ruined. Then in the 1930s a Scots vet' (I had to get in a plug and keep up their regard for our ability) 'took blood tests from a hundred cows suffering from milk fever. In every case the blood-calcium level was too low, so what we do now is simply inject calcium. Mind you,' I went on with utter sincerity, 'I've seen this hundreds of times and it still seems like a conjuring trick, a miracle really. Your cow would have died by this afternoon without treatment, but as you saw, within half an hour she was up on her feet. I know of hardly anything in all medicine quite so dramatic as this.'

Seemingly inconsequentially, Mrs Hopkins murmured, 'Once I was blind, now I see.'

I nodded, bade them good-day, and to vociferous thanks went out to the car. I arrived there at the same time as Miss Browne with an 'e'.

'Oh, Mr Vet'nary,' she gasped, 'I'm glad you're still here. Your office phoned me to say would you please call at the Rectory. The Rector, dear man, had called up to say that he had a bullock gone quite mad – "maze as a brish" were his words – and could you go right away?'

This was another new client, so I inquired where the Rectory might be. They proceeded to direct me, one booming and two twittering voices, with much arm-waving and correcting one another. Finally Mr Hopkins, now quite recovered, said, 'Look ee here, surr; it be nigh about a mile and a halve over by. I'll show ee,' in his anxiety lapsing into the rich Devon accent which I loved, while Mrs Hopkins, with a different anxiety, that for her huge man, announced, 'If you go, Perce, I go too.' So his name was Percival, I mused. She went on, 'You might come over all queer-like again.' I wasn't sure if the little lady was more concerned about his physical well-being or the possible spiritual taint of hobnobbing with Church, but anyway they both piled into the little van, while Miss Browne with an 'e' waved us goodbye. After sundry wrong turns, for Perce and his missus had different ideas about right and left hands, eventually I pulled up in front of an old, large, rambling house, with quite a few outbuildings to be seen beyond. We were met by a wild-looking figure striding rapidly towards us. He had one elbow sticking out of an old jersey, his hair was considerably dishevelled, and incongruously his clerical collar was only fastened at one end, so that the other stuck out in front like a direction-finder.

'Quite extraordinary!' he announced. (He certainly was, but I don't think he meant it autobiographically.) 'Oh, hello, Mrs Hopkins – Percival, good-day to you,' he said, proceeding to raise a hat, then finding there was none there. He tried to fasten his clerical collar to its retaining stud and appear presentable. I gazed fascinated as the collar-end came away again with a 'Ping!'. The poor man grabbed it in one hand and me in the other.

'Look here, Mr . . . er . . . er . . . Cameron. I put a call through to my own vet, Mr Darnaway' (I didn't mind him; he was a cheerful old chap, and co-operative, unlike the vindictive Warman), 'but he is out on a case; then I telephoned you, to discover you were actually here in Fardley. It seemed quite providential, but whether you can do anything, I doubt. The poor animal seems stark, raving mad.' 'Ping!' went his collar yet again, as he tried in vain to fasten it with one hand.

'Is it a cow, or a bull, or a young beast?' I inquired.

'It's a two-year-old heifer,' he explained as he led me to his shippen – his recalcitrant collar periodically pinging merrily as he led me on.

'See, in here,' he whispered, lest the mad beast would hear us, and he peeped in the top half of the stable-type door. 'Quite, quite gone,' he said, pointing to his head. It wasn't clear whether he meant himself or his heifer, it being a moot point which was looking the wilder, but I gave him the benefit of the doubt. 'Have you ever seen anything like that before?' he demanded.

'Yes, a few times, but this one's a beaut!'

'Really.' He paused, and further exclaimed, 'Extraordinary!', as if it was beyond the realms of understanding that there should be so many mad bovines in the world. Then he asked rather piteously, poor man, 'Can anything be done?'

'Mr Cameron just brought our Grizelda back from the dead, Rector,' said little Mrs Hopkins. 'I'm sure he'll put you right too.'

I looked at her quizzically and wondered if she was having a wee theological dig, then decided that was unworthy, that at that moment I really was her hero. I explained to the distraught cleric: 'Your heifer has staggers, Rector.'

'Good gracious!' he exploded, 'who has been giving her alcohol?'

I really couldn't restrain myself any longer. Here were two staunch Chapel-goers looking suspiciously and wonderingly at one distraught High Churchman, dressed in rags and half a clerical collar, while from the shippen came thumps and bellows reminiscent of a Malemute saloon when the boys had come to town and were whooping it up – and all this in quiet little Fardley.

I recovered and apologized for my unseemly mirth, and said, 'No, no, Rector. Alcohol has nothing to do with it. Staggers is variously called stomach staggers, mad staggers, grass staggers, but really it is a hypomagnesaemia.' I was rather maliciously pleased with that. I bet when it came to quoting Aristotle he could beat me to a frazzle, but clearly hypomagnesaemia had him beat. He looked bewildered, so I hastily went on. 'A magnesium deficiency. It affects the brain, and it can and often does kill an animal; but if we can get some magnesium into her we might pull her round, provided there is no brain damage. The difficulty will be holding her steady, for it must go directly into the bloodstream, into a vein, in an acute case like this.'

I nipped through the door and was soon out again, as she charged me – a characteristic of the condition, on occasion. It seemed a hopeless proposition to get in there and restrain her without loss of life or limb. I looked around.

'Is there any other way I can get in?' I inquired.

'Only from the hayloft above.'

'Then, Vicar . . . ah . . . Rector, if you have a rope handy we'll prepare for a heavenly visitation.' He looked at me doubtfully. Did I seem too flippant, I wondered? I hastily went on to explain.

'We have no hope unless we can restrain that heifer somehow, and what better way than from above? Now, I'll go up into the hayloft and drop a noose over her head. When she charges she'll pull the slip knot tight, and it's up to you and Mr Hopkins here to get in beside her and secure her by that rope to a post, stanchion, anything. It'll be hot work ... maybe you should take your collar off.'

So the pinging collar ceased to ping, but there followed an equally mad fifteen minutes. Several times I had the dangling noose almost over the beast, but always she dodged. Finally I suggested the Rector should call to her over the stable half-door, and from the loft immediately above, when she headed for the door, I would try to lasso her. Thankfully, it worked, the rope pulled tight and flew out of my hands, but the big, burly farmer and the lean, rangy churchman were in there like a flash, grabbing the trailing end of the rope and securing it round a post. I swung down from my lofty abode to lend a hand. That heifer struggled like mad. I tied another rope round her horns, gradually releasing the lasso, which by now was all but throttling her.

'Now, Rector, you pray that I can hit this jugular vein pretty soon, and that the magnesium will be in time to work, but I warn you, it can also kill sometimes. Mr Hopkins, I suggest you look the other way.'

I wasn't so expert with jugular as mammary veins, having trained on Ayrshires, where the mammary vein was about an inch in diameter. However, at the third jab I got it, and once again the flutter-valve routine was repeated, but this time much more slowly, as I watched the respiratory rate with care. The beast quietened a bit, its flutterings beneath us lessening.

'Now for some chloral hydrate to quieten her a bit more, then a spare supply of magnesium under the skin, and I think you'll find – I hope so, anyway – that the combination of Church, Chapel and infidel Scots Presbyterian has worked wonders.'

'Amen to that,' came from a perspiring parson.

The young beast was quivering but little now; the madness had gone. We guided her into a loose-box where for the rest of the day she could be watched, but I was pretty sure she'd be OK.

'Do come in and have a wash,' invited the Rector. I followed, so did the Hopkins, and in the next ten minutes we gave ourselves over to some hearty and very necessary ablutions.

Presently Perce Hopkins boomed, 'You know, Rector, I reckon that ther yiffer was jus' like the man in the Scriptures as was allus cuttin' himself with knifes, or like that thar Gardenin swine.'

'Indeed you're right, Mr Hopkins, though I think it was Gadarene – an instant cure, a miracle — and from above too.' He smiled.

He really looked quite a different man without his collar. He apologized that his wife was out and so he could not offer us tea. 'Will you have a little refreshment?' he inquired. 'I can soon get that.'

I thanked him; no — I didn't indulge. The Hopkins shook their heads resolutely.

'Well, I think I will,' said the man of God. 'As the Scriptures also say, "Take a little wine for thy stomach's sake and often infirmities." ' And he did. By the size of the noggin, his stomach was pretty bad or his infirmities very frequent!

I dropped off Perce and Mrs Hopkins and went on my way, well satisfied. That was one of the joys of being a vet, I thought: you saw an immediate result for your work. Two animals rescued from death in quiet little Fardley that morning, thanks to medical science and a modicum of skill in the operator. So different from the poor old Rector, I thought. Apart from his glebe-land, which he farmed as part of his living, what results could he show? The thoughts passed idly through my mind, with no realization then that I would often return to these very questions in my next vocation — but more of that anon.

I've quite often noticed how you've seldom been near a place, and then suddenly you seem never to be away from it. So it was for a time with the little community of Fardley. Two weeks after their milk fever, the Hopkins had milk trouble again. This time it was reported that a sow named Jemima had farrowed a litter of fourteen – and had no milk. Could I come? I grabbed that one for myself before Bernard could volunteer, for we both especially loved that district of the practice. As the Austin headed once more for the Grange, I thought ahead, as vets do, to what was likely to await me. Almost certainly this was agalactia, which simply means, of course, no milk. Again, as with milk fever, it is a misnomer. In fact, the sow delivers her piglets, and nature provides her with a requisite number of teats and milk enough to feed her hungry brood – but something has gone wrong with the mechanism. There's a spanner in the works, an infinitesimal fault, but with disastrous results. The 'letdown hormone', as it is called, produced by the tiny pituitary gland in the brain, triggers off the mechanism – releases the trapdoor, if you like – to let the milk flow. Without that hormone functioning, the udders can be bursting with milk, to the sow's acute discomfort and the piglets' utter despair, yet not a single drop will come and the piglets will starve to death.

Two pictures always came to my mind when I thought of this condition. One was of a lecturer we had, a bumptious Englishman – though I'm sure the two facts were coincidental! – and a man, moreover, given somewhat to exaggeration. He had a habit of speaking out of the side of his mouth, so that the words were squeezed out seemingly reluctantly, giving a peculiar timbre to his utterances. In describing this condition, he said to us: 'You stick the needle in, then jump back quickly – or you'll get your trousers splashed with milk!' I had never seen that quite happen, though I had seen some pretty prompt responses. The other memory was of my student days, visiting with my old boss a farm near Barr, in Ayrshire. That evening two sows had farrowed, one with twenty-one piglets, the other with fifteen, and neither had any milk. I'm sure it was some kind of productivity record, matched only by the volume of despair that permeated the place as we arrived. In the mother of twenty-one, the injection of Pituitrin worked like a charm and all was well, except that queues were forming for the available teats. But in she of the fifteen piglets, no amount of the hormone availed. The drug had no effect, as sometimes happened. Clearly in these instances there was some other, unknown, factor, but that farmer's wife set to and bottle-reared fourteen of the fifteen pigs, getting up every few hours day and night to do so, and in fact winning a prize at a local farming show with one of them. I vaguely wondered, as I journeyed onward, if Perce or Mrs Hopkins would do that, if need be; I rather thought they would.

I was received with open arms — it's marvellous what an initial success does for a vet with a new client — and was led immediately to Jemima's abode. She was one of two sows (the other being introduced as June) on this little farm, where they had something of everything, but generally found the summer B. and B. visitors their best source of income. I looked at Jemima and her squealing, hungry piglets, told Perce to shut his eyes again, jabbed Jemima behind the ear — the easiest place to pierce a sow's needle-bending hide — told him he could look now, and at his expectant glance said, 'Now we wait a little. How's Grizelda?'

They took me to the little one-acre orchard where she was grazing, whistled her up to the gate, and the gentle creature stood there, placidly chewing the cud and regarding me with her big brown eyes as I stroked her head. Mrs Hopkins twittered, 'Here's Mr Cameron, Grizel — he saved your life, you know.' Grizel chewed on. Life was good now, why think of the past! The reunion over, we went back to look at mother and piglets. I knew before we reached the pen that all was well. No longer was there the squeal of hungry piglets, but instead that lovely deep baritone grunt of a sow suckling its young, while from each little knob came a contented sucking note, like a line of bellringers pulling their ropes in turn.

'Well, I do declare,' said Mrs Hopkins, 'if I didn't know you for a Chapel-goer I would say you were a wizard. Do you never fail, Mr Cameron?'

'Often,' I said. 'You just haven't found me out yet!'

I was presented with a jar of Devon clotted cream for Mrs Cameron, and pressed to take the service in their little Methodist chapel sometime. I promised I would, with pleasure, and I meant it. They were the salt of the earth, these simple, straight, homely folks.

I thought I'd have a quick call at the Rectory. I was met by the Rector in full clerical attire, just off to a diocesan meeting. 'Would you have a quick look at a lamb?' he asked. 'It's a late one,' he explained, 'and is all crippled and poorly.'

I looked at the pathetic wee beast and gave him a rapid synopsis. 'Joint ill, for certain – infection through the navel at birth, localization and swelling in the joints, either will die or won't thrive – unless you're prepared to spend something on it and a lot of time with it, and even then I can't promise.' He said he would try. He was a kindly soul, and he knew what it was to have frequent infirmities himself! So I gave the lamb a massive dose of serum, left him a bottle of penicillin with orders to inject daily, to poultice or otherwise heat-treat the joints, and to make sure it got its full milk ration from the ewe. It took time, but it worked. Three weeks later, when I was out visiting Miss Browne's cat, which had ear canker, I called at the Rectory and saw my patient, now virtually whole, if fractionally stiff, but putting on weight and *doing* – that word beloved by shepherds and so descriptive. Doing! I congratulated the Rector on his patience and perseverance.

'You know,' he said, 'I've been thinking of your visits. The first one was dramatic, exciting, a quick and visible result, all over in no time and a beast made whole. This lamb has taken weeks of treatment and coaxing, but it's whole now too. I think I've been learning a lesson. Before, I used to scoff at the sudden convert – the Billy Graham approach wasn't mine – but your curing that heifer from its madness made me see that things *can* happen in an instant. Probably most of my work is like treating that lamb. Some people' – he paused, searching for the right words – 'maybe find wholeness, that's what the Greek for salvation is, you know,' he twinkled at my ignorance, 'slowly, bit by bit. But the end result is the same, and the Person treating them, the source of healing, the same.'

He knew more than Aristotle, did that gentle soul. After years in the ministry, I've good cause to remember his words. One fold – one Shepherd – but many ways to both. A sudden finding of Him in a blaze of noontide heat, or a slow progression, following and finding maybe as the evening shadows fall. But both are equally real experiences of the Shepherd, by His sheep.

15

Variety Pack

'Bernard, what's a coypu?' I asked as I put down the phone.

'Haven't a clue,' came his prompt reply.

'I think it's like a rat, only bigger,' said Ann. We both looked at her in admiration, not only because she was easy on the eye, but regularly our new secretary would surprise us with the scope of her knowledge. Two weeks ago she'd put us right on an ocelot.

'Charlie in trouble again, then?' asked Bernard.

'Well, his coypu is. It doesn't sound very much, and if it's only a kind of rat, I reckon I can manage. If it had been those black bears, Bernard, I'd have remembered a calving in the middle of Exmoor! Besides, there are a few things he would like me to see, so I'll get a free conducted tour of the zoo — maybe if I'm in luck I'll get a choc-ice going in!'

It was a glorious warm, early summer afternoon, just the kind of sleepy day for a leisurely zoological expedition – plus a choc-ice, to which I am somewhat partial. Bernard hadn't a lot on his plate, so I didn't feel too bad on this occasion at exerting my prerogative as senior partner in selecting my cases.

Charlie Trevelyan and I had three things in common:

1. We were both fond of animals – actually he was animal daft and a Fellow of the Zoological Society.

2. We both earned our living from animals.

3. We were both perpetually hard-up, since his zoo and my practice were both at the 'ploughing money back to reap the benefits later' stage.

The one big difference was that he was acquainted with a far greater variety of animals than I was, and was liable to appear in his car or on television with almost any kind of beast. In recent years I, who had been trained on horse, cow, sheep, pig, dog (including cat), and a little bit on poultry, had been asked to treat creatures of whose existence I had been in total ignorance till I found Charlie thrusting them at me for my expert diagnosis and treatment! And I didn't even know what a coypu was! Needless to say, in many of my cases I had been singularly unsuccessful, not always because of the rarity of the species, but for one of two very good reasons – always assuming, that is, that I was a moderately competent vet. My lack of success sprang firstly from the fact that in those days there was no literature whatsoever on diseases, diagnosis, or drugs of choice (let alone dosage) for the exotic creatures at Charlie's zoo, and there were probably at most four experts on such animals in the whole United Kingdom to whom hapless vets like me could turn for advice. Black's *Veterinary Dictionary* had nothing to say on the restraint of a hippopotamus, nor could Heare's *Veterinary Therapeutics* advise me on the dosage of digitalis – or any other drug – for a coatimundi. So literature being nil tended to cut down success rates. The second reason for my high failure rate was almost as old as creation, and I imagine plagues present-day practitioners as of yore; for it concerns a law as ancient as time, as immutable now as when beasts first walked our planet – that the weakest goes to the wall. So animals, even in captivity, would often mask symptoms of illness from their fellow creatures and from man till they could hide them no more, and by then, from the vet's point of view, it was too late. Case after case could be quoted to illustrate this law of the wild.

I remember being gripped urgently by Charlie at the gate one day and rushed to the puma's cage. I knew a puma was a mountain lion and was therefore a member of the cat family, but my life hitherto had been completely puma-free, and as Charlie hustled me cagewards that day I felt that doom had come upon me. I was in mortal terror of either disgracing myself by fleeing from the cage, gibbering with terror – or by not making it to the door before the puma had sampled me! As it happened I needn't have worried, for I could see as we reached his cage that the puma was breathing his last. I reached for the adrenaline bottle, but before any stimulant could be given our patient had gone, his final gesture being a despairing lunge with one paw at us – at man, the ancient foe. I looked at that great cat lying there, and if there was – I admit – a sense of relief in my heart, there was also a feeling of great pity. He was beautiful, so sleek and graceful, even in death. I suppose he had been happy there – he had certainly been well cared for – but every sinew of his legs, his powerful hip and shoulder muscles, his proud eye, now unseeing – all had been designed for him to wander the high uplands of his homelands . . . and he had died, far away, in a cage.

'There didn't seem a thing wrong with him till yesterday, when he was a bit off colour, and then today he wouldn't eat at all,' said Charlie.

'Sure?'

'Certain sure' – and you can't be surer

than that in Devon.

'Let's see then, Charlie, what killed him.'

I carried out a post-mortem there in his cage, the great cat's body still warm, and almost at once found the trouble. You couldn't miss it. A massive great fur ball, about the size of a cricket ball and compacted together so that it was almost as hard, was lodged in his small intestine. All cats lick themselves, all cats get small fur balls, but usually so small that they are passed without the owner ever knowing of their existence. I had certainly, on occasions, treated cats for the condition, and all had recovered uneventfully because all had shown symptoms in time. Never had I lost one. Truly the law of the wild seemed to be: 'Thou shalt show no weakness.' For this was enormous — and all the intestine around was massively inflamed and even gangrenous. That fur ball had been growing for weeks as more and more fur bound itself round the initial small nucleus, and in his last days, with the gut completely blocked, the pain must have been intense, yet the puma had borne it without visible sign.

'Poor li'l ol' thing,' Charlie was sighing. 'He must have suffered with that.'

'He surely did,' I agreed.

We both felt humbled, and somehow better men, for having witnessed what one creature of the wild could endure. Charlie stroked the soft coat of this, one of his prize exhibits, but in that moment he was not thinking of the cost, but of a friend lost. That was the great thing about Charlie. Always he was full of new plans, new schemes, further extensions; costs were prohibitive, money was tight, but these animals were more than money-earners – they were his charge, his concern, his friends. His enthusiasm was boundless and infectious. He had earned his Fellowship of the Zoological Society.

But today it was a coypu, not a puma. I found indeed that it was a kind of rat, to be exact a South American aquatic rodent. There wasn't much wrong with it, though I let Charlie do the handling. It had a skin condition for which I prescribed a shampoo of sorts, to be followed by a cream of the same ilk. The beauty of many skin conditions is that they are delightfully vague, and even for the expert, treatment is often a case of trial and error.

The coypu dealt with, Charlie took me on a conducted tour; he had time on his hands. He wanted to show me new additions and get some advice, and since I also had time I was content to wander round the whole zoo. Almost every cage, every enclosure, brought back memories of battles won or lost, and everywhere were creatures I had seen before and treated for injury or disease. First we went to the aviaries, where Charlie had about the best and biggest collection of birds in Britain at the time – hundreds of them. The overriding impression when you entered was one of colour and sound. It seemed as if some artist had been busy and made merry with every known colour. Bright reds were equalled by vivid greens; softer orange matched gentler pink, while pastel shades abounded. Over all was the chatter of sound: the screeching of parrots, the call of the mynah bird, the soft intimate murmurs of dozens of pairs of budgerigars; there were macaws, chaffinches, cockatoos, canaries, dozens of species, the noise inside being augmented from time to time by the quacking of muscovy ducks outside, the scream of a peacock or the hissing of a goose. It was here in the aviaries that I'd had my greatest failures. These birds, I soon found, are very subject to nose, throat and chest infections. I kept peering suspiciously for psittacosis, but it was always straightforward chills, croups, bronchitis, pneumonias, or so it seemed, and naturally I had used, where I thought it necessary, penicillin. I might as well have given potassium cyanide. For what reason I know not, penicillin was fatal to or useless for my avian patients. So we switched to chloromycetin, a broad-spectrum antibiotic, and it was as dramatically successful as penicillin had been lethal. We loitered long in the aviaries;

you could have spent an afternoon there. Then we moved outside to the children's corner. There I spotted amidst its friends a kangaroo, whose leg, one of the little front ones, I had once encased in plaster. Ducks waddled about, bantams proudly strutted, lambs lay in the sun. There also were my two goats. When I had first seen them in their own paddock, they had resembled two bundles of old rags borne on thin sticks of legs. A faeces sample had revealed a quite astonishing concentration of round-worms. So they had been dosed a few times, their pen moved, the ground ploughed up in their 'goat sick' paddock. Now they were sleek, and growing fatter weekly on children's titbits. We came to the enclosure of the Dead End Kids, whose exploits I recounted earlier. Opposite, the ostrich was out taking the air, his head turning like a periscope on top of his long neck.

'Remember him?' grinned Charlie.

'I surely do,' I smiled back.

I could afford to smile now, but there had been few grins around when first our paths had crossed. It was almost my first visit to the zoo, I recalled, a Sunday afternoon. Word reached me via the minister's wife as I taught my Sunday School class of eight- and nine-year-olds that I was to phone home as soon as class was over, and then proceed to the zoo to stitch the ostrich's neck. Immediately my class volunteered to accompany me *en masse*, but since that wasn't on, one lad, Barclay Beer (now a pillar of the Established Church of England), for some reason was selected. Probably he had just got in first. Lesson over, Barclay and I went back to the surgery, from where I phoned home, merely to have the message confirmed, with the additional instruction to take plenty of thread because it was quite a big cut. Thread, indeed! I'd have a word with Charlie about my suture materials. I filled a tray with needles, nylon, forceps, scissors and all the necessities, as I thought, for suturing an ostrich's neck. What I unfortunately omitted to take was a hammer! We arrived at the zoo, my nine-year-old assistant proudly carrying the black bag while I carried the tray. Barclay swung the bag at the gate meaningfully, to show he was with the vet – like showing your ticket in some soccer battleground to demonstrate you are one of the combatants.

Charlie was waiting for us at the ostrich pen. Since it was Sunday, all his assistants were off-duty. I walked in and stopped dead – 'quite a big cut' was a conservative description. In fact at first sight it seemed to me it was all cut and no whole. Closer inspection showed that the ostrich had ripped its neck from top to bottom, exactly like a zip coming undone. Apparently a protruding nail had been the cause. I looked at my patient in bewilderment, and probably it showed, for Charlie reassured me that all I had to watch was his feet. I glanced down. I believed him; the ostrich's feet were bigger than my size 11s and equipped with useful-looking nails on the end of each toe. I then looked up, and realized what big birds ostriches were. I had never been this close to one before and it towered above me. I had been well instructed on how to cast or otherwise restrain horses weighing a ton and bulls weighing about fifteen hundred-weight, and had proved these methods reliable many times in practice, but nobody had ever told me how to restrain this bundle of feathers weighing but a fraction of my horse or bull.

Anaesthetic, I thought, but what? I had never tried any form of general anaesthesia on birds before, and didn't think I ought to practise on the biggest of them. So, with more confidence than I was feeling, I announced, 'I'll spray the edges of the wound with this to take some of the pain away', and proceeded to scoosh half a container of ethyl chloride on to the ostrich. Now the great thing about ethyl chloride is that you can see where it is because a layer of frost forms, but its drawback, as with all local anaesthetics, is that it only freezes the surface. To get deeper I'd need to inject all round that wound, and somehow I didn't think that was the best way to get acquainted with Mr Ostrich – besides, I was sure I detected a definite twitch in the feet as though he was flexing the muscles preparatory to having a go. After a moment I approached the patient, whose neck looked as if it had recently been removed from a deep freeze.

'There's a good boy – good boy – good boy – atch, you brute!' as a foot whistled past me. So we tried again, stroking the back, getting nearer to the neck, when to my delight the ostrich suddenly sat down.

'Now's our chance, Charlie; quick, let me have that water and disinfectant.' The ostrich continued to sit as I cleaned the wound as best I could. Then for good measure I gave him another nozzle-ful of ethyl chloride, stuck the needle in to begin the stitching, and in a twinkling that pen was the scene of furious action. At the first jab of the needle, the bird took off, with me after it, my junior assistant headed for the door, and Charlie ran around the pen. Since the pen was not large there was a limit to where you could go, and for a time it looked as if I was chasing the ostrich, hanging on grimly to my needle, and the ostrich was chasing Charlie. We went round and round in this merry fashion for some time, when lo! just as suddenly as before, the beast sat down. I think this sudden sitting movement must be a characteristic of ostriches, probably to get their heads down out of sight in the long grass when the feather-hunters are spotted on the horizon!

Charlie said, 'I'll sit on his back and hold him down.' The first part of his statement was absolutely spot on, for Charlie sat on the ostrich's back, but the second part of the prediction was way out: at the touch of my needle, the ostrich got up again, Barclay headed for the door once more and the whole mad circus act continued, me pursuing the ostrich, hanging on by a needle, while Charlie galloped merrily round on its back! Something would have to be done, but what?

'Get a sack,' I suggested. Charlie obliged — that is, once he had leapt or fallen from his mount. 'Now when he sits down again, put that over his head. It's just too bad if some dirt drops in the wound, but at least I'll maybe be able to creep up on him without being seen and make a start.

In time, the ostrich did its celebrated flop and was blindfolded, and while I emptied the remains of my ethyl chloride spray on the wound, I commanded my assistant-acting-unpaid to return with the suture tray, which he did with the greatest reluctance and a murmured 'Oh, Mummy, Daddy . . .' over and over again, like some African incantation. Perhaps that's when the lad gained his first liking for liturgy! Whether it was the sack, the extra ethyl chloride, Barclay's spoken plea, my unspoken one — or just the sheer exhaustion of the bird, I know not, but it sat still for the remainder of the proceedings. Feeling like a seamstress who has just completed a particularly long stitching stint, I inserted the last suture, packed the wound around with sulphonamide powder, and with Barclay safely out of the door, whipped the sack off the head. The ostrich sat on, seemingly now at peace with the world, while Charlie and I wearily made our way from its pen.

'It should be all right, I think, but you understand I've never stitched an ostrich before, so I'll look in for a couple of days to see how the wound's healing. Meantime, Charlie, for Pete's sake get a hammer and knock that nail in, so that it doesn't un-zip itself again. Come to think of it, a wee tap on the crown with a hammer might have let us get the job done more quickly. I'll remember to bring one for general anaesthetic purposes next time!'

We departed for what I felt was a well-earned tea, while Barclay went happily home with two ostrich feathers and many a tale to tell. The wound healed perfectly, and the scar was almost invisible in the flabbiness of ostrich-skin neck. As for Charlie, I don't believe he ever knocked that nail in, or else another sprang out, for some two years later the creature repeated the process. I didn't see it that time; I reckoned Bernard needed to gain experience!

'We had some fun that day,' chuckled Charlie as we continued on our tour, coming next to the lion cages where resided Mary and Butch. Mary had recently had another litter of cubs.

'That makes forty-six now, a European record,' said Charlie with great pride.

I liked Mary, and recalled how once we had treated her for milk fever, but I thought that the strain of perpetual motherhood was now beginning to show and maybe they should stop. They had no more cubs. We talked of a previous litter, named Shem, Ham and Japheth. I don't recall which of these sons of Noah had the abscess in his ear, but I well remember the struggle to net and treat one large lion cub.

Next we passed by the black bears' cage, my step quickening at that point because I knew what Charlie was going to ask – and he did.

'Don't you think their claws are a bit long?'

I peered at them. 'No, I wouldn't say so. Bit longer maybe than in the wild, but nothing to worry about.'

Charlie had brought up the subject of clipping bears' claws before and I had always sidestepped it, for in those days before the knock-out dart I didn't much fancy a wrestling match with his bears, roping the legs one at a time, pulling them up to the bars, and clipping the claws. But I could understand his anxiety; he was sensitive to complaints from the public, and these every zoo attendant knows well. Charlie paused in his stride, as if divining my thoughts.

'You know, I think the only reason some people come here is to find fault.' That was condemnation indeed, coming from Charlie, who was the most benign of men, in my experience seldom saying anything about anyone unless it was good and to the credit of his brother man (or person!). We paused a moment by the chimps, not knowing then that Bernard and he would spend a whole night trying to recapture one which had escaped and which refused point blank to re-enter its cage, and I looked at Lulu and Fifi, the star attractions of the time, totally ignorant that glorious day of the pathos that was to come for one of them − but that's another tale. So by devious routes we had come again to the main entrance gates, where, in his enclosure, a healthy, fat sea-lion was taking a cool dip. Again we paused, and again memory took us back.

'Do you remember?' Charlie began.

'Fine,' I replied.

The sea-lion was being sick, had lost weight, and was listless and generally off colour. Since sea-lions were again an untaught species at college, I contacted Oliver Jones, the famous London Zoo vet, who tried for years to breed from the giant panda at his zoo. But if he was unsuccessful in that venture, he was successful in many others, and a mine of information for the uninformed like me.

'Has he recently lost his mate?' he asked at once when I gave him the sea-lion's symptoms. I'm sure I held the phone away from my ear and looked at it in wonderment. This man was hot stuff!

'As a matter of fact he has, but how did you guess, and what's the condition?'

'Almost certainly an ulcer – peptic or possibly duodenal. I've seen it a few times here after one of our sea-lions has lost its mate. Only answer is a new mate; he's pining, anxious – typical syndrome.'

I reported the expert opinion to Charlie. That particular type of sea-lion was about £300 at the time, and Charlie, I imagine, had already overspent on other species.

'I can't possibly afford a new mate just now. Can you try something?'

So we did. We put the ailing creature on to Vitamin B, gave him the usual bismuth/kaolin type of white stomach mixture, and tried tastier morsels of a finer fish. In fact we gave him pretty well the standard treatment used for a peptic ulcer in humans at that time – Vitamin B, stomach mixture, lighter diet. And he responded, started to pick up, stopped pining, and in a short time was his usual sleek self again.

'You know,' I said to Charlie, 'peptic and duodenal ulcers are very common in people; as a matter of fact I had the beginnings of one myself a couple of years back. I've sometimes wondered if Oliver Jones's cure is what we need. What do you think, Charlie?'

He looked at me blankly. 'How do you mean, Alex?'

'New mate was what the man said,' I grinned.

He roared with laughter, slapped me on the back, said 'Come and have a choc-ice' (I'd thought he was never going to offer) 'and sit over here.'

'Over here' was a seat that gave us a most magnificent view right over Bristacombe harbour, and away across the Bristol Channel to Wales. The sea was deep, deep blue that day, with lighter patches here and there and ever-changing patterns as light clouds scurried overhead. I've always associated such colours with the sea off the North Devon coast. Around us the trees were in full leaf, the scent of blossom was in the air, and the birdsong of our native species as they flitted among the branches merged perfectly with the sounds coming from the 'variety pack' behind us. We both fell silent and just let all this loveliness wash over us. Then Charlie said:

'The world looks very beautiful
And full of joy to me . . .'

'Indeed it does, very lovely,' I agreed.

'I used to play that hymn, Alex. I was a church organist at one time.'

'Well, now, Charlie, that I didn't know. So was I; or rather, I should say I played a church organ. Got me £80 a year and helped to put me through college.'

'What church would that be, now?'

'Oh, a wee country church – Church of Scotland,' I said.

'Mine was a country one too – but C. of E. But Alex, when you look at a view like that, what do denominations matter? You just want to sing together, in harmony, in praise to the Almighty. You know, Alex, we can learn a lot from the animals. Look how many there are living in harmony, some of them natural enemies too. It can be done. Did you know that I once had, as the Bible says, "the lion lying down with the lamb"? They were called Leo and Persil. Word got around about them, natural enemies being great pals – of course they were both young, you understand. Anyway, I was asked to take them and any other animal to a service for animals in St Paul's, Covent Garden. Canon May took it. Went again the next year and took a monkey and Jill, an African grey parrot. She disgraced me. The Canon was a big man – weighed about eighteen stone. He had to stop for several rests going up the pulpit stairs to get his breath. When he finally made it, Jill shouted, "Cor!" The Canon, the verger and the congregation exploded. Later in the service the Canon stopped to mop his brow, and up pipes Jill with "There's a pretty boy!" It was a good address, about being kind to God's creatures and what we could learn from them, but I was on edge with my wretched parrot. She kept butting in. When Canon May said, "Let us consider the king of the beasts," up she pipes again with "Pretty poll!" But the Canon took it all in good part. He was a fine man, gone now.'

So we sat on, reluctant to take our eyes from the view before us or shatter the peace that wrapped us round that day. I felt I would be content to live in this glorious country overlooking the Bristol Channel and tend animals there all my days, but it was decreed otherwise. Bernard remains in practice. But there is no zoo on the hill to visit; the zoo, with its variety pack, where Virginia McKenna filmed, where Johnny Morris and other notables visited, and where tens of thousands found pleasure, is no more. The view remains, enjoyed by the visitors to the holiday centre there. But Charlie is still busy in the town park with a miniature zoo, continuing to prove that a variety pack can co-exist, content and in harmony, in this best of all worlds entrusted to us by God.

PART TWO
In the Vestry

16

The Monkey on my Back

We moved into Moorton's old, large, but
homely Manse a month after I had preached
for the charge. It was a house that seemed to
say 'Welcome' as soon as you crossed the
threshold. Many generations of ministers had
lived there, going back 300 years to the first,
who had been ejected from this very house by a
dozen dragoons on the order of the Bishop; for
King Charles II, like his father and grandfather, was determined to be head of the Kirk of
Scotland and impose episcopacy. After all, he
reasoned, he ruled by divine right . . . But
Scotland's people worshipped a higher divine,
and in consequence many, like Moorton's first
minister, were forced from their homes and
church buildings to shelter in caves and worship behind a dyke, with their guards posted to
warn of any approaching Redcoats − the
guards were later to form the Cameronian Regi-
ment. I prowled around the house, and with

my love of history I felt it a tremendous privilege to be in this place, so steeped in the lore of ages. I wondered in which room the minister, with amazing courtesy and forgiveness, had treated his captors to a meal, and prayed for them . . . amazing grace indeed!

The last painters and plumbers had moved out, the furniture was in place, the boys had surveyed the passing scene already from the branches of every one of the fifty climbable trees in the garden, trees dotted still with the remains of rooks' nests. I had walked round and round the acre of ground − or rather wilderness − and tried to picture it laid out in strawberry beds, vegetable plots and rose gardens, as it had been, we understood, forty years before. A series of ministers who, though excellent in other respects, had clearly not been gardeners had allowed Nature to take over, and Nature had, with samples of every known weed. All that remained of the fine walled garden was the wall . . . and a patch of rhubarb. But, for our coming, farmers had already been in, ploughed the whole garden up and cut the grass − my love of gardens, like so much else, having somehow filtered through the grapevine. I should have been content. After three years of preparation, I should have been glad that I had reached the culmination of it all, that in one more day I would be ordained and begin this new life for which I'd been trained. The kids were thrilled by it all, Janet loved her kitchen, we were well satisfied with our new home, and had already received so much kindness. I should have been very pleased by it all, but I was wretched. I still had the monkey on my back! He had been there ever since I'd left Devon.

That monkey had clung to me, chattered in my ear, and generally made life troublesome for me every single day since I'd given up practice. Many times he'd told me I was a fool. A herd of cattle in a field on a winter morning, their breath rising in clouds in the frosty air – and I was back calving cows or treating milk fevers and a host of other conditions, out in the open air. Even more nostalgic was each spring, with the shrill call of lambs and the deeper bleat of the ewes in many a field. My fingers would start to itch, for perhaps above all I'd loved the lambing season, never ceasing to marvel at this annual miracle: the unfading wonder of delivering a lamb, saving a life, and seeing a contented mother nuzzle her lamb, while the little creature, on shaky legs but with unerring, inborn accuracy, would head straight for the source of food. Driving past fields of lambs was the hardest thing of all, but even a cat curled up on a sunlit window ledge, or a couple of dogs romping in a park, stirred the memory. Animals I loved – treating them had been not only my livelihood, but my life – and, fool that I was, I'd given it up. 'Idiot!' the monkey continually chattered in my ear. Then there was the financial side. After years of building, the practice was really taking off, and just when I could look forward to taking on another one or two colleagues, being the senior, and being comfortably off, I'd given it up. 'Madman!' said the monkey. I couldn't argue about it. From a secure future with our own house, a spare car for my wife and a considerable income, I was going into a 'tied' house, an uncertain life, for congregations could be fickle and easily tire of their minister, and all for the low salary for which most churches expected the wife to serve as well as her husband. What had I done? By every human standard the whole thing was sheer lunacy, and my decision would result in years to come in my family being denied many things they would otherwise have had.

Again the monkey had whispered (a very insidious argument this . . . he really was an intelligent ape): 'You are throwing away five hard years of study in a course infinitely more difficult than theology, years for which your parents sacrificed much for you.' That, too, was undeniable. My mother had kept hens, ducks, geese, turkeys; she had sold eggs and, every Christmas, fowls for the table, when the whole family and two old friends would sit around in a cold outhouse, the air thick with feathers and down, as we plucked hundreds of birds — all to educate my brothers and me. Now, said the monkey, that sacrifice had all been in vain. I had thrown it all away, for nothing — for a veterinary, medical or dentistry course was not equivalent, said the University, to an MA course half the length of those others. So, at the end of the Divinity training, despite doing a BD course, nothing was awarded, and one was doomed to remain an oddity, a freak, a minister with no apparent ministerial qualifications, for ever a vet in the vestry! The monkey had nagged at me day after day. But lately the monkey had changed species, had grown horns and a forked tail, and the demon doubt was seen in his true colours, and was having a real go at me as I sat in the study, head in hands.

'If you were a son of mine, I'd advise you against this change,' said old farmer Conibear, and he was a wise man. 'You're a passable preacher, but you're a good vet.'

'How can you possibly leave sunny Devon and its kind folk, and go back to cold, wet Scotland?' another had asked, and added, 'You'll live to regret this.'

'You'll get more bites and scratches from people than ever my old cat gave you,' said Miss Inglewood, and very likely this would be so.

So blow after blow thudded in. I was on the ropes, punch-drunk, and Old Nick was fairly hammering in the uppercuts, straight lefts, and thumps to the solar plexus. But was it really Old Nick? Was it not just plain common-sense? Humanly speaking – from a family or financial point of view – there was no possible way I could justify this daftness. My actions hadn't been rational. Why had I done it, then? Was it some kind of wish-fulfilment of my father, who had wanted to be a minister, and was a far more worthy man than I was? It had just not been possible for him, for his mother had died when he was young, he was the youngest of a fairly large family, there were no university grants and, in the post-war years of depression, wages were low. There was no way he could realize his wish, so he had taken any job he could get and had become a railwayman. Moreover, he would never even see his eldest son as a minister because he had been snatched away in his fifties, just before my course commenced. I was far from clear about all the whys and where-fores of my move. In the cold light of day they didn't seem to make much sense, nor could they be explained to others. I just knew that, willy-nilly, I seemed to have been gradually propelled along this path. Kenneth, as a lay preacher, had inveigled me into it, and my involvement had grown until I was preaching every second Sunday in one or other of Devon's many little Methodist, Congregational or Baptist chapels. I'd always been keen on youngsters, and took part in different kinds of youth work. I had been taught to believe – and proved to my own satisfaction that it was true – that life's surest foundation was a sound Christian faith.

'But why did you become a minister?' Francis Gay of the *Sunday Post* once asked me on the phone. How could you cram all the forces at work, the issues involved, into a short, snappy answer on a telephone, to an unknown voice at the other end? I'd answered something like this:

'In North Devon, with its many small farms, the vet was treated very much like the family doctor, so you came to know your clients well, not just as clients, but in many cases as friends. Your advice was asked on all kinds of things, quite apart from their animals. As time went by, I came to see in this life there are really only two kinds of people – not Scots or English; rich or poor; Labour or Conservative; black or white, but those who had this strange, intangible thing we call faith, and those who hadn't. The former might not be in church every Sunday, but it seemed to me, as an outsider looking in, that this faith was very real, something that worked, an anchor that held them in

319

life's storms. Those without it appeared to me to be poor in comparison – not only had they no anchor, they had missed the boat! So eventually I, who never in my life had thought of becoming or had wanted to become a minister, felt that this "faith thing" worked, and that I should try to share it with others.'

That statement, I suppose, about summed it up. It sounded pi to say one had a Call, for people could have a call to be doctors, nurses, teachers, or anything, almost – even vets. None the less it had been a Call. Like Masefield's 'Sea Fever', 'A wild call, a clear call, that may not be denied,' I had repeatedly, over several years, heard this voice say, 'This is the way; walk ye in it.'

I had felt that my conscience would never let me rest again unless I at least tried the door, so I had written to Tom Allan, just about the best-known minister in Scotland at the time, asking for his advice and inquiring how a vet might go about becoming a minister. Busy man though he was, he'd replied, and passed my request to the powers that be; secretly hoping that the doors wouldn't open or that I would be classed as unsuitable, I'd gone on, step by step. The Old Testament had a record of men who had been reluctant prophets, who had been called against their wish, almost. I was no prophet, but I understood now how they had felt, for one by one the doors opened before me. I was accepted, and felt as if I'd been taken by the scruff of the neck and thrust into this whole thing. We'd had various signs (at any rate they were signs to us) along the way, directing us on. I say 'we', for from the beginning it was a joint venture. It had to be, and I recalled how I had come home from surgery one evening feeling I must really broach the question of giving up practice to Janet; but before I could speak, she said, 'I think, my dear, it's time you were seriously thinking of the ministry.' I'd gasped! Was this telepathy, ESP, or was it something higher? As for sacrifice, Janet had always emphasized that she'd married Alexander Cameron, not a vet or a minister, but the man — bless her!

So I wrestled in my study that day. The voice whispered: 'There's still time to turn back!'

If I'd been a swearing man, I would have said, 'Go to hell!', and even if this might not have been accurate geographically, it would certainly have been sound theologically concerning the wretched creature on my back. I just groaned aloud, and held my drooping head.

'Now, now,' came the voice in soft, soothing tones, 'stop worrying and fussing. You're just being prudent. You can do far more for the Christian cause as a layman than in a dog-collar. What's happened is simply the concern any person brought up in a good, devout Christian home would have for helping others, and telling others about your God. Well . . . you've just let it go to your head a bit. Besides, as a vet you would have more money to give away to charities, churches and missions. Pull out now!'

The arguments were subtle, the battle hard, but Gethsemane cannot be avoided. Tomorrow night one of the questions at ordination would be: 'Are not zeal for the glory of God, love for the Lord Jesus Christ, and a desire for the salvation of men, so far as you know your own heart, your great motives and chief inducements to enter into the office of the Holy Ministry?' No man can answer that without a clutch at the throat, and great heart-searching. But it's a question that cannot be ducked or glossed over.

So, when the family were in bed and the noises of the world were hushed, like King George VI on the night before his Coronation slipping into Westminster Abbey to be alone, I went quietly by myself into Moorton's lovely old kirk and there in the silence faced up to that question. All around me were the influences of the past. The very hush of that place seemed to carry an echo of many voices, of men and women to whom this house of prayer was the dearest spot on earth. The soil of this parish, more than any other in Scotland, had been stained by the blood of the martyrs for whom zeal for the glory of God had been life's chief end. In the quietness of that darkening building, which tomorrow would ring with songs of praise, whispers of the past seemed to come to me from those for whom love for Christ and concern for their fellows had indeed been the chief motives for entering the ministry. I thought of all they had given up – security, family life, even life itself in some cases . . . and then I thought of One who had given up everything, coming from heaven's glory to earth's gloom, out of His vast love. By comparison, I was not giving up anything; and there, in the deepening hush of that ancient church, the monkey at last jumped off my back – the devilish taunts ceased, at least for a time.

I knew I was no great shakes. I was certainly no plaster saint, and I was aware of a fair old number of faults and failings, but I believed that truly it was love for Him, for others, and zeal for God's glory, that had brought me here. Others might understandably laugh or criticize. I would doubtless falter many times still, but in that precious moment I knew I was where He wanted me to be. That meant everything, and on the following night, in an atmosphere that was very special and in a service that was unforgettable, the people of Moorton and I plighted our troth to one another — and to God. If I had now, as the lovely old phrase put it, 'the care of souls', I had also around me many souls that cared. The marriage was complete. The monkey was not present, being shut up in his cage — at any rate for a while!

17

Welcome

'I regret to have to tell you that your new minister is not the man you think he is. In fact he has a past – quite a past. He's been in trouble with the police.'

The congregation was silenced. There were gasps here and there, and the looks we had been getting all evening hardened into stares. What was this? On the platform Jimmy licked his lips. He was enjoying himself in anticipation of further revelations. Jimmy Duncanson and I had gone through Trinity College together, and because he had been in agriculture, there was a common bond between us. We were more or less on the same theological wavelength; we were both married with a family; we normally sat together at lectures and had endured many a weary hour side by side, both doodling on our note-pads when the lectures were especially dry . . . and now the blighter was spilling the beans on his closest friend!

'Yes – with the police,' he repeated. 'John Stevens, your minister and I were driving along Bath Street one afternoon when we saw these three big fellows laying into one wee fellow. The odds didn't seem fair, so we stopped the car with a screech and leapt out. The fight was taking place on the steps leading up to a terrace house, where the big fellows had the wee chap down. Alec was first up the steps and wondering which big fellow to tackle, with us close behind him, when one of the big men said, "Police! Dial 999 for help and give us a hand!"

'We stood and stared, not quite sure what to do. The wee man was fighting like mad, throwing the big fellows about, but before we could join in the battle a police car came roaring up, out piled some bobbies, and eventually the little chap was handcuffed. It seems he was a wanted criminal, actually had a gun on him, and the three policemen, off-duty and in plain clothes, had recognized him, tackled him . . . and we had been going to help a criminal!'

The company in the church hall relaxed. Their new man was maybe all right after all . . . as far as the police were concerned, anyway.

The Welcome Social was in full swing. The tables were groaning under their weight of food, with the kind of spread that only a country congregation supplies . . . scones, pancakes, sausage rolls, sandwiches of every kind and cakes of every conceivable variety. Tables were arranged all round the hall, and on the platform was the top table, where the minister and his wife, their friends and all the various speakers were seated. Our four little sons were tucked up in bed, cared for by a baby-sitter, but we were on public view, being eyed, in kindly fashion of course, by everyone in the hall. What would this new man be like? A vet . . . well, at least he was different . . . But could a vet make a minister?

Janet was undergoing equal scrutiny, for the minister's wife was at least as important as her man. We were trying to be on our best behaviour, but I had already disgraced myself. In front of me was a plate of huge meringues, a delicacy I love; I had picked one up, bitten into it, and it had more or less exploded on my face, covering me from ear to ear in a sticky mess . . . a plastered minister!

The night before, in all the solemnity of a Presbyterian ordination, I had taken my vows in the hush of Moorton's lovely old kirk . . . a service whose atmosphere lives with me to this day. But the following night was for socializing, for presentations to various people who had helped during the short vacancy, and for a mutual 'getting to know you' by the minister, his lady and the congregation of Moorton. It was also a time for revelations about the Camerons by their friends, and words of advice from senior colleagues.

'You will find your new minister a grand preacher' (praise I certainly didn't deserve), said the Rev. Andrew Eastham, the Interim Moderator or acting minister during the vacancy.

'He's up-to-date, modern, but not too way out, not like the man who was always trying new gimmicks to get his congregation's attention. One Sunday he instructed the Beadle to be up in the church loft at the sermon, and when the text was announced, to throw down one of the pigeons which roosted there. The preacher announced his text: "Oh for the wings of a dove and I would fly away and be at rest" ... but nothing happened. So he repeated it, twice, the second time bellowing out the words. At last the trapdoor opened and the Beadle's face appeared.

' "Minister!" he shouted, "the cat's been up and ate the doos! Wull I throw doon the cat?" ' (Loud laughter.)

Andrew went on: 'He's not a blood-and-thunder preacher either, like the man who every week pounded the book-board and gave his people what for. One Sunday he was preaching on "The Day of Judgement". "There shall be wailing and gnashing of teeth," he thundered, when from the back seat there piped up a man without a tooth in his head.

' "Fit happens tae them wi' nae teef?" he inquired.

'The minister glared, then announced, "Teeth will be provided!" ' (More laughter.)

Then Rev. Andrew paid a lovely tribute to my father and mother, who had latterly been members of his church. I was glad of his words, for I knew this was a hard night for my widowed mother. Before the Social, she had said, with tears in her eyes, 'If only father could have been here. He would have been so proud.'

Andrew gave place to the Rev. George Meek, after a duet by the two sisters Agnes and Mary Black. George had helped during the vacancy too, and he spoke up and said how glad he was that the new minister had a young family, for there was nothing like a family for making a man humble and keeping his feet on the ground. He went on to tell of a certain family who were sitting in the Manse pew one Sunday when, to his horror, the minister noticed one of his boys plunking paper pellets at the congregation in the middle of the sermon. The Manse pew was at the front row of the gallery, so the boy had a good view of most of the congregation. In full flow, the minister stopped his oration and glared at his son. The wee fellow was not one whit abashed, but merely waved at his dad in the pulpit and called out, 'That's all right, Dad! You go on preaching and I'll go on wakening them up.' (More laughter and glances at the minister.)

'But,' went on George, 'remember your minister is also a husband and father. He has to give time to his family, and don't expect Mrs Cameron to be at everybody's beck and call all the time. She will do her part, have no fear, but she has her hands full with four wee laddies. Give them time to settle in.'

I was very glad of George's words, for in the few brief days we had been in the Manse, Janet had already been asked to be President of the Woman's Guild, President of the Mothers' Circle, and to take over as Girl Guide Captain. It seemed the Mothers' Circle were in dire straits, for 'the President has a wee boy now, and you can't expect her to carry on'! I had decided to put my foot down right at the start, and pointed out that my wife had *four* wee boys to look after, that she would do her share in church life, but one organization at a time. I don't know if I was too popular, but I was determined to clarify things right from the beginning, and hit this curious notion that many folks have – that because she is the Lady of the Manse, it is somehow the duty of the minister's wife to do everything that is asked of her.

George then went on to give me some advice. 'Despite what some folks think about ministers only working on a Sunday, you will find the ministry every bit as demanding as your vet life. You must learn to take a day off . . . go fishing, or take up golf. That's a good way to get you out, away from your parish, and rid yourself of a lot of frustration. You will no doubt find one of your Elders who will take you with him to a golf course. When I was a young minister, I used to play with my senior Elder, who, although well up in years, was almost a scratch golfer. I was just a beginner, and as the Elder won every hole I got more and more discouraged and embarrassed. To cheer me up with his way of it, the old man said to me, "Never mind, Mr Meek, one day you will have the burying of me." That was no help, for I pointed out to him that even then it would be his hole!'

George paused to let the laughter die down, then went on, 'Mind you, you've got to be careful golf doesn't get a hold on you. A certain minister's manse was right beside a fine golf course, he was a keen golfer, and one glorious summer Sunday he was up early and went out to have a look at the course. It was deserted, and he was sorely tempted to have a few holes before anybody was about. He was tempted and he fell!

'It so happened two angels were watching the scene, one a new recruit, the other an old, experienced angel. The young angel was shocked. "Look at that," he said, "a minister playing on the Lord's Day. You'll have to punish him."

' "I will," said the venerable seraph.

'The minister teed up at a short hole, swung the club sweetly, the ball soared in a perfect arc, landed on the green, bounced twice and went into the hole. A hole in one! He was overjoyed. He'd never had an ace before.

'The young angel was puzzled. "I thought you were going to punish him?" he said.

'The old angel smiled a sweet smile and replied, "I have! He'll never be able to tell a soul about it!" ' (More laughter . . . the company thoroughly relaxed now.)

So the evening wore on with song and story, presentations to various people and to us. I thought, as I looked at the assembled vast throng, that I had seldom seen a happier bunch of people, and thought also what a lot of nonsense was talked about kirk functions being wet, wishy-washy, goody-goody, drab, boring affairs. I had listened to some fine speeches – sure, some of the jokes were old, but all were good and wholesome . . . I had enjoyed some excellent singing and music . . . and as I looked out from the platform at a host of happy, smiling faces of young and old, I felt a warm glow inside me.

These were *my* people. This was my little flock. No doubt there would be difficulties from time to time, perhaps criticism at times, but that night there had been a resounding 'Welcome!' from one and all. We were wedded together, one family in the service of God and His Church. That strange creature, a vet in the vestry, had been accepted.

18

A World of their Own

'Is it all right for you, John, if I pick you up about seven tonight, and you can maybe take me round some of your district?' I asked on the phone.

'Fine, man,' replied John. He had been in farming and we had mutual acquaintances, so there was no reticence or reserve between us as can exist (indeed often has to exist) between a minister and his people, for a variety of good reasons. But from past knowledge, John and I were free and easy together. I was gradually getting to know my flock, being conducted by each Elder in turn and introduced to his complement of maybe twenty to twenty-five families. John was Elder in the Waterfoot area of Moorton.

'I'll take you to so-and-so' – John reeled off a few names – 'and we'll end at Low Blackpark. Man, be prepared for a shock; you never saw anything like that. They live in a world of their own out there – prehistoric!' He rang off, chuckling.

'A world of their own – prehistoric.' The description had a familiar ring about it. My mind went back ten years as I sat at my desk musing. Ken had used that very description when first he sent me to the Tuckers' farm at Keystones in a fold of the North Devon hills. 'Expect anything, and be ready for anything,' he said. It sounded intriguing, even slightly sinister.

I duly arrived at Keystones, after driving down a rough track which meandered across a few fields. I was a bit late, which I didn't like for a first visit, but COD 330, my ancient Morris van, had played up again that morning. New cars were virtually unobtainable in these post-war years, and old ones that were only fit for pensioning off were still in use and commanding high prices. COD had been paid Cash on Delivery all right, but it lived up to its title in other ways too – it was a proper Cod indeed. That morning it had refused to budge; I had swung the starting-handle till my hands were raw, and finally, not for the first time, had to be towed to get her started; hence the delay. I thought as I approached it that the farm had a pleasant enough setting, sitting as it did in the cleft of a hill overlooking the blue waters of the Bristol Channel far below. It would be exposed in winter, no doubt, but this was a fine spring morning of soft winds and scudding clouds. The good earth, one felt, was just having its last short snooze before awakening in the glory of spring's new life. There weren't many buildings about the farm, I noticed as it drew nearer, and the dwelling-house looked very bleak and bare with its slate-covered exterior. No neat gardens, palatial barns, silos and all the rest that there had been in my native Ayrshire, but I had got used to this by now in Devon.

I noticed as I pulled up, leaving 'Coddy' conveniently on a hill for an easy start, that there were five ponies tied to a rail and five characters lounging on the wall beside them. I couldn't spot John Wayne among them, but otherwise it was a perfect Western set. I looked carefully but could not spot any guns − but I had been warned to expect anything, so you never knew. After all, this was the family to which Basil belonged, a cousin of the present lot. Everybody knew Basil. He was none too clean, generally had a drip at the end of his nose, and was only ninety per cent or maybe less, as the local saying had it. He attended a tiny independent chapel near one of the other Tucker farms, and on one occasion was out with the pastor for a day's shooting. Suddenly Basil's 12-bore blasted off, the shot so 'adjacent' to his companion that the latter leapt heavenwards like a startled grouse.

'What – what did you do that for, Basil?' he demanded.

Basil didn't believe in using two words if one would do, and merely grunted 'Magpie – bad luck!'

'But your shot wasn't anywhere near it,' said the petrified parson.

'No matter; fire anywhere breaks the bad luck,' explained Basil patiently.

'Well, look here, don't do that again, for you nearly blew me away.'

I knew Basil quite well. He was a friendly soul, but was the plaything of anyone who wanted a laugh, on the receiving end of much hurtful hilarity, and the butt of many a hundred per cent, consciously superior mind. Yet he had a grasp of life's basic realities and was happy with what little he had. Despite the innate superstition of many country folk he had still a real piety, a sincere if simple faith, and a heart of love for all mankind as big as his large, craggy frame. I also knew cousin Donald, who was a different kettle of fish – a rogue of the first degree who would have cheated his granny, and who did cheat many, but generally managed to steer clear of the law. He was, physically, all angles; a lean individual with sloping shoulders, long arms, and a nose and chin which seemed almost to meet. He never smiled, and communicated with snorts, grunts and sly looks. He kept sheep, anybody's he could annexe, and when his flock was not grazing on the sides of the road it was in somebody else's fields; Donald was sorely troubled with bad fences round his own fields and never had time to mend the gaps, for he had other nefarious pursuits which kept him busy. Thus he eked out a fairly comfortable existence with a life of busy idleness. Donald had a collie dog which followed him everywhere, a wall-eyed creature which he kicked, beat and continually abused, yet the dog would have given its life for this unworthy object.

But Basil and Donald were not in the welcome committee of five, whom I took to be the sons of old farmer Tucker, gathered here for the occasion at the parent farm of Keystones from the other Tucker strongholds of Brindacott, Buttersby and a few others. Those were farmed by the various sons, all bachelors, who had their sisters as their cooks and housekeepers. There seemed to be a happy haphazardness about their methods because, as I later discovered, you never quite knew which son would be where or which sister would be the resident cook for that period. As I walked down the little hill towards the reception committee, I became aware of five female forms gathered in the porch of the farmhouse, eager, it seemed, to catch a glimpse of the new 'vet'nary'. I smiled towards them and gave them a hearty 'Good-morning', whereupon they disappeared like rabbits down a burrow. I wondered if I had sprouted horns since morning or if they were bereft of the gift of speech, but it transpired they were all so shy, retiring and modest beyond belief that a strange man addressing them before they had been properly introduced was enough to send them scuttling for safety. I tried the men, shouting as I approached, 'Good morning! Sorry I'm a bit late, but the old car wouldn't start.'

'Aar!' they responded, continuing to prop up the wall.

I sidled up to my five cowpunchers very deliberately, in my size 11 wellington boots. I had my own 'Colts' plainly visible, belted over my long black waterproof coat and carried high on the hips for instant action, each gun loaded with twenty shots – in one, avian tuberculin, and in the other, mammalian. I had come to do the annual tuberculin test.

'I'm Mr Cameron, the new vet; you know, the Major's partner.'

'Us knows,' grunted one, while they continued to stare in an offhand fashion.

There followed a long pause. The conversation was distinctly languishing, so I ventured, 'Nice day!'

'Aar!' said the previous speaker, evidently the talkative Tucker.

'Ar – I mean er – can we make a start? We've quite a few beasts to do.'

'Reckon us'd best wait till vather comes,' said the speaker of the house.

Now I'm by nature a friendly soul, but what with females disappearing as soon as I hove in sight, and four males who had yet to open their mouths, though they continued to scrutinize me closely, I found it all a bit unnerving. I felt it only wanted Basil to appear waving a gun to send me scuttling for the car, but I tried again.

'I don't think we've met; I'm Cameron –'

I was interrupted. 'So ee jus' zaid,' confirmed the spokesman. He was sharp!

'Yes, but I haven't met any of you. Who's the oldest?'

The brother who talked was about seventeen, and he introduced himself as Kingsley; he nodded towards the others, who were respectively Ivan, Bernard, Cyril and baby Arthur, aged about fourteen.

'Do ee like it here, en?' asked Kingsley, providing a positive rush of conversation.

'Love it,' I said.

'Aar,' they nodded, with the obvious assumption that nobody could fail to like it. 'Hyer comes vather now; us'll get started,' nodded Kingsley in the direction of an old man slowly climbing the hill towards us. I noticed the loungers pulled themselves erect at the advent of father. I shook hands with the old boy, who gave a few 'aah, aars' in my general direction, which I took to signify welcome. 'Vather' had only one eye, but I thought it was not unfriendly, with maybe even a twinkle in its blue depths.

'Where do ee want to start then?' asked Kingsley.

'What about the cows, then you can let them out for a bite. I've kept them long enough, with being late.'

'Oh, no matter; us had nothin' much to do, like' – which I was to find was an excellent summary of the Tucker philosophy. They would have been absolutely at home with a West Highland crofter for whom there was 'always tomorrow'; but who's to say that their outlook on life was not the most comfortable?

So we started with the cows, tied up in the murky dark shippen. I clipped the neck hair and injected the tuberculin, while Arthur was despatched for a torch, a rag and some meths so that we could clean the ears of the beasts and read the numbers tattooed there. I soon found that Ivan, the oldest and quietest, was also the most responsible, but even so, on this occasion I thought I had better mark up the book myself. The cattle were a scrubby lot, badly

wintered, but having them tethered to a stanchion was half the battle and they were soon
done and turned loose. I noticed that they took
their time on the way to the bite of pasture, in
keeping with the leisurely outlook of their
owners.

'Now where?' I asked.

'The bull, I reckon,' said Kingsley. I was
conscious, in the casual way he said it, and in
the eager looks young Arthur was darting at me
(he had not learnt to present a deadpan countenance on every occasion yet), that this was a
test case for the new vet. Now I am no braver
than the next man, and have my own particular
fears and phobias, but fear of bulls is not one of
them. Respect for them, yes; care in handling,
by all means; but not fear. Besides, having dealt
with Ayrshire bulls, the most treacherous of
any breed, I had found the Ruby Reds, as the
North Devon breed was called locally, docile
big creatures up till now.

'One of you come in with me, and stand
behind me till I inject him, then when I grab
his ring, get that ear number.'

So, accompanied by Kingsley, I braved the
bull in his loose-box, gently rubbed his back,
and then with a couple of quick jabs had the
tuberculin in his neck. I was conscious when I
rejoined the others that I had clearly passed
some kind of test. It was only later, much later,

that I learnt that my nice quiet beast had more than once had a go at a Tucker, and generally they approached him with pitchforks at the ready.

'Where now?' I asked.

'The yiffers and steers, us reckons,' said Cyril, finding tongue.

I was conducted to a smallish shed, which housed the 'yiffers' and steers. Never before had I seen anything like it — a world of their own indeed, for in that confined space some thirty-five to forty young beasts were milling around, treading in what had once been straw bedding but was now many feet deep, indeed half-way up to the roof. It was impossible for me to stand erect in places. There was no ring, stanchion, crush or any other means of restraint such as all the best veterinary books describe. But the Tuckers had their method, and it was sheer mayhem. I noticed 'vather' wisely retire outside, and all of a sudden we were at a rodeo. Keystones Farm, I thought, was well named, for never outside the silver screen had I seen anything quite so like the Keystone Cops as what followed now. Here we were, right back to the slapstick, custard-pie days, though when I opened my mouth to speak, what hit me slap in the face was anything but custard. This had hurtled in my direction as a direct result of Kingsley leaping on to the back of a 'yiffer' —

or it might have been a steer – with a loud 'Ya-hoo!' It was impossible to determine which it was, for the only light in the place came from two slits in the wall. It was true, there was a large hole for a window, but this was com-pletely boarded over; once a year, when the beasts were turned out to graze, the board came down and the residual dung was forked out into the yard. Again I thought of my veterinary hygiene books and how they had emphasized the need for proper ventilation, extolling louvre windows and the like. I stood there, my face covered in mud of a particularly repugnant flavour, and watched 'like stout Cortez, silent upon a peak in Darien, and all his men in a wild surmise' as Kingsley rode his animal round and round till it collapsed under him. That was the signal for me to dash in, guns at the ready. The animal was then marked with a piece of marking crayon – a keel mark – to show it had been done. To find out ear num-bers was hopeless; that would have to wait for three days, when, if any reactors showed, we would be compelled to scrub through layers of dirt to find the tattoo.

Soon the shed was a maelstrom of steaming, sweating beasts and flying dollops of dung, as the Tucker boys made whoopee and rode their beasts to a standstill. It was at this point that I discovered they could in fact all speak, and that

Arthur, presumably to show his manhood, had learnt an oath or two. So the battle progressed. Perhaps you have, like me, watched those saloon fights without which no good Western epic is complete, and wondered how the contenders could pick themselves up again and again and head back into the mêlée. I saw it all happen that day, until, covered in mud from head to toe and with rivers of sweat coursing down my back, I decided to join in the fun. As a 'yiffer'/steer passed me at a trot, I grabbed hold of it, one hand on a horn, the other grasping its nostrils, and with a heave, as I had often seen my old boss in Scotland do, I threw it to the ground, put a knee on its jaw and jabbed in approximately the approved areas — when lo! there was a great calm. It was just as if, in the middle of the aforementioned saloon fight, somebody had suddenly said, 'Whoa, there!', or the James brothers had walked in, and everybody paused, chairs ready to crash on an opponent's skull, fists drawn back for the right uppercut, or bottle about to be hurled at the large mirror which all good saloons seem to require — presumably so that a bottle can be thrown at it. It was something like that, and I was suddenly conscious that the whooping had ceased and I was being closely scrutinized by five pairs of eyes.

'Darn me, but Oi nivver saw that done

before,' said Kingsley. 'How was it you did it?'

So I showed them again, picking the smallest animal I could see, and in that moment I knew I was accepted as an equal, a true, fully-paid-up member of the Tucker brotherhood. From henceforward over the years our relationship was grand. I could say anything to them and they would take it, and by golly they said plenty to me in return. They could speak, all right!

I don't know how long it took me to test those few bullocks – a whole morning easily, when normally, with animals properly housed and restrained, I would reckon to get through around 200. I only know that eventually the torture was over. I fought my way through the steaming mass of bodies, human and bovine, all covered in dung, ninety per cent proof, and reached fresh air and father, who surveyed us as we came out, uttering a few expressive 'aars' and 'uurs'. I was absolutely limp and glad to avail myself of the offer of a wash in the house, having first divested myself of my once black, now greenish-brown, coat, and scrubbed my wellingtons. Various maidens fled before me as I was conducted into the kitchen, where with a dollop of hard soap and cold water I did my best to look human again. As I was clearing the soap from my eyes, I became aware of a large form standing in front of me, proffering me a jam-jar containing some of Devon's famed clotted cream. Having seen the state of hygiene that prevailed in the Tucker establishment I was a bit doubtful about taking it, at least until I was sure the cows were TB-free. But I could hardly refuse, so took it in the spirit in which it was offered – and lived to tell this tale! I also looked with great interest at the figure in front of me – Mrs Tucker. She was a large, raw-boned woman whom you could hardly now call beautiful, yet she undoubtedly had a presence, a bearing, and I had no doubt that her will was law at Keystones and beyond in the other Tucker outposts, an influence and power that was all the more real because it did not seem to require enforcing; it was just somehow accepted. If father was respected, mother, I was sure, was loved.

That was my first contact with this family who lived in a world of their own. There were to be many other encounters. I thought of some of them as I sat at my desk, remembering. I remembered a number of gymkhanas where I was honorary vet in attendance. Well did I recall how the landed gentry would come from miles around, plus the horsy types who did the circuits; of how they had to pass under my measuring rod to be eligible for the under-fourteen-hands class, and how young ladies whose accents you could cut with a knife would stretch out ponies that were patently too big, to try to squeeze them in – and of the unladylike retorts I received when I excluded them. And I particularly remember Kingsley Tucker on an old grey mare, a working pony, riding bareback over the jumps and beating the young Harvey Smiths and David Broomes of the day. He was a magnificent horseman, and just seemed part of his mount as they flowed over the fences. I recalled, too, how a postman friend had gone one cold winter day to deliver the Keystones mail, and had been astonished to find the front door open and a tree trunk sticking out of the doorway. He followed it in over the stone floor of the living-room, and found to his amazement that the other end of the tree was actually blazing in the enormous, ancient fireplace; every so often some muscular Tuckers would slide it in a bit further, all to save them sawing it up. I dare say they managed to get the door shut by night.

The odd thing was that the Tuckers seemed to prosper. They never seemed in a hurry, but, apart from gymkhanas locally, they had little interest outside their work. I don't know if the sons were paid wages or simply given their keep, but 'vor zurtain zure' they made money, acquired more land, and even bought a town house, where the young ones occasionally lived, and had to acquire two television sets because they could seldom agree on which programme to watch. For a time they broke out into a positive rash of spending, and reminded me of a story currently going the rounds of a farmer who came in from Exmoor and plonked a biscuit tin on the bank counter, instructing the teller to check it, for there was, he said, £1,000 there. The teller unfolded the crumpled mass, laboriously ploughed his way through it and said, 'Nine hundred and ninety-nine pounds, sir.' The farmer maintained there was £1,000 and insisted it be recounted. Still it came to £999, whereupon the farmer's wife said, 'Dang me, 'Erb, us's brought the wrong tin.' Thus the Tuckers – wild, untameable, unpredictable, rough and ready, yet intensely loyal to their friends, sympathetic to anyone in need. I suppose that they were the stuff that the old pioneering families were made of, and they had the same piety and godliness, despite their rough ways. This was not a natural thing for them, but acquired from mother, who, quite late in life, had found a real, personal faith, an anchor to hold her in life's storms, and longed that each of her children should find that same sure anchorage. If ever there was an example of the power of a mother's influence and a mother's prayers, it was demonstrated here. Orthodox Christians they could never be, and being Tuckers, some favoured the Baptist Church, others the Church of England, a few the Plymouth Brethren, and one or two a little independent mission right on the crown of a windswept plateau, where he who had almost met an untimely demise from Basil's shotgun exerted a considerable ministry amongst these pioneering families of the wild uplands. I knew them well; I remember them with considerable affection, even though their world was not mine, but a world of their own.

As I picked up John my Elder, I wondered what surprises awaited me in the 'prehistoric' Low Blackpark. After several calls at other homes, we eventually turned the car up the farm road to the two Blackparks, the first of which was our objective. If possible, I like to know a bit about the folks I am going to visit, but I only knew that there were two brothers Baird, Davie in his eighties and John a mere stripling of seventy odd; that they resisted change, holding out against milking machines for cattle for years on the grounds that if the Almighty had intended beasts to be milked by machine He would have seen fit to provide tubes on the teats; and that only that year John had finally, to keep the peace with his son and maybe to provide an interest to keep him out of trouble, for he was 'a wild loon', allowed a tractor on the place.

'They will like be sitting one on each side of the fire, puffing their pipes and going "poop, poop".' (Here John imitated a spitting sound and action.) 'Man, it's amazing the distance they can spit. They'll maybe have a bottle between them too, sitting on the table. Have a look at one of the table legs; it's gey near scratched richt through wi' the cats.'

The car swung into the yard, a typical old-style Ayrshire steading with the house forming one end and the farm buildings two sides of a square, of which the entrance was the fourth part of the square.

'Look in there,' said John, clutching my sleeve. 'Leave your lights on!'

I obeyed and beheld a most ancient Morris with canvas hood, and beside it a large, modern Rover. On both, hens were roosting.

'John drove that old car for near thirty years,' I was informed. 'He would just chase the hens oot, gie the seat a bit dicht wi' his sleeve, an' away to the market. He's only had the Rover about a year an' he's been in the ditch wi' it three times already, blind drunk, but aye blaming it on this new-fangled machine. I think the auld car kent its way hame by itsel'.'

This, then, was my background knowledge of the Baird brothers, who, as John the Elder had predicted, were indeed sitting on either side of the fire, with their feet up and their pipes drawing nicely. I only got one glimpse of their amazing prowess at unfailingly hitting the target from a great distance as they spat towards the fire, but on the strength of that one demonstration I should say Davie, the older brother, was the champion – after all, he'd been longer at it!

John introduced me as the new minister, and they received me with courtesy and gravity, ushering me to a chair. All the chairs were ancient straight-back wooden models. I looked surreptitiously around me, and John Baird's eyes spotted my glance alighting on the table. 'My grandfather made that,' he announced. Sure enough, there was one leg very much thinner than the rest, with a cat even at that moment sharpening its claws on it. The room was bare, carpetless, with of course a stone floor. The fireplace was ancient, enormous, like many I had seen in Devon when first I went there. Beside the fireplace sat a huge three-legged pot, a bit like a witch's cauldron, I imagined, and various other iron kettles and pots, which when required were hung on the hooks or 'swees' over the fire. John had been known to bemoan the fact that you couldn't buy three-legged pots any more and it was hard to get a blacksmith to repair one. The only other items of furniture or equipment in this large, bare room were a dresser, with plates arranged along it in approved traditional fashion, and a very old sink. All this I took in while the brothers Baird were taking me in. John was officially a church member, appeared generally at 'the sacrament', and was 'very generous, putting £5 in the plate', an Elder had informed me. Davie had no church connection, but in that rural parish I tried to visit everybody, regardless of persuasion, or even if they had none. We were one community, and the church in a very real sense was at the heart of it.

I noticed that Davie had been reading a book, while John had the *Glasgow Herald* stretched out around him – no gutter press for them!

I was just wondering where to begin when John took the first of me and asked, 'What do you think of Free Trade?'

I was astounded, and I'm sure I showed it. What I thought about it was nil, for I only remembered it as a phrase in a history book, but I didn't dare show my ignorance. Soon John was in full flow about the respective policies of Gladstone and Disraeli, Lloyd George, the Irish question, bringing us up-to-date and castigating the iniquities of the present government. At some point in this monologue, Davie shuffled off to bed – presumably he had heard it all before! I nodded and grunted, and realized that here before me in these primitive surroundings was a man of considerable knowledge and no mean intellect. Then, while John my Elder and I just listened, John Baird turned his attention to the kirk. He had been a great sermon-taster in his youth, and could tell me the 'heads of the sermon' that James Black had once preached.

'Man,' he said, 'in these days the preacher took you by the scruff of the neck and dangled you over the pit o' hell, till you could smell your clathes singein' and decided you would do onythin' to get oot o' landin' there.'

I was mightily impressed by this armchair theologian. I ventured to ask if he'd been at Moorton kirk lately, and he fixed me with his eye and said, 'I've heard you.' Clearly my preaching, which some thought too evangelical, was milk and water to John Baird, compared with the 'real preachers they had long syne'.

Then John turned to his schooling in the tiny one-teacher school at Waterfoot. What an amazing 'dominie' had been there! I knew from the records that from that little country school had come two doctors, three lawyers, half-a-dozen ministers, an MP and a New Zealand Cabinet Minister – and these 'country loons' like John, who had stayed on as a farmer where his father had farmed before him, yet whose knowledge, grasp of world affairs and home spun philosophy were the fruits of seed sown by that lone schoolmaster in one tiny out-of-the-way hamlet.

Now and then as he talked, John's sense of humour would shine through, and I realized for myself what others had already told me, how in the old Waterfoot discussion group he had been such a live-wire and doughty debater. But the night was drawing on . . .

'You'll put up a prayer afore ye go, meenister?' asked John.

I did, as was my wont, but after the flow of eloquence I'd heard my words seemed poor, stumbling things. So we departed for the car, with John's solemn 'Good-night to you both' speeding our departure.

'Well, what do you think?' asked John the Elder as we got into the car.

'I think you might have warned me to swot up my history!' I grinned. 'What a man! How long has he been a widower?' I inquired.

'Man, he's no' a widower. His wife and family live in a wee hoose in the village. They've never lived wi' John. It seems his folks thought he was marrying beneath himself, and they wouldna' have the wife aboot the place. He looks in to see them whiles.' (Since there were six of a family, that presumably meant he called at least six times, I calculated.) 'But they hardly ever see each other now, never go out anywhere, though one of the lassies keeps hoose for him and the youngest boy works at the farm. John's a clever man, but a gey lonely yin.

His regular companion noo is the bottle!'

I dropped John at his house, and slowly made my way Manse-wards, trying to remember those lines about 'the tragedy of might have been'.

As it happened, I was called back to Low Blackpark a few months later. Davie was ill and sinking fast, and could I call? I found the kitchen shining, a few rugs on the floor, and a bright young woman busy at the sink. It seemed one of John's sons had moved in with his wife to look after the old men. I was taken upstairs to see Davie. He lay in a poor little room, a room that seemed crammed full of books – but Davie was beyond where I could reach him. Unconscious, his mind was roaming in distant places, probably back to the days of youth when life had been uncomplicated, un-tarnished, and full of hope of all that was to be. I sat in that dark room for a time with the dying man, silent in prayer as I commended his soul, so soon to fly away, to its Maker. I buried him a few days later, and afterwards visited John, all alone again, for he had fallen out with his son and they had left him. There was little I could do for him either that day, for by his elbow was one empty and one half-empty bottle. I knew John would not lack the 'solace' of John Barleycorn, for the Bairds were worth tens of thousands, their own earnings augmented by a legacy from a brother who had made good overseas.

I mused long before the study fire that night on my two 'prehistoric' families. One ill-educated, ignorant even — the other well-educated, knowledgeable. The one close-knit as a family — the other fragmented. The Tuckers with their simple piety and code of living — John Baird with his considerable theological and philosophical knowledge. I thought of them long, and as I went to bed I had a picture of an old man facing the years, with only a bottle for his companion. There was no doubt in my mind which family had won, in this race of life.

19

Each in its Season

A certain Bishop, years ago, was travelling on holiday in the Scottish Highlands, journeying on one of those trains that give the passengers their money's worth. It stopped at every station, and at many places where there were none, but where passengers still got on or off; and it made many other halts where a loaf of bread, or a leg of pork, and in one case a wee pig, were handed over to folks waiting beside the line. At one such halt in the middle of nowhere, a shepherd accompanied by his dogs joined the Bishop in his compartment. The shepherd was a friendly soul, and was soon deep in conversation with his companion, who, being on holiday, was disguised as a normal layman, and might have been anybody. After a time it became clear to the Bishop that his companion was puzzled as to who or what he could be, so he remarked, 'You know, I'm in the same line of business as yourself.

I've got a flock too!'

'Iss that so now?' replied the shepherd. 'And how many sheep would you be haffing in your hirsel?'

'About half a million,' replied the Bishop, without batting an eyelid.

The shepherd was greatly astonished. 'Haff a million! Haff a million! Whateffer do you do at the lambing time?'

While not possessing gaiters or other clerical attire comparable to that of the Bishop, I too had my little flock at Moorton. We didn't have anything quite the equivalent of the lambing season of my vet days (a period in my former life I miss to this day); none the less, there were particular seasons in the life of one's flock and in the yearly round.

There was, for example, the Wedding Season. This tended to be split into two distinct parts: in spring, before 1 April, or early autumn. In the early days, I assumed in my innocence that spring weddings were due to the romance of that season when 'a young man's fancy lightly turns to thoughts of love'. The autumn I presumed to be a practical time of year in a farming community, when the harvest was safely gathered for another year. My sentimental notions were speedily shattered when I learnt that romance or expediency had nothing whatever to do with it. It was simply that these, then, were the times of year when maximum rebate of income tax could be reclaimed by a married man, and I was astonished to learn of a city colleague who actually married ten couples on the optimum Saturday of spring. How sadly do our dreams depart!

The Manse door-bell rang, and there, looking somewhat apprehensive, stood George Reid and Betty Thomson, with their attendants. They had come for a rehearsal of their wedding of the next day – a quite unnecessary proceeding, for we had already been through the whole service and subsequent reception festivities on several occasions. But couples, or more correctly, brides, like to savour the great day to the full, and in advance ... bridegrooms, on the other hand, sometimes give the impression of a double dose of doom!

I led the way to the study and paused at the door to ask, 'Sure you want to go through with this? I don't advise it.'

They looked at me, completely taken aback, glanced at each other, then Betty stammered, 'What do you mean, Mr Cameron?'

'Let's go for a wee walk,' I said, and, even more mystified, they followed me across to the adjoining church and its old burial ground. We paused at a particular ancient gravestone.

'Read that!' I said.

Betty read aloud: ' "In memory of John Calderwood, Farmer, Clanfin, died 1856 aged 51; his brother Robert Calderwood, Farmer, Craigneuk, died 1863 aged 55, and William Calderwood, Farmer, Meadowside, died 1864, aged 62." '

Betty's eyes travelled to the bottom of the gravestone, where she read the one brief line:

' "And their respective wives." '

'That's marriage, Betty,' I pronounced solemnly. 'The wives are not worth a mention!'

They looked at me uncertainly. This vet-minister was surely a queer fellow, I could see them thinking, but at last they saw the twinkle in my eye, laughed heartily, and the ice was broken. It was a much more relaxed group that filed into church for the rehearsal, which proceeded smoothly enough, and in the course of which I emphasized to the attendants that when it came to the blessing, only the couple should kneel on the stool. After all, it was the couple's day . . . besides, the stool only accommodated two.

Their great day dawned fair, the guests assembled, the bride joined her groom before the table, the first hymn was sung; then, as the ceremony continued, the door opened and a man clutching a handkerchief passed right behind the wedding group, and handed the handkerchief, with a few whispered words, to the person at the end of the pew which held the bridegroom's family . . . parents, brothers, sisters. The hankie was passed from hand to hand with the same few words of explanation, while I, somewhat curious as to this wedding version of 'pass the parcel', continued with the words of the service. Eventually the handkerchief reached the bridegroom's father, who was right at the end of the row, next to the wall, and he took the proferred hankie and casually put it to his mouth. His teeth had arrived! Judging by his slick, wristy action, I would say it was not the first time he had carried out this public procedure with his molars, managing somehow, with splendid camouflage, to get them right way up in his mouth.

We came to the vows.

'Do you, George, take this woman, Betty, to be your wedded wife, and do you promise to be to her a loving, faithful and dutiful husband till God shall separate you by death?'

George thought a moment while I peered at him and nodded, indicating that his turn had come. I thought I'd need to kick him, but finally he nodded and murmured, 'I do.'

'Do you, Betty, take this man George to be your wedded husband . . .'

I paused to take a breath, and the bride immediately, cheerfully, chirruped, 'I do.'

I completed my question, and the girl again

made her affirmation, surely making clear to her bemused bridegroom her undying fealty! But the look he gave her tended to suggest, 'Trust you to use four words when two would do!'

Then came the moment for the couple to kneel in that most lovely part of the service where the Aaronic blessing, the oldest in the Bible, is bestowed on the now man and wife. The trouble was that George's younger brother, the best man, tried to get on the stool beside them. Had he succeeded poor Betty would have been tipped off the other end, but he didn't quite succeed, being elbowed in the ribs by George, who advised him in a stage whisper, and with real brotherly love, to 'Get up, you fool!'. Ministers are supposed to keep going despite snags and not to betray their feelings over-much, but at times, as with George and Betty's nuptials, it can be somewhat difficult. However, despite the hitches another marriage was solemnized . . . if that's the right description on this occasion . . . and the wedding party departed for their reception. Each week of the Wedding Season saw its marriage, each one was different, and for the couple and their guests, special, and for me, moving, as two young lives set out on the adventure of sharing everything on life's journey.

But spring was not only the Wedding Season. It saw the start of the Wandering Season.

'Daddy, there's an old gentleman at the door wanting to see you,' announced Neil one day. Aged nine, and gravely courteous, everyone to Neil − still happily innocent − was a 'gentleman'.

'He's a poor, poor, poor old man wif no coat,' added David the tender-hearted, aged four.

'I expect he's a tramp!' pronounced Ian, from a not inconsiderable experience of tramps in his seven years.

'Twamp! Man! Old!' added baby Alan, thumping his spoon in his high-chair, while the dog, Bruce, who made Alan his special charge, wagged his stump of a tail in agreement.

The boys were all correct. He was an old gentleman ... he had no coat ... he was undeniably a tramp, one of the many 'gentlemen of the road' who called at the Manse from time to time. Our present caller peered up at me from beneath a downcast countenance, and asked, 'Are you the minister ... him that was the vet?'

What difference the vet title made, I'm not clear, unless the caller thought vet-ministers had more ready cash than ordinary ones, but I acknowledged I was the minister.

'Well, you see, Father ... er, Reverend ...

I've been walking frae Liverpool wi' just some lifts, to get tae Glesca' tae see ma auld mither. She's in a gey bad way, and I wondered if you could help me.'

I pondered a moment. He was probably an old rascal and I was a ready 'touch', but maybe, just maybe, his story was true; Glasgow was not far away, and we were, as Christians, to 'be not forgetful to entertain strangers unawares'.

'I dare say we can manage a bus fare,' I responded, handing over half-a-crown.

'You widna' hae a cup o' tea? I hivna ett since yesterday.'

'Come in and we'll give you something.'

'That's rale kind o' ye.'

Janet gave him bacon and eggs, while the boys looked on with big eyes and the dog with suspicious ones. He told us his name was Willie McCafferty . . . told us again that his mother was very poorly and not expected to last long . . . confessed, as he leaned back in the chair picking his teeth, that he had not been a very good son, and had not seen his old mother for five years . . . recounted, almost with tears, what a mess he had made of his life but would like to make a fresh start, and could I give him a book to help him? Much moved, I gave him one of Professor Barclay's books of daily Bible studies, and another half-crown, and eventually he left.

A month later he called again, wondering if I could help him with something as he was on his way to Birmingham to look for work.

'How's your mother?' I asked.

He looked completely blank, then muttered, 'Oh . . . ah . . . she's a' richt.'

He got another five shillings, called down blessings upon us, and left.

Throughout the summer various other wanderers called seeking help, and with the most harrowing stories of ill-fortune. It seemed some poor souls had never really had a chance in life, so the half-crowns and cups of tea were regularly dispensed. One suggested he could do with the kind of coat I had on, and though I remembered the bit in the New Testament about those with two coats giving to those with none, I really only possessed the one coat. By the late autumn the Wedding Season was almost over, and so was the Wandering Season, or so I thought until one last incident.

Returning from a visit to my mother one cold, wet, dark evening, we found the fire almost out, and while the family took off their coats I headed for our huge coal-house, once a stable, to get an armful of logs. There was no light in the place, but even in the pitch dark I knew my way to the pile of wood. As I groped warily towards the corner where the fuel lay, I stepped on something softish, squelchy, something that was firm yet yielding. I thought of a sack with straw in it, perhaps. I picked up some logs, but as I reached the door it dawned on me there was nothing like that in our coal-house. I felt the hairs on the back of my neck stand up as the realization came: that was a body!

I dumped the logs on the fire, grabbed a torch and the poker (I am in most ways a pretty traditional being!), and, leaving Janet and the family standing at the back door of the Manse as reinforcements, headed trembling back to the coal-house. It was a body right enough. Yelling for Janet to phone for the police, I advanced, poker at the ready, and demanded to know what the body thought it was doing, lying there! There was no reply, and I feared the worst . . . but eventually there was a stirring in the corner. Now, there had been a couple of burglaries in the parish in the past week, and, convinced I was facing a desperado, I kept my distance and shouted, 'Come out of there! Don't you dare move!'

How he was to do this (I had now ascertained the 'body' was male) he clearly didn't know, so compromised by sitting up on the pile of logs where he had been lying. In the light of the torch, I recognized Willie McCafferty. He seemed placid enough, and so, feeling some-what sheepish at my overreaction, I invited him into the house.

'What were you doing in there?' I asked sternly.

'Och, I came to see if you could help me, but when there was naebody in, I just went for a sleep till you came back.'

Feeling sorry for the poor shauchly creature now, I put the kettle on to give him a cup of tea, which he had just started when the village constable, plus a colleague from the neighbouring town, burst on the scene, demanding, 'Have you got him?'

'I've got him, Jimmy, but I think maybe I've wasted your time. He's a tramp kind of body called Willie McCafferty, and he's been here before, but when I stepped on him in the pitch black of the coal-house, I have to admit I got a fright.'

'He'll likely be the burglar,' said the policeman, coming with his colleague into the kitchen where sat our wanderer.

'What's your name?' demanded PC McCluskey.

'Hugh Murphy,' replied our 'guest'. I gaped!

'What were you doing here?' shouted the bobby. I thought he was about as excited as I was, but I suppose if you have had two robberies in a week in a district where a forgotten dog-licence is about the only regular crime, you might be excused for getting a bit uptight.

The tramp protested that he had been doing nothing, only waiting to see the minister.

'Some story!' snorted the officer of the law.

I didn't know how the KGB went about these things, but I thought our two large men in blue were pretty impressive in their interrogation. There was no brutality, far from it, but under their rapid barrage of questions I'd have confessed to anything! Eventually Willie McCafferty, alias Hugh Murphy, was led off to the Police Station. Next morning a fingerprint expert arrived and dusted our doors and windows, finding his 'dabs' on the kitchen window where our tramp had tried to force an entry; alas for the police, the prints did not match those at the burgled coal merchant's or the Post Office. The prisoner appeared in court, and to my relief he was let off with a stern warning. I didn't like the idea of having landed a man in jail for sleeping on a pile of logs. It seemed that Willie McCafferty, alias Hugh Murphy, was really a Daniel Hodges, with a record for vagrancy, another for never having worked in his life, and was possessed of no mother in Glasgow.

My faith in mankind was somewhat shaken, and no matter how I looked at it I had to admit my attempt at reform or conversion had not been a notable success!

The wanderers kept coming each season, but

the supply of half-crowns gradually dried up. I also took steps to obey the scriptural command when seeking logs: 'Let there be light!'

20

The Wud You've Got

In my early months as a minister I spent long hours in the study, not only preparing for meetings, Sunday School, Bible Class, Youth Fellowship and the Sunday sermons, but just thinking, planning, and examining my ministry. Early on I came to the conclusion – which has remained with me – that I was not a committee type of man. I could cope with the Sunday congregations, I loved visiting people, young, middle-aged and old, in their homes, but when it came to Session meetings and the like, I was uptight beforehand and drained afterwards. I was abundantly blessed in my wife in a host of ways, and on committee nights she was a tower of strength with her quiet support and understanding.

I came out of a Kirk Session meeting one night early in my stay at Moorton very upset. Things had not gone well. Elders had argued, decisions had been deferred, work I wanted to see begun had not been agreed upon – in short I felt it was a mess. As we left the meeting-room, Duncan the Treasurer came up to me and said, 'Dinna worry, Mr Cameron! Things will work oot. I ken you're anxious to see things done, but you canna' change folk; you've got to work wi' the wud you've got.'

Duncan was a joiner; he knew all about 'wud' (wood), and I sat long at the dying study fire that night thinking of his words. In many ways I was blessed in the kind of wood I had to work with. There was Duncan himself, strong, deter-mined, a prodigious worker, and as long as he felt a thing was right, quick to get on with it.

There was dear little Andrew Phillips, my Session Clerk, of all things a pawnbroker to trade in Glasgow, but a saint with a beaming face, a gentle, kind, loving, understanding man with whom I shared many of my dreams and problems. He had been twenty years in Moor-ton but was still regarded as an 'incomer'. Not long before my coming, an old lady of eighty-two had died, and Andrew, speaking to one of the locals, had said, 'Well! That will be one of your oldest Moortonites gone now!'

He was answered with withering scorn. 'She wisna' a Moortonite! She was twa year auld when she came here.'

There was the other Andrew, Andrew Crom-bie the Beadle, an old soldier who had faked his age to join up as one of the early volunteers in the Great War . . . a man who lived for his church, kept it shining, and was in every sense the 'minister's man'.

I had two stalwart supporters in Jimmy Aitchison and Maxwell Watson, who, like me, felt that changes were necessary if the church was to thrive and who, in their enthusiastic way, supported me to the hilt. Great men! There were the two senior Elders, Robert Murchison, in his nineties, but in church every Sunday, and John Brown, a lovely man with a wonderful family, all thirled to the kirk and supporting the minister in anything he might try. There was my own Elder, Jimmy Rodgerson, quiet, understanding, loyal, true. My thoughts turned to my two golfing partners, Tom McMichael, a retired policeman, and Ian Bryce, the local vet and a good friend. Then there were farmers like Jimmy Gibson with his quaint, old-fashioned ways and pawky sense of humour . . . Jim Shankland and Jim Grant, who were great practical helps, and ploughed and worked the enormous Manse garden every year.

As I thought round them all, and many others, I came to the conclusion that I was really a lucky man in my office-bearers, and maybe my dissatisfaction at times was entirely my own fault in trying to rush change. Andrew Eastham had said to me, 'Always remember . . .

quick in the town, but slow in the country. Take your folk along with you and hasten slowly.'

I concluded that night that he was right — that there wasn't much wrong with the wood, only with the man trying to work it, and I should leave things to evolve slowly and just do my weekly work. For there was plenty of that, as varied as ever my vet's life had been.

'Mr Cameron! Can you come right away?' said the agitated voice on the telephone. 'Mrs McMinn has tried to commit suicide in the butcher's shop.'

The oddest thought came into my mind . . . 'What an appropriate place for the deed!', but aloud I replied, 'I'm on my way.'

We had no resident doctor in the village and most of the men were away at work, so I imagine they felt a vet-minister was the best person available. I had visited the McMinn home twice. They were the poorest family in the parish, and although they had never been in a church in their lives, I tried to visit every home in the district. The first time I called, they were breaking up the sideboard to fuel the fire, because they had no coal. The second time, the house was in darkness and I had to nip up to the Manse for an electric bulb before I could see them. Well, not completely in darkness ... in the corner was a light: the television set, just about their only piece of furniture ... a sad comment on the times, if one was looking for a sermon.

Mrs McMinn was bleeding from the wrists, but not too badly. She had a dazed look on her face and clearly did not know where she was or what had happened. We dressed the wrists, bundled her into my car, and I headed for the nearest town and the first doctor I could find. His examination was brief. 'Drive straight on to the mental hospital,' he said.

It was a harrowing journey of fifteen miles, and I fearfully watched that she would not throw herself out of the car. In fact she did try to commit suicide on the way, but at last, to my great relief, we reached the hospital and I handed her over to proper medical care.

She had a stay of a few weeks, and returned, apparently sound in body and mind once more, to the same dreadful housing conditions, large unemployed family and abject poverty. I could help financially to a small extent, though I could do little to alter their situation radically; but at least I could show concern and demonstrate that the church did care.

I met him by accident when I went over to the church one afternoon. Young he was, and clearly greatly upset, with tears streaming down his cheeks. I didn't know him, and asked if I could help. He said he didn't think so as he had already spoken to his own minister about his domestic problem, but he wanted to sit in the quietness of a church and pray, and ours was the only one in the area that was always open. In fact I'd had to fight hard in the Kirk Session to have the church kept open, for we had many visitors who wanted to see our historic building, but the Elders were afraid of vandalism. (No act of vandalism was committed over the years, but once during the night the building was broken into and our Property Fund box, which had little in it, stolen. He must have been a clean thief because he had then proceeded to wash his hands in the vestry wash-hand basin.)

My young visitor just wanted to do what many have done: call for higher help in a domestic situation that had got beyond him. He came again – and again – and I like to think that he at least found peace there. I was reminded of the old man who used to go into a large city church every day and just sit there. One day the minister asked him what he did each day. The old man smiled and said, 'I look at Him, and He looks at me.'

That's real prayer!

'You've got a visitor,' my wife informed me

when I came home at tea-time from a round of visits. 'He's been here for two hours.' The poor girl had been plying him with cups of coffee and conversation until my return.

He proved to be an alcoholic called Jim, who had just happened to get off the bus at Moorton, he didn't really know why, and had made his way to the Manse to look for help. He didn't want money, simply somebody who could maybe help with his wasted life. For it was wasted: he was jobless; his marriage had broken up; he had a wife and four children somewhere who couldn't put up with his drinking any longer. He had a prison record for violence, had been 'dried out' innumerable times in mental hospitals, and was now a broken, beaten wreck of a human being, scarcely able to eat, only drink – even meths. He had been employed in the family business of monumental sculptors, and had served in the war with distinction, becoming a sergeant-major, but after years of sponging off his parents he had finally been thrown out of the business. Now he was a wanderer – a poor ruin of what had been an intelligent man, a skilled worker and, in the early days, a good son, husband and father. What could we do?

We kept plying him with coffee; we discovered he once could play table tennis, so I phoned Jimmy Aitchison who, willing soul that he was, came round and we played with Jim till he was weary and ready to sleep. I didn't feel like risking him in the house with my wife and four wee bairns, but felt we must help somehow, so we gave him a bed in our caravan, and there he stayed. He was almost a full-time job in the early days when he had 'the shakes' and the craving was strong in him, but he kept off the bottle. In time we found him a job on a farm and I recall his tremendous joy when he was able to send his first wage to his wife. The weeks passed, and the months. Once he crept off to the pub and I pursued him, and literally dashed the glass from his hand. I thought he was going to strike me, but he came home quietly. So the time went on – six months without that fatal first drink for the alcoholic. Jim ate with us, the boys accepted him as one of the family, and gradually a normal human being arose from the wreck that had been. Janet was absolutely marvellous in the way she treated him and cared for him, and one evening he said (though older than Janet), 'Mrs Cameron! I wish you were my mammy.'

It was pathetic, yet moving, and we felt we were doing what Christ would have us do. Indeed, nuisance that he was at times, we had grown really fond of Jim. Then we went off on holiday – the 'crutch' was removed, and we came back to find Jim had broken out, assaulted a policeman, and was in prison.

We tried again and again, sometimes winning, sometimes losing, but finally Jim moved on in his wandering, out of our orbit. He left behind in us a sense of failure, but a little consolation in that we had tried, and for a short time he had been a human being again.

Jim is but one of many alcoholics I've tried to deal with over the years, usually with little success, and the tragedy is that many of them deep down are very likeable people. But it has coloured my thinking . . . and actions. I accept that many finer Christians than me enjoy a drink, and in no way do I stand in judgement on folks who like a glass with friends and can control their drinking. Often I've been misunderstood, laughed at or downright condemned because I don't drink . . . but Jim and his like, and a string of broken marriages caused by the bottle, always come to mind . . . I feel – who knows? – that maybe I or some youngster watching me at a wedding or other social occasion could become another Jim . . . and I've always felt, with deep compassion for these poor souls, 'There but for the grace of God go I.'

I was given an extra task for six months – to be chaplain to a large geriatric hospital some distance away, until another man nearer at hand could be appointed. I visited every week, moving amongst the beds of old folk, some completely helpless, some just weak and weary, some mindless. On Sunday evenings some of the choir and Youth Fellowship would come with me and we would take a little service in two of the wards.

One day when I was visiting I came across a new patient, much fitter than most.

'How are you?' I asked.

'Fine, thank you, who are you?' she replied.

'I'm the chaplain.'

'But *who* are you?'

'Oh, my name's Cameron and I'm from Moorton.'

'Hah! so you're Cameron! I've no time for you,' she went on in a very correct, indeed very affected, voice.

Now I don't like affectation, and while I'd often had my leg pulled about being a vet-turned-minister and suspected that must be the reason for this madam's condemnation of me, for the first time I felt my hackles rise, and thought, in rather unchristian fashion, 'You old besom! Lying there condemning somebody you don't know!' But I managed a smile and asked why she had no time for me. I was right in my conjecture.

'Vet – minister – can't make up your mind, can you? A man is one thing or another and shouldn't change boats in mid-stream.'

'Oh, I don't know,' I said. 'I have the best possible example for doing what I did.'

'What do you mean?' she inquired.

'Well, our Lord was a working carpenter to the age of thirty before He became a wandering preacher.'

She shot up in bed and looked at me as if seeing me for the first time. 'You know, I never thought of that!' she exclaimed in surprise, and from then on she couldn't have been nicer!

I discovered there had not been a communion service in the hospital for sixteen years, so I decided to hold one. I have never known an occasion like it. My faithful Elders Jimmy Aitchison and Maxwell Watson came with me to assist. We asked no questions – whether Protestant or Catholic, whether Church member or not. Whoever wished communion (and that was nearly everybody) was given it.

It was a moving occasion of great peace, and quite different from the more formal celebrations in church. Many of the patients had to have the cup held for them. Somehow, I felt in its simplicity it had been like the 'upper room' where it all began. We left one old Highland woman of ninety-four, almost blind, singing softly to herself in Gaelic, 'I to the hills will lift mine eyes'. For a short time she had been transported to the hills of home, and communion seasons she had known there in the happier days of youth. At the end another old dear, well advanced in years, exclaimed to me with shining eyes, '*He* was here – *He* really was!'

An unforgettable experience of – as our fathers called it – 'the Real Presence'.

'I hear you're a minister now,' said Leslie in the train one day. I replied that was so.

'Man, I thought you had more sense!' he said. 'A quarter of a vet's salary, nothing but criticism, and tell me, what good has Christianity ever done for the world?'

Leslie had been at school with me; he was brainy, and was now a lecturer at university. We had a rare old discussion, for there's nothing I like better than getting the jacket off, so to speak, and getting down to basics. I told him that the first hospital of which there was any record, the first home for the blind, the first free dispensary, had all been founded by Christians . . . surely that was some good Christianity had done in the world? I might have told him, though only thought of it afterwards, that in various ways the work of caring was still going on. I should have told him about our 'battle' and my honourable scars.

The week before had been Christian Aid week and with ten others, ministers and priests, of varying ages, shapes and sizes, I had taken the field to play against the Stirlingshire Police at football. They seemed giants compared with our little shaughly, bowly-legged team, but, feeling like Christian martyrs facing the lions, we performed in the arena, a large football field surrounded by a very big crowd carrying banners saying 'Come away the clergy' and cheering our every effort. I don't know if they were pro-Christian – but they were certainly anti-polis! My first encounter with the police centre-half knocked me half-way across the park, and it looked as if we would be slaughtered. But as time went on, it was obvious we had some hidden talents. Our goalkeeper was performing heroics, though sorely troubled with his bonnet falling off; two of the young priests had a fair turn of speed; our right half, a rugby player, was sailing in with great gusto, and the inside trio (total age 120) were showing an ancient craftiness which produced goals. Yes, we actually won, and the police took it in good part. Though I had skinned knees and aching muscles for weeks afterwards, it was all in a good cause and some needy people across the world benefited from the large sum collected.

In the early summer of my first year at Moorton, we had a similar encounter when the men of the church took on the Youth Fellowship at football, and all the village turned out to see the minister in shorts! After a stern battle, which the lads took seriously and the men did not, and with some help from the referee (one of the stars of a big First Division team), we gained a creditable draw – and the kirk was shown as a place where people really could enjoy themselves.

Every week I visited one of our village schools and the very large Academy in the town, to conduct school assembly and take RE in some classes. I particularly liked the wee one-teacher school at Waterfoot. What a welcome I always received! There was young Jeannie anxious to show me her handwork ... Sarah proudly pushing into my hand a painting which might have been anything, but which you had to agree was like a cow ... and Billy telling you in his gruff voice that the mare had a foal last night. Eventually we would get down to the short service, or the story for the day. They liked the stories best and were full of questions. Come to think of it, the Master teacher had lots of questions for his stories too.

There are many learned people in places of authority who would close the little country schools. I emphatically disagree with them and with the contention that children get a better education in a larger school. Of course, so much depends on the teacher; but from that little school at Waterfoot, as I've mentioned elsewhere, in the lifetime of one schoolmaster came doctors, lawyers, several ministers, an MP, and a Cabinet Minister of New Zealand. In addition, and perhaps more important, each child was taught well, given a love of poetry, and taught to use words, so that in later years they formed their own debating society. Farm children, all of them, and taught by a wise teacher on their own wavelength – like the schoolmistress in one school who was trying to teach the doctrine of the Trinity, a mighty difficult subject.

'Imagine, Angus,' she said to one boy, 'you have three sheep at home. Call one Father, one Son, and one the Holy Ghost. They are all the same, but yet all different.'

A few days later she was revising the lesson. 'How many persons in the Trinity?' she asked.

'Twa, miss,' said Angus.

'Oh, Angus, do you not remember me telling you about the three sheep?'

'Aye, miss, I ken, but you see the Holy Ghost chokit on a turnip and he's deid.'

Unassailable logic, if not theologically sound!

The lesson over, on each visit I would be seen off by the whole school with waves and cheers. Yes, I like the 'wee schoolies'!

I had come to Tom Longmuir's farm one

April day on just a routine visit. It happened to be milking time in their dairy herd, and as was my custom, I had a walk up the byre before going to the house. I loved the sight and smell of the cattle, something I miss to this day. Tom was nowhere to be seen, but I found his teenage son busy with the milking.

'Faither's in the hay-shed,' he informed me. 'He's busy trying to lamb a yow.'

I made my way to the hay-shed, which was divided by bales into partitions, with in each little section a ewe and lambs. I found Tom down on his knees with his hand inside a ewe. He greeted me with enthusiasm, and a measure of relief.

'Just the man I need!' he said. 'I've got a right corker here and I'm beat with it.'

'I'll have a feel, Tom, but I'm a bit rusty. It's a few years since I lambed a ewe.'

So I got down on my knees, having taken my jacket off and thoroughly soaped my arm. It was a big lamb with the head well back, and not too much room in the ewe. I'm blessed with a long arm and fairly slim pair of hands, and I was able to reach the head, but couldn't bring it round into the correct position.

'Tom, could you get me some fresh warm water, put some Dettol in it, and three bits of binder cord?'

The years had rolled back, and I was doing

what I had done many, many times, and loving it again. The water and cords were fetched, I gave them a good swill in the antiseptic water, then proceeded to put one on each of the lamb's fore-legs. I then pushed them back to make a little more space, and after some difficulty managed to get the third cord through the lamb's mouth and round its head. Then, with my hand still inside the ewe's womb, I said to Tom, 'Now pull on that rope, but not too hard,' and as Tom did as I asked, I managed to guide the lamb's head round.

'Now the leg ropes, Tom,' and up came the legs into position. It was now a simple matter of traction, and in a short time we had a big lamb lying on the straw, spluttering its way into the world. Tom busily rubbed it down with a wisp of hay, but the ewe was already round at her lamb, licking it dry, and 'talking' in that lovely, deep, throaty way to its new-born. It felt good . . . and it was good to see the instant reward for a few minutes' work, a live lamb and an undamaged ewe.

'Meenister! I'm right grateful to ye,' said Tom, 'and while you're here, maybe you would take a look at a beast. She's off her grub, doon in her milk, so there's something no' richt.'

So we headed for the byre, and I had a look at his cow. I had no thermometer, but checked her pulse and respirations, which were normal.

I had a listen at her rumen, the big first stomach, and though it was a bit sluggish, it was still churning over. But I was certain what her trouble was, for while up at her fore-leg taking the pulse, the smell of acetone came to me strongly.

'She's got acetonaemia, Tom, or as maybe you would say, she's stawed. You'd better get Ian Bryce out here to give her a bottle of glucose, or a shot of insulin, or whatever he uses.'

I, of course, didn't possess any of these remedies, and I was already feeling guilty at doing a fellow vet out of a job. Tom Longmuir looked at me long and earnestly, then his face broke into a big grin.

'Man, you're a handy fellow to hiv for a meenister. If you canna' cure a beast, you can aye say a wee prayer ower it!'

I smiled too, but didn't say anything; yet I thought back to the many times when, in the middle of a hard calving, and, like many vets, I'm sure, I had indeed breathed a prayer.

We finally got to the farmhouse, saw Mrs Longmuir, had a cup of tea and a chat, and then I went on my way, feeling that maybe a vet-minister had his uses. The Longmuirs, though by no means regular churchgoers, were in their pew the following Sunday. Ah well, I thought, there's many a way to get folk to the kirk!

Christmas Eve – surely the most magical, happiest night in the year! Moorton was silent under a December moon, the roofs of the little cottages glistening from the touch of frosty fingers, the windows bright with the twinkle of fairy lights.

Eight o'clock found the carollers assembled at the Church Eventide Home, about fifty of them ... mostly young, but augmented by some seniors like Jimmy Aitchison and Joe Gibson, the Cubmaster, a tower of strength in the background of any church activity. Carols ancient and modern were sung with great gusto, if not always in the right key. Then out into the streets, feet crunching on the snow-clad roads, breath steaming in the frosty air, faces aglow in the light of lanterns carried by the excited youngsters. Up and down the village we went, sped on our way by shouts of 'Happy Christmas!', and singing of the good king Wenceslas and the Child born to be King. Into the 'big hoose' where a party was in progress, but where they stopped to listen and smile, and where the collecting cans were generously filled. At Mary Clanachan's house, 'Child in a Manger' was very appropriate, for a babe had been born that week. Outside old Andrew's home we sang very softly (even the grunters in the company muting their bass notes), for Andrew, all knew, was not long for this world. 'Sleep in Heavenly Peace' we sang to the old man, like a benediction at the end of a long life.

Then into Mrs Beaton's house, all fifty squeezing into her little living-room; for there, lemonade and shortbread were laid on for the singers, and the heat of the room was welcome. Then on again, youngsters skipping ahead, collectors rattling on doors, voices becoming a bit cracked in the night air, complaints of 'We're ower high,' and grins for pyjama-clad bairns peeping from behind curtains, waiting for Santa to come with his exciting bundles. Finally, the pub. Would we go in? Why not? Jimmy and I did, to the great consternation of some of the customers, who tried to hide behind their pints from the august presence of the minister. But they all stumped up for charity.

Last of all, the Manse, a heat at the fires blazing in every room, hot soup and sausage rolls prepared by Janet, the Manse boys hopping about in excitement at this invasion. A final rousing sing around the piano, then the climax of it all . . . the Watch-night service, carol-singers in jeans, wellingtons and Rangers scarves augmenting the great crowd assembled for this service with its unique atmosphere. A great peace seemed to wrap us all around as we heard again the wondrous story of the Child laid in a manger, and felt ourselves one with shepherds, wise men and angels as we brought our worship; at midnight we sang that loveliest of all carols, 'Still the Night'.

Only one night in the life of our little community, but a night of nights, when hope was abroad in the world and in every heart the feeling of goodwill to all men, because of the One who came to bring His peace to every longing soul.

There was one man in our little community I visited every week – Davie. His wife helped at the Manse one morning a week, and when I ran her home I would stay and have a chat with Davie. We both cherished these talks. He had few visitors, and was pleased to see me, and I always learned something from this good, God-fearing man.

Davie had been a shepherd, and a good one, but long before retiring age he had to give up his work because of a bad heart. His flock was now composed of statuettes of sheep on the mantelpiece, photographs of prize tups he had bred and a few hens which his faithful collie had to content himself now by rounding up. He made crooks as a hobby, and I will always cherish the two he gave Janet and me just before he died. For Davie has come down from his last hill, and gone home to the great sheep-fold where all kinds of breeds gather at the last.

I will always remember these talks we had, and in particular one story he told me. As a young lad he was apprenticed to an older shepherd up in the hills of Ayrshire. One night there was a tremendous blizzard of snow, and the old man felt he would have to go out and bring down as many of his sheep as he could to the safety of the lower ground. But before he went, he had his moment of communion with his God. He took his fiddle down from the wall, and slowly, meditatively, like a prayer, played, 'Nearer, my God to Thee, even though it be a cross that raiseth me'. Then out into the violent storm he went, refusing to let the lad Davie go with him. The old shepherd saved many sheep that night, but he himself did not return. In the morning a search-party found his body in a snowdrift, his faithful dog beside him. The good shepherd had given his life for his sheep.

Davie never forgot that experience, and grew up to be a man like his old teacher. He and his wife were a happy, cheerful couple, but Davie sorely missed his flock, and I like to think our 'cracks' round the fire about sheep and shep-herding, pulpy kidney, lamb dysentery, dip-ping, clipping, lambing and all the rest gave him an interest week by week.

We laid him to rest on a wild, stormy day, having sung his hymn in church. A good man had gone to his reward. The shepherd was home from the hill.

So the weeks and months passed at Moorton, each week bringing its joys and sorrows, and as I thought around my flock of a night, I was well content with my task in life – and with 'the wud I'd got'.

21

The Cure for All Ills

Going back to the vet world, written on the heart (or at least on a bit of paper) of every vet's wife, housekeeper, receptionist or anyone entrusted with the taking of a message is a list marked 'Very Urgent', 'Urgent' or 'Can Wait'. While it is almost certain that in the minds of all animal owners each case comes into the 'Very Urgent' category, in fact there are comparatively few which can truthfully be so described. Bloat, choke, staggers, some calvings, lambings, foalings, farrowings, etc., and the list is almost exhausted. But there is one other condition which may well appear, and indeed, be ringed around. It is known by a variety of names – urticaria, hives, blaines or nettle rash, and it is listed as 'Very Urgent' for a different reason.

'If ever you are called to a case of urticaria,' said our old Prof., 'drive like blazes or the beast will be better before you get there!'

The symptoms of this condition, particularly in cattle, can be startling, even alarming, and since it is of such rarity that most farmers come across it but once in a lifetime, almost all rush at once for the phone. Young Derek Hocking of High Deane was typical as he begged me to come with all possible speed.

'Hur vace be swollen somethin' terruble, hur eyes is near shut, an' she's blowin' like the dickens.'

I smiled to myself and said I would see her in an hour.

'An hour!' wailed Derek. 'Can't ee cum quicker, like? I tells ee it's 'orrible an' I reckon if hur head keeps growin' like it is, hur brains will zoon be comin' out hur ears!'

It was a graphic description and a pretty gruesome thought.

'Derek, this looks far worse than it is, but don't worry, I'll come right out. Anyway, you know fine that Friesians have no brains, so her ears are safe.' I, an Ayrshire fan, was always ribbing him about his Friesians.

I had intended to do another call on the way, but often, in practice, you have to treat the client as much or more than the animal, so I was with him in ten minutes.

The case was exactly as had been described so vividly – face swollen, eyes puffed up, lips sticking out, and a general hangdog expression.

'I don't know what you call it here, Derek, but the technical term is urticaria. She's allergic to something. Have you changed your cattle cake lately?'

I wasn't treating it too seriously, for it simply isn't a serious condition. Untreated, it will disappear in twenty-four to thirty-six hours; with a shot of some anti-histamine drug, a bit less. As I talked with Derek and his father, purely from habit I was going through the routine of temperature-taking, pulse, respiratory rate, and the general look of the cow. The temperature was 105° (normal for a cow is 101-102°). 'Must have forgotten to shake the mercury down,' I thought, gave the thermometer a vigorous shake, and still one minute later came up with 105°. Cows with urticaria had a normal temperature. Taking the pulse up at the radial artery of the fore-leg, I was able to kill two birds with one stone, for at the same time I could count her respirations. Pulse was 80 (normal is around 50), while her respirations at 30 were about twice as fast as normal. There was something more than urticaria here. I looked at her – 'Always study the way a beast looks and the expression on its face,' the voice of old Geordie Dykes, our Professor, came back to me. We had thought it amusing then, even ridiculous, as my medical friends do yet, but I had found old Geordie knew more than we gave him credit for; perhaps we used to be a bit put off because every lecture was sprinkled liberally with his experiences in the trenches in the First World War. Yes, this cow looked ill. She had an anxious expression, maybe. The normal urticaria expression is embarrassment, like a woman being caught with her curlers in at tea-time!

The Hockings, Senior and Junior, were studying me as I studied their cow.

'Us hasn't changed our veedin', like; only thing I can think is it was the red drink.'

'Red drink?' I pounced. 'Why did you give her that, and when?'

Veterinary diagnosis is a bit like a jigsaw, putting together the pieces that you can pick up from patient and owner till all fits, or even like a detective drawing clues from unwilling witnesses. Sherlock Holmes, if he hadn't been so taken up with his wretched fiddle, could have been a first-class vet, as a lucrative sideline from his other work!

'Us drenched hur last night for she was dowie, like, off her grub, an' hur milk was down.'

'Well, ten to one your red drink caused the urticaria — something in it she was allergic to. I'll give her a jag which will soon put that right, but that swollen face was putting us on the wrong scent. We've got a sick cow here.'

Out came the stethoscope, and right away I

could hear the squeaks, whistles and gurgles that signified broncho-pneumonia. I thought I could also hear the 'creaking leather' sound associated with pleurisy.

'Pneumonia, Mr Hocking,' I said to the old man. 'It's still serious, but before penicillin' — I jabbed her in the neck — 'it might have killed her. As it is, her milk will go right down. Put a rug on her, or stitch some sacks together and put them over for some heat, and I'll see her tomorrow. Why on earth you keep giving this red drink beats me, for it doesn't help pneumonia, and I don't know what it does help except constipation. Do you know what's in that drink? Epsom salts, ninety per cent, plus some ginger and a bit of colouring! Wouldn't be surprised if some of it didn't go down the wrong way last night and make the pneumonia worse.'

I was laying it on. Derek was a good and progressive young farmer, but his father was of the old school to whom so-and-so-'s red drink took second place only to the Bible for reliability and authority. After all, 'if vather and grandvather had used it for their cattle, why not us' was the attitude, but I thought if it got about that the red drink which adorned every shippen in the shire was shown to be just a waste of money, and maybe even dangerous, I'd have done some good. But the old man wasn't giving in so easily. I suppose he must have felt as if I was blaspheming his gods. He fetched a packet.

'Read that,' he stabbed triumphantly at the well-known label. Probably he hadn't his specs! I read it. ' "A proven remedy for all chills, fevers, pneumonia, stoppage of the bowel, founder of the feet, rheumatic pains and swollen joints, a purifier of the blood and the perfect remedy for almost all conditions in horses and cattle." '

'See?' said the old man, 'didn't I tell ee?' He spat eloquently. 'But read on – go on,' he urged. So I obliged, and read aloud the quote from Mr A.G. of Wiltshire who'd used the drink for thirty years and never needed a vet (probably he kept hens, I thought). Mr W.C. (that at least was appropriate) from Berkshire declared that his father and grandfather had never been without it. My mind boggled at what three-quarters of a pound of Epsom salts would do for father and grandfather, but assumed it meant their stock.

'They can't all be wrong,' said the old boy, poking me in the chest.

'Cures sunstroke – also excellent for frostbite,' I muttered.

'What's that? Speak up!' said old man Hocking.

' 'Twas nothing; I was only recalling a cartoon I saw once,' I assured him. 'Look, Mr Hocking, look what your red drink has done here. If Derek hadn't phoned me, you'd probably have given her another dose, and that would have killed her – one way or another.' The alternative methods were messy even to imagine! 'If you want to have a stomach mixture or a laxative by you, for that's all your drink is, OK – or, better still, come to my surgery and I'll give you some powder at half the price; but if *you* had pneumonia, would you take Epsom salts to cure it?'

I'd said more than enough about the folly of trusting in patent medicines and using them indiscriminately, yet I knew almost every farmer in my practice bought these by the dozen from the purveyors of quack remedies. Faith, I thought, is a fine thing – but blind faith can sometimes be utter folly.

As I drove on to my next case I recalled my old boss, who had made up his own stomach mixture for cattle, called it '1001' and sold it in considerable quantities. It was an excellent prescription, and as an assistant it was some time before he let me make up any of the mixture, indeed he swore me to keep secret its contents. I remembered too the old vet who used to retire to an inner room, there to make up some of his own special brews, safe from his assistants' questing eyes. But these, handed out by vets for specific conditions, were very different from the mass of tonic draughts, blood conditioners, all-in-one mixtures, three-in-one powders, red drinks, black drinks and, for all I knew, tartan drinks sold by the purveyors of cure-all-ills; they were often sold as such, and bought in vast quantities by the farming community. For the most part, the sales reps of the various firms were friendly men and they had a living to earn, but beyond a basic knowledge of the ways of the country they made no claim to be experts. Much more serious was one particular man, representative of a very well-known phar-maceutical firm, a household name, which both dealt with vets and sold certain products over-the-counter to farmers. Kenneth had trusted John Pusey and given him large orders; even now, most of our vaccines, sera, antibiotics and so on came from his firm, and presumably he earned considerable commission. John hung about the markets, was familiar to the farming community, and had established a sound foot-hold in at least some veterinary practices. But I had, from various little bits of information, a suspicion that the same man was running with the hares and hunting with the hounds, and not very long after Kenneth departed to prac-tise in his native Kenya and I took on Bernard as partner, events moved rapidly to a climax and produced a showdown.

John had been going into a certain farm one day, one of our clients, and noticed a cow from his car which had bloat, or was 'tinged up', distended with gas. Now this is a common condition, can be caused by a variety of factors, and on occasion can be cured by some reliable bloat remedy – *on occasion!*

John told the farmer about his cow, persuaded him he didn't need a vet, and forthwith sold him a couple of dozen 'bloat cures' and instructed the farmer to pour one over the cow's throat. This, he maintained, would scatter the gas and all would be well. Who needs vets? Some hours later I got a panic call – a re-direction from my wife from one farm to go at once to the other, for 'the beast was like to burst'. Well trained as she was, she had told them to try to keep the cow on the move and not to allow it to lie down, or very likely it would burst. (In fact the condition must be absolute agony for the beast, as the gas builds up in the rumen, or first of the cow's four stomachs, and eventually the stomach wall does, like a punctured balloon, burst. Mercifully, the pressure through the abdominal wall has usually caused such interference with breathing and the heart circulation that the animal may be unconscious or dead before the explosion.)

In the case in question, I was just in time. I

had to 'stick' the cow immediately, pushing a trocar and cannula right through the stomach wall. The trocar is a sharp-pointed stilette which fits closely inside a hollow tube (the cannula), and once the poor beast has been stabbed and the trocar removed, the gas comes bubbling out of the cannula. Needless to say, this is only done when deemed absolutely necessary, and, barbaric though it sounds, the instant relief to the cow is immense. I then rounded on the farmer and, good client or not, asked him what he had been playing at, what had kept him, and a few other things beside. He was a decent sort, a good, and be it noted, an intelligent farmer, yet he had believed the bloat cure would do all, since John Pusey said so.

By now I was calming down a bit, so I grinned at him and said, 'Put not your trust in princes, even if called John Pusey.' Had to get in a dig! 'Now let's see, Mr Zeale, if we can find what caused that gas to form.'

'Reckon it was just the young clover,' said Mr Zeale.

'And I reckon not. Feel that – put your hand on your cow's throat.'

'A lump – what is it – well, dang me, I bet it's one of the last of the winter's turnips we scattered this morning to the milk cows.'

He was right. Tympany, or bloat, can be

caused by various things, including young, succulent clover, but it can also arise mechanically when the cow, which burps every half minute or so without ever a 'Pardon me', just can't do it because of a turnip or potato stuck there, thus preventing those hearty rumbles as the cow's cud and gas come up. There are two ways of removing a turnip: by putting your arm over the cow's throat and bringing it up (provided you've still got an arm left), or by passing a long tube or probang and pushing it onwards down the gullet into the stomach. This is by no means as easy as it sounds, and many a probang has punctured many a gullet wall. However, that night one of the many implements and instruments the vet has to possess for only one specialized function did what it was made for, and within moments of the turnip hitting the stomach wall, we were enveloped in an aura of gas as the cow made up for lost time and regurgitated with considerable rapidity. I knew that the next bloat at the Zeale farm would bring me a prompt call. Actions that night had spoken, as they mostly do in practice, a heap louder than words.

The next day I phoned John Pusey and asked him which college he had attended. He laughed.

'The best of all, the college of experience, lad.'

'So you reckon you know it all, John?'

'Well, not all, Alex,' more guarded now, 'what's biting you?'

'You are, John. You took it upon yourself to advise a client of mine yesterday on what was wrong with his cow, without even seeing the beast, except from your car. You told him he needed no vet. That cow, John, is going about this morning with a hole in its side and it's very lucky to be going about at all. We've been good clients to you and your firm in the past, man, and you have your job to do, but John, if you ever try to do mine again and advise on individual cases, so help me your headquarters will hear about it!'

Before I hung up, he managed to say he was sorry and it wouldn't happen again. My family, I hope, would agree that the old man isn't often roused, but when he is, it's like the summer storm, soon past — at least I like to think so!

But this one was not to pass so soon, for within days I was on a farm out on the fringes of the moor investigating the deaths of lambs. I did a post-mortem on two — typical cases of pulpy kidney.

'How many have you lost?' I asked the young farmer, who was a very new client and not yet well known to me.

'Reckon about two dozen,' he said. 'Yus, someways about a dozen before we asks Mr

Pusey to look in, and 'bout the same since.'

'Mr Pusey?' I questioned. 'He was here — because you asked him?'

'That's right. Folks reckon he knows more about sheep than any vet'nary,' the young fellow replied rather hesitantly.

'And why have you not called him again? I expect he gave you something.'

'Oh, aye, he cuts open the lambs, bit like you, likes, only he was quicker maybe, said it was worms and gave us stuff to dose them all. He said that would do the trick.' He looked up aggressively. 'But missus reckoned we ought to give you a chance.'

I ought to have been grateful to 'the missus' for her consideration, but felt one of my summer storms coming on, so swallowed hard a few times and said, 'Look, John Pusey is not a vet. He knows a fair bit, I admit, the same way as a car salesman knows a bit about cars, but he isn't a mechanic!'

I could see I wasn't getting through, so said bluntly, 'Look, if your wife was at death's door, would you ask the chemist to call, or the doctor?'

'The doctor, I reckons.'

'You sure would unless you happened to be trying to get rid of your wife!' I hoped I wasn't giving him any ideas! 'Do you know that John Pusey isn't even a trained chemist? Yet when he said "worms" you believed him, spent pounds on his mixtures, and you've lost another dozen lambs.'

'Well, you always reckons to lose a few, like, an' I just thought the worm drenches hadn't had time to work.'

'They're your lambs, lad, and you can do as you please, but I'm telling you they are dying of pulpy kidney, which is so common that nearly everybody injects them when they're born, and it's near enough a hundred per cent effective. Sure, there's a few worms about them, but you'll find that in almost any sheep you open, and I don't say but what John's drenches mightn't help later. But if you like, I'll send one of these lambs up to the Ministry laboratory. It won't cost you anything, and that will tell us for certain.'

He thought that would be a good idea, or rather his wife did. She had joined us half-way through my talk, and clearly was much more progressive than her husband. The lamb went off, the report came back a few days later confirming the diagnosis, and I gave him the necessary amount of serum and vaccine, telling him to come to me at the beginning of next year's lambing and I would fix him up with what was needed. I wasn't back at that farm for a year, and then it was simply to do their annual tuberculin test.

'Had any trouble with lambs this year?' I asked, as we went round his few cows.

'No,' he assured me, 'us had Mr Pusey here and he fixed us up with same stuff you gave us last year. He really knows a lot, does Mr Pusey.'

He knows which side his bread's buttered on, I thought. He had cashed in on my work, and sold this young chap all the vaccine and serum he needed, and it was more expensive, I knew, than the brand we used! But I kept quiet. You can't win, when the Puseys of this world know all the answers and can cure all ills. In the meantime I'd written to his firm, as I'd warned him, complaining of his interference and un-ethical behaviour. We got a letter of apology and presumably he got a rocket, so, for a time at least, he had to walk more carefully.

Of course, this faith in a person or product is far from being confined to veterinary medicine. Give a cure-all-ills enough TV advertising, and the public is crying out for it. There is plenty of quackery about, and I find a deal of ersatz religion too. It comes in all kinds of packages, attractively labelled. There's the fellow who believes that an hour on Sunday is his weekly insurance payment to the Almighty to protect him from life's troubles, or reckons an atten-dance at communion and maybe Christmas is all that's needed to keep his Santa Claus kind of

God happy and ensure similar Santa Claus-type benefits. I've seen dozens of this persuasion over the years. Then there's the person who has latched on to a new faith, has found in a twinkling the remedy he has long sought, and zealously seeks to bring others into his sect — for there is the truth, there alone.

I recall two instances of this at Moorton. One day two young fellows came to the Manse door, and asked if they could see the church. I showed them round, telling them something of its history. Then they came round to the real purpose of their visit. They had, some months before, become Mormons, and were now, with all the freshness and keenness of the new convert, seeking to set my feet on the right path.

'Do you prepare your addresses?' one inquired.

'I do.' And I quoted the old saying about sermon preparation being ten per cent inspiration and ninety per cent perspiration.

They shook their heads sadly.

'You don't believe in preparation?' I asked.

'Certainly not,' one of them replied. 'I just go into the church and say what the Holy Spirit puts into my mouth there and then.'

I was naughty enough to ask if the Holy Spirit could only guide in a church and not in a study, and recalled a man who had gone into his pulpit and waited for the Spirit to speak.

'I'm sure He did,' said one of the youngsters with an emphatic nod.

'He surely did. He asked why the preacher hadn't thought about what to say before he dared to stand up and preach to others.'

Now there is much to praise in Mormonism. Who can but be impressed by the upright lives, the morality, the tithing of their income by such well-known figures as golfers Billy Casper and Johnny Miller so that their Church gets a tenth of their earnings? Who can but admire the crusading fervour of young students and others who give one or two years of their lives, without pay, as missionaries? But if there is much to admire in the Mormon ethic, and a great deal in their singing, youthful approach and shining sincerity that is very attractive, I cannot accept that the teachings of their founder Joseph Smith and his famous successor Brigham Young are the truth, the whole truth and nothing but the truth. As I thought earlier of the Hockings and their red drink, faith is an admirable thing, but blind faith can sometimes be the most utter folly. So we agreed to differ as the two young men and I bade each other goodbye.

I was well used to being put in my place and my feet set right, for each Friday in the village a meeting for children was held which sought to correct the errors of the Church as perpetuated by me and my fellow clergymen week by week. To the originator of this meeting there were few – if any – truly Christian ministers. He was a member of the Plymouth Brethren and ministers were anathema, blind leaders of the blind. Now I have a number of friends in the Brethren, and it is but right to say that not all hold this view, clergy-wise. Equally, I freely admit that a university education in Divinity does not necessarily make a Christian. If a Divinity training was a must for the practice of Christian living, then Jesus would be a non-starter, for degree He had none. I do believe, however, that to an already committed Christian, a college or university training is an aid in their future ministry. I had often chuckled over the story of the old minister who died and went to his heavenly reward, where, to his surprise, he was asked to get in the queue at the pearly gates. He was somewhat put out that he, after forty-five years of service in the one parish, should have to wait his turn – and not even a back number of *Punch* or *Country Life* to hold his interest! His chagrin turned to wrath when a stunning young blonde swept past him and was at once admitted. He demanded an explanation, to be told by the recording angel, 'That young lady passed her driving test but one week ago, but in that week she put the fear of

God in more than you did in forty-five years.'

'The Fear of God' – that was the theme at the children's meetings in the village hall. I went along once or twice to show interest, but my presence was manifestly ignored. There were choruses, quizzes, sweets for prizes, all of which we had in our Sunday School. Then the twenty or so youngsters, aged from about four upwards, sat through a long address where the book was freely pounded – and a bar of chocolate given to the one who had sat most quietly. We sent one of our lads along, David, feeling we ought to support and not discourage any good endeavour. In time, he started quizzing us about death, and where he would go, or we would go, afterwards. He was at the time aged five. Then his nightmares started. So I went along to the children's meeting the next week, and heard these kids told repeatedly in the talk that if they did not accept Jesus that very night, they might be knocked down by a bus while crossing the road, or take some deadly disease before next Friday, and they would go to hell. The fear of God indeed in children of four to eleven years old! Our lad stopped going, the nightmares ceased, and as far as I am aware he has grown up to hold a strong, sure and reasoned faith.

Shortly after my Friday tirade, I happened to be visiting a family in the village, the only

Brethren family in the parish. They welcomed me graciously, then the wife proceeded to say what a fine thing it was that somebody was doing something for the young people (I thought it should have been *to* them) each week. I thought of all our Sunday School classes, our devoted teachers, our youth clubs, three church-based football teams for the young, and all the other work, but only nodded. I was saddened that this version of the Gospel was being propagated, that children were being told to take this 'red drink' because it, and it alone, was the cure for all ills. I once asked one of our Sunday School youngsters, aged about ten, why she went to the meeting, and was promptly told 'To get a bar of chocolate.'

I thought that about summed it up.

22

Just a Bit of Sport

'I hear John Pearson has got himself into trouble,' one of the Moorton Elders said to me one Sunday after morning service.

'In what way?' I asked.

'Gambling! Mind you, it's his wife and bairn I'm sorry for.'

I was sorry for Mary Pearson too, but also for John. I was also absolutely astonished. Although they lived some distance from Moorton, they belonged there originally, John was a regular in our church, and I had always thought him a steady sort of fellow, and knew he was a good husband and father. His parents were in church nearly every Sunday, and I knew they would be deeply disturbed.

So I went to visit John and Mary, and found Mary alone with their little girl in their small pre-fab house. I was shocked at Mary's appearance; she was normally a plump girl, but she had lost weight and her usually round, smiling face was furrowed with hurt and worry. She looked haggard, and just drew herself along in a hopeless fashion.

I found it difficult to talk, and also did not want to seem to be intruding in their private affairs, but clearly Mary was at her wits' end and very badly needed to share her load with someone.

'It began, Mr Cameron, with just the odd bob on a horse. Then the bobs became pounds, and it got more and more until the whole wage was gone every week. We're hundreds of pounds in debt and the Electricity Board are threatening to prosecute us. We owe so much to different folks – the grocer, the milkman, the rent – that John's wage is being confiscated before he gets it to pay off these debts.'

'And how are you living, lass?'

'Oh, John's folks and mine are helping, and we get by, but I don't know where it's going to end. It's like some terrible disease that's got hold of him – and it all began with just a bit of sport, with his way of it.'

'You know, Mary, I can hardly believe this of John. He's always seemed such a sensible fellow that I find it difficult to understand that he could let it get a hold of him like that.'

Mary sat silent for a while, then quite suddenly burst into tears – great sobs that came from deep inside her and wracked her whole body. I let her cry uninterrupted for a time, for there can be healing in tears, but I also felt terribly helpless and not a little angry that anyone should cause his wife such misery. After a time the poor woman pulled herself together and apologized 'for making such a scene'. She gathered the little girl to her, who had been looking on, completely mystified, and crying with her mother.

'It's like some drug that he's hooked on, Mr Cameron, and I can't see how we're ever going to get out of the mess.'

'He needs help, Mary. Have you thought of Gamblers Anonymous?'

'Funny you should say that, Mr Cameron! He's going up to Glasgow tomorrow with some man to a meeting of that. I'm hoping and praying that it can help, but it seems to me it will take a miracle to save us from the awful trouble we're in . . . him and his sport.'

'Well, lass, miracles still happen. We must go on praying for one.'

And there and then we did, in simple words that came from the heart.

'Mary — don't be offended, but we have a wee fund in the church which I can use to give to anybody I think needs help. It isn't very much but it will at least keep you in food for a few weeks, and nobody but me knows who gets the money.'

So I left a little bit with the poor girl, which she promptly hid in a tin 'where John won't be able to find it'. I left her, promising to come back, and as I looked at her drawn face I felt a cold fury about the whole unholy business.

On the drive home the words 'just for sport' kept going through my mind like a chorus, and I found my thoughts drifting back to a scene from Bristacombe and my vet days.

It began when three dogs met late one evening. One was a wild, half-trained alsatian cross that came from a tinker encampment; the second was a farm collie, a well-trained, faithful animal which brought the cattle in for milking twice a day and was gentle in its handling of sheep. It slept in a barn, and could come and go as it pleased. The third was a corgi, the pet of a little girl, which had been turned out for its evening run and normally just played round about their country cottage before coming in for the night. The three dogs met up on the High Road between Bristacombe and Morte-combe, frolicked along the road together play-ing the canine version of 'tig', and in their joyous abandon getting further and further from their respective homes. Bye and bye they came to a field, and in that field were some interesting woolly creatures. Tired of their game, they went over the dyke to investigate these other animals ... which broke before them, and ran for their lives. This was better sport and soon the chase was on ... just a bit of sport ... but in time a chase wasn't enough. It would be more exciting to catch these woolly bundles ... and so it began ...

Early next morning I had a phone call from Geoff Gascoigne. Geoff was a young farmer, struggling to get going, heavily overdrawn at the bank but determined he would make a go of his small upland farm. Geoff was not only a client but a friend, and he had shared his problems and his hopes with me.

That morning there was a catch in his voice as he pleaded, 'Alex – can you come out right away? I've had dogs among my lambing ewes. I tell you it's like a battlefield out here.'

I bumped my way in the old van up his farm road, the roughest and most twisting in the whole practice, and found Geoff standing in the yard, his shoulders slumped, his whole attitude one of utter hopelessness and despair. Behind him was a trailer piled high with the bodies of dead and dying sheep.

'There's twenty-seven of them, Alex – almost half my flock,' said Geoff. 'See if there's anything you can do for them.'

I moved among that pile of suffering sheep. I had never seen anything so terrible before. Their wounds were horrific ... throats torn open . . . legs hanging off . . . abdomens ripped open and there was a feeling of utter helplessness in me as I went from sheep to sheep injecting penicillin here . . . stitching wounds there . . . and sometimes with the humane killer bringing a merciful release to the remains of what had once been a sheep.

'It'll take a miracle for us to survive this, Alex. We were counting on their lambs to keep the bank manager happy and give us a breathing-space.'

We moved from the sickening scene out to the field where the slaughter had taken place. The remainder of his sixty ewes were huddled together in a corner . . . stunned, shocked, terrified, exhausted after their night of terror. As we walked up the field, I spotted something white lying in the bottom corner.

'There's one you've missed, Geoff,' I said, and we headed towards it.

'It's Snowy!' exclaimed Geoff. 'She was young Billy's pet lamb last year. She's just a hogg. Poor lil' ol' thing . . . she must have been hunted into that corner and couldn't get out.'

The little hogg was far through, lying with its neck stretched out and a dreadful gash in its throat. Somehow that little hogg, trapped there by three dogs, unable to escape or fight back, brought the obscenity of the whole dirty business home to us even more than the pile of bodies. As I looked at the little animal, I realized to my complete astonishment that she was also in labour, and before our wondering eyes she gave birth to a tiny little lamb with the last of her strength. We pulled the lamb round to her head, but her eyes were already glazing in death. Yet somehow, in a strange way, this lamb from his dying hogg seemed to lift the young farmer somewhat.

'She's given us her lamb,' muttered Geoff. 'Imagine that! With her dying breath. I've never seen anything like it. You know, I think Snowy has been trying to tell me something . . . a life from the dead, in a way.'

He knelt beside the dead mother and its little lamb, already struggling to get on its feet, and as he stroked the dead little Snowy the tears flowed down his cheeks, and he kept saying over and over again, 'Dear li'l Snowy! Dear li'l Snowy!'

Then his head came up, he got to his feet, squared his shoulders and said, 'I'll struggle on – and Alex . . . I'll win through!'

When we got back to the farmyard, after having inspected his other ewes, we found the police had arrived, a sergeant and a young constable. They looked at the heap of bodies on the trailer and the constable was promptly sick. The sergeant was white too, but with anger.

'This is damnable,' he said through clenched

teeth. 'I've seen sheep-worrying before, but never anything as bad as this. I know it won't help you, Mr Gascoigne, but we'll get these dogs.'

Well, they got two of them. The culprits had been spotted by a farm worker on his way to the early morning milking, and he gave a good description of them. That afternoon the police came into our surgery, followed by a farmer with a collie, and a couple with a little girl carrying a corgi.

The child's father was highly indignant at the very suggestion that their dog would ever harm a sheep. 'Look at her! Can you imagine her ever hunting anything?'

'We'll soon see, sir,' I retorted.

I had little sympathy, after the scenes in the farmyard that morning. Both dogs were given a shot of apomorphine, which immediately made them violently sick; the vomit was composed of masses of wool and strips of flesh. They were undoubtedly guilty, condemned from their own mouths, and the penalty for sheep-worriers was carried out there and then, after the owners had been removed to the waiting-room where the police explained this was the law and that 'once a worrier, always a worrier'. It was hard, particularly for the little girl, and the policeman's statement may seem a sweeping assertion, but in my experience it is correct. I never liked taking life, but felt, as I gave the two dogs the specially prepared strong anaesthetic, that they were having a painless death, something very different from what they had inflicted on little Snowy and the other ewes. The alsatian cross was never found. The tinkers had moved on, so the chief culprit did in fact escape – no doubt to cause further killing elsewhere, when it felt like a little bit of sport.

For Geoff it was a struggle, but somehow the lesson of little Snowy had seemed a sign of hope to him. Her lamb was reared, the bank manager proved sympathetic, and Geoff fought on and won through, moving some years later to a bigger farm.

I called to see Mary Pearson from time to time, and she told me that as far as she knew John was not gambling, and that 'the meetings in Glasgow seemed to be helping'.

Then one evening John came to see me at the Manse. As I showed him into the study, he gripped my arm and said, 'Mr Cameron, you see the biggest fool in creation here – but I've learned my lesson. I haven't had a penny on a horse for three months, and it's all thanks to GA. I'd like you to come up with me to a meeting and see what they're doing up there.'

So it was arranged, and John and I drove up to the hall in Glasgow one evening where

Gamblers Anonymous met in one room, the wives in another. Mary was not with us because she had their little girl to look after, and perhaps she was still a bit sceptical. I had my eyes opened that night as I saw and heard speaker after speaker tell their story. They were from every conceivable background – a company director, the manager of a large furniture shop – from well-dressed men right down to the latest recruit, who was practically in rags. He had been sleeping rough in a kind of night shelter, and pleaded with someone to go from GA to where he, and others like him, some of them also alcoholics, slept on newspapers at night. Two of the best-dressed men in GA volunteered to go to the shelter and see how they could help, and I realized that a real sense of camaraderie and caring existed between these mutual sufferers and addicts, which I found touching. All, that night, spoke of the mess they had made of their lives, and as I heard stories of stealing, embezzling, furniture being sold, houses being repossessed, marriages breaking up, my thoughts flashed again to that scene in Geoff Gascoigne's yard and the heap of casualties there, all in the name of a bit of sport.

I don't know that I would have cared to bare my soul in public as these men did, but clearly there was strength in this mutual sharing and fellowship, and encouragement for the new boys in seeing one of their number get his two-year badge – two years without a bet. Each man had a book, a book that was, for whatever religion, a kind of prayer-book. I drove home with John, having greatly enlarged my experience and modified some of my views, and thinking of One who in His life on earth had compassion for the outcasts and dregs of society, and all who had made ruin of their lives.

Some months later I happened to be at a Youth Fellowship meeting in a church hall where the speakers were two men from Gamblers Anonymous. One of the two was John – a different John: a man able to look the world in the eye again; man trusted once more by his employers; a man clearing his debts; and a man who had not gambled for many months. He wouldn't say he was cured, for an addict would seldom say that, but he had been addiction-free for a good period of time. He told me privately after the meeting, with a thrill in his voice, that in some months' time he was to become a father again.

Clearly the marriage was saved. Life was good again. We had had our miracle.

23

With Dignity and Daring

'How are you today, Mr Mackenzie?'

'I canna' complain.'

He had silicosis, making every breath an effort; he had a failing heart and kidney complications so that fluid gathered in his legs and lungs; when he wasn't in bed, he was in his chair by the fireside; he was completely limited to the four walls of a room, the outside world but a view from the window; he knew he would never be better. Yet always his reply was, 'I canna' complain' – and he meant it. It wasn't bravado, it wasn't an attempt at some kind of stoic philosophy, a shrug of the shoulders that indicated you had to just somehow put up with it all – it certainly wasn't a wish in the slightest degree to be thought gallant. He really didn't, and wouldn't complain, for he genuinely reckoned he had many blessings to count. Not an old man, he was aged far beyond his years by suffering and weakness, yet for him, his wife beside him, his family's regular visits to their dad, the warmth of a coal fire, a drink of cool water, clouds scudding across the sky, a storehouse of happy memories, the dawn chorus of the birds heralding a new day after a night of suffering . . . all these were glorious things that outweighed in the balance of life the weakness and struggle that were his constant companions.

I visited John Mackenzie often, for ministers were supposed to bring comfort and cheer to the suffering, yet as we talked, he was the one who did the cheering. I would leave his house humbled, and ashamed that a twinge of rheumatism had me moaning and sighing all over the place.

The time came for him to go into hospital to give a temporary boost to his tired heart, and ease his laboured breathing a little. He was a sick, weak man, scarcely able to lift a hand, but what a welcome he gave me in his hospital room!

'I'm awfu' glad to see you, Mr Cameron. Sit doon and tell me the news. Whit's fresh at Moorton?'

'Nothing much except the wind – it was fresh enough when I left.'

He laughed at my feeble joke as if I'd said something clever, and our talk ranged far and wide, every sentence he uttered punctuated by long pauses while he gulped in air. Here was a man who walked close to God, so it was as natural as talking *to* John to talk *with* John to his Father and commit home, family and future into His safe hands. John was content to leave it all there. But before I left, he asked, 'Would you do something for me?'

'Surely.'

'Would you go into the room next door and talk to the man there? He's frae America an' hasna' many visitors. He's got a lot o' money but I doot he hasna' muckle else.'

John's summing-up of his hospital neighbour was about right, I decided, after five minutes during which the American had given me a rapid picture of himself painted in glorious Technicolor. He was a Scot, really, who had gone to the States as a young man, and had now returned to his birthplace to retire. He told me of his many financial deals — about some of his clever dodges — the people in high places he knew — even his success with women: three American wives and now a Scottish one. He was able, he told me, 'to beat the hide off' anything or anyone that stood in his way. A big man physically, he was big, it seemed, no matter how he looked at himself.

'Good of you to look in, padre, but there's not a lot wrong with me, and I'm gonna ask the chief guy here to tell me straight from the shoulder just what it is, so that I can get outa this place.'

Now and then I tried to get a word in, but he kept going like a tape-recorder on his favourite theme, himself. Yes, a big man, I thought; in the phrase we had used as boys, 'a big blaw' (boaster).

'Would you like me to ask a blessing?' I inquired.

'Come again, padre?'

'Will we have a word of prayer together?' I asked hesitantly. He was amused . . . hilariously so.

'Suit yourself, padre,' he chuckled.

In prayer I felt I was talking into a void. There was no sense of a Presence here as there had been next door.

'I'll see you next week,' I said, and made my departure, glad to breathe some fresh air again.

A week went by and I saw John again. He was a little better, but greatly disturbed.

'I wish you'd see what you can do for the Yank. He's in an awfu' state, puir man!'

He was indeed. Huddled down in the bed, his large frame seemed to have shrunk and his eyes had a tortured look. He was mouthing curses at doctors, nurses, padres, his wife and the world in general. It really was a very terrible picture. It seemed he had insisted on the truth, and got it. He had advanced, inoperable lung cancer, and a life expectancy of perhaps a few months. I felt deeply sorry for him — for who can say how any one of us would react to such news? — yet I felt somewhat nauseated too. The man next door had lived with death as his companion for a long time and he knew there was not long to go, but John had a Companion stronger than death. This poor creature seemed to have no companion, no friend to share . . . not a soul, because he had turned against the one in life nearest to him, his wife. For the first time in his life he was in a situation where all his money, power, clever-dick dealings and important acquaintances were as nothing, and he couldn't cope. It was a desolate scene. The room seemed cold and empty, and I felt very, very helpless.

'Is there anything I can do?' I asked.

'You can go to hell . . . you, and all your kind!'

As I finally left, I felt he was already in his own private hell. I could only say, 'I'll be around next week, if you would like to see me.'

On the drive home, I thought of the two scenes, the two adjoining rooms. In the one was dignity, in the other, desolation. I recalled others like John I'd known, who had this same, strong anchor in life, who knew the calm in the eye of the hurricane. This was one of the things that had made me a minister, noting over the years and in different lives the tremendous difference faith made.

Incidents of the past came drifting back to me — odd, seemingly unrelated things — and strangely, I thought of Lulu. Lulu, you will remember, was one of Charlie Trevelyan's chimpanzees, a gentle beast who was a favourite with all visitors to his zoo, and with millions of children through his appearances with her on 'Blue Peter' and other TV programmes. I remembered well his call one evening.

'Alex? Could you come up and see Lulu? I don't like the look of her.'

Neither did I, when I walked into his house and saw the chimp. She was huddled in an armchair by the fire, and with her outstretched arms gripping the sides of the chair and her wrinkled face resting on a cushion, she looked like a wise old grandmother watching over her family. I examined her with a sinking heart.

'I don't know what it is, Charlie, but she's dying.'

'Never! Are you sure, Alex?'

'As certain as it's ever possible to be. How long has she been like this?'

'We've noticed her getting a bit thin,' said Charlie. 'Maybe a fortnight ago we first suspected there was something, but today was the first time she just wanted to stay in her house.

We brought her in here to watch her.'

The law of the wild again, I thought ... never show weakness till it can no longer be hidden, for the weakest goes to the wall.

'Charlie, I wish I could do something, but I'm afraid it's far too late. I honestly don't know what she's got, but since monkeys are very susceptible to TB, we'll give her a big shot of streptomycin and hope for the best.'

Lulu watched me with her sad eyes as I opened my case, and scarcely moved as I injected her. She was far through, but suffering in silence, with a strange dignity about her.

She died in the night. A post-mortem showed that she had indeed tuberculosis ... She was riddled with it, more than any animal I'd seen. Yet she had borne it with the quiet gallantry of wild things, doing at the zoo her job of making people happy and smiling, right to the end. Contact with the vet at the zoo, where she had lived till about twelve months before, revealed that they had lost many of their chimps with TB, the human strain, and the outbreak had been traced to some filthy character spitting at the animals. (Thereafter zoos found it necessary to put glass fronts on their monkey cages.) Lulu had clearly been infected then, all those months ago, and the disease had spread till her whole body was affected, yet no one knew ... no fuss, no refusal to work, no complaints, dignified to the end.

But people are not creatures of instinct, like wild animals. They are logical, thinking beings, able to reason, knowing the end of a thing, and thus knowing fear or apprehension. John Mackenzie had a similar dignity to Lulu's, but he had something more, much more. He had lived with disease and weakness for years, and, as a thinking, reasoning human being, had recognized death as it slowly came towards him. Yet in it all was faith. Here was a man who *dared* to believe, for faith has to dare. There was no repining in him. Rather it seemed to me, as the months passed, the dignity of his bearing became more marked, and as the shadows gathered round him, serenity and calm seemed to enfold him. A few months after his hospitalization, I saw him for the last time on earth, in his own home. He smiled and said, as matter-of-factly as if it was only a trip up the street, 'I'm going home, Mr Cameron. It's no' far noo.'

'Don't talk like that, John!' his wife protested.

John just smiled, gripped my hand and asked, 'Will you put up a prayer?'

There were tears in my heart that I daren't show in my eyes, yet a great peace too as we spoke, so naturally, to the One who is always near, and who said, 'In my Father's house are many dwelling places. If it were not so, I would have told you.'

John said, 'Thank you, Mr Cameron,' then, in a lower voice, '. . . you'll help mother, I know.'

I nodded and left him. In these moments, this humble man had shown not only dignity, but daring . . . the daring of great souls in every age who have looked beyond life here to hereafter, and known that just as surely as the sun would set here, it would rise on the other side. Known that over in the far horizons of eternity, there would still be oneness with friends on earth, and with the great Friend.

I never saw the American again. He had moved to another hospital well beyond my orbit. There was a chaplain there, I knew. I could but hope that the sick man would some-how come to terms with himself, find the peace John knew, and even in weakness be able to say, however hesitantly,

> Let me no more my comfort draw
> From my frail hold on Thee;
> In this alone rejoice with awe,
> Thy mighty grasp of me.

24

The Greatest Thing in the World

'You must make time in your ministry to read, to study, to keep up to date with the latest thought and developments.'

So we had often been told by our professors at Divinity College and University, and while I suppose they were right, I was finding it mighty hard to do, for two reasons. Firstly, there just wasn't time in a busy church without something else in one's work, like visiting people who were suffering. True, they had said *make* time, but my life seemed too full to do even that. The second reason was that, after a veterinary course of five years' very hard study . . . *very* hard study . . . and having just completed another three years studying for the ministry – less difficult, but still demanding – I felt I had done enough concentrated reading for a lifetime. Of course I dipped into books, but mainly for help in preparing talks and sermons, and I confess it seemed a luxury just to read with no particular end in view.

One book, however, that I did study early on was Henry Drummond's *The Greatest Thing in the World*, and it set me thinking. I agreed with the famous professor about the greatest thing in the world . . . love, for I had frequently seen it in action in my ministry, and also in my life as a vet.

I recalled an incident at Hill Barton in dear old Devon. Hill Barton came about bottom of my list of favourite farms, not because of the farmer, Fred Bowden, for he was a decent young chap and good farmer, but because the farm was perched on top of a hill, and there was no road to it. You drove up a track as far as you could and then walked the rest of the way over several fields. I was re-directed by our secretary to it one day by means of a phone call to another farm I was visiting, and I had no information about the kind of animal I was to see, let alone what was wrong with it. It made life a bit difficult because I didn't know what drugs or instruments I might need, and at Hill Barton you couldn't just go out to the car and collect whatever you required – you had to trudge back over the fields to your car a long way off.

So on that bleak, cold, wet, early April day, before I left the car I checked my two cases . . . yes . . . I had most of the regular drugs and tools of the trade there. But to make sure, I stuffed the pockets of my old black waterproof coat with more bottles, draped a stomach-tube round my neck, and set off, wondering, not for the first time, who would be a vet, as the rain poured down and soon was running down my neck and stinging my eyes in the driving wind. I did some more wondering when I got near the farm and it seemed to me that half of Devon was gathered there. I suppose, to be more accurate, there were about ten people huddled on the side of a little hill just down from the farm buildings, all looking at a cow stuck in the middle of a bog. It was up to its belly in the water, and there was a rope round its horns with which the assembled company had been trying to pull it to safety. A tractor was parked nearby, with the ground at the edge of the morass churned up where its wheels had just spun on the boggy, sodden ground. Everybody looked at me expectantly, and I did yet more wondering – what did they think one solitary individual could do where all that manpower and machine-power had failed?

'How did she get in there, Fred?' I asked the young farmer – as if it mattered, but I had to say something.

He just shrugged his shoulders and said, 'Don't know. Hur calved yesterday, like, but she seemed a' right this mornin' and was turned out to get a bit of grass. Us found her there at milkin' time this afternoon.'

'Calved yesterday, eh? Could have a touch of milk fever on her then.'

So I plunged into the bog, sinking over the tops of my wellingtons, and had a look at the cow, a big Shorthorn cross. Temperature was down, pulse slow and lazy – chilled, I thought, in that perishing swamp. I gave her a bottle of calcium into the bloodstream, and another mixed calcium, magnesium and phosphorus subcutaneously.

'Now we wait a little,' I shouted to the crowd of spectators. It was mighty cold waiting in that marsh, almost up to the knees in water and with the rain still sweeping down. Calcium given intravenously usually works in about fifteen minutes, but it seemed to make little difference that day. I pricked the cow with a needle, rubbed the base of its tail between two sticks, poured some water into its ear – old-fashioned tricks to try to stimulate a stubborn animal. But nothing worked, and it looked as if nothing would work. The cow's head was down, its chin resting in the peaty water; it had given up trying – it was doomed.

'Have you a horse?' I shouted to young Fred.

'Aye, us 'as,' he shouted back.

'Well, bring it, Fred, and we'll see what it can do.'

So a big carthorse was brought, the rope from the cow's horns attached to its harness, and the horse led forward. At least that was the idea — but after a few yards to take up the slack of the rope, the horse also stuck. It staggered and plunged, but its feet kept slipping in the mud and the cow stayed as it was. What on earth could we try next?

Then far back in my mind a little bell tinkled, advice an old farmer had given me, yet really very obvious. I called to the young farmer to go up to the farm and bring down something. He looked at me with surprise but did as I asked, and eventually came back carrying the something, something quite small with four legs, which was giving tongue in a high-pitched voice and, since it didn't like the rain much, doing plenty of shouting. It was, of course, the cow's calf, which after the fashion of dairy herds had been removed from the mother at birth. Fred Bowden stood on the edge of the swamp holding the struggling calf ... and almost at once the cow pricked up its ears. It gazed at the bank, and at its calf. It was then the miracle happened. The cow gave an almighty sprachle, heave and splash, and pulled itself out of that clinging, cloying muddy water. In no time it was clear, and nosing and licking its calf. We all looked on in wonderment and thankfulness. What brute force — ten men, a tractor and a horse — and scientific know-how in the shape of a vet's treatment had failed to do, love did . . . the love of a cow for its calf.

I sat back in my study chair and thought . . . that's it . . . that's my main function as a minister . . . to speak of and show a love . . . not just the love of a cow for its young . . . but a greater love, the love of God. Because it was love that sent His son into the world, to teach, to heal, to show compassion for all, yes . . . and to go the whole way to a Cross and give Himself for all mankind. Was there ever such a love, one that embraces all, good and bad, saint and sinner? And the glory of our faith — love incarnate conquering death, and showing the power and extent of His love that not even the last great enemy could defeat.

For God so loved . . . He gave His son. 'Never forget that *so*,' said a famous conductor to the choir about to sing Stainer's 'Crucifixion', 'for it says it all.'

'Now abideth faith, hope, love, these three, but the greatest of these is love,' wrote Paul.

Aye . . . the greatest thing in the world indeed, as Henry Drummond had said in his book. I felt very humble, but also proud, that somehow the great Father had entrusted me who had tried to heal animals because I loved

439

them (and will to my dying day) with the message of His matchless love, and so had led a vet to the vestry.